COMPLETE
A-Z
Physical
Education
HANDBOOK

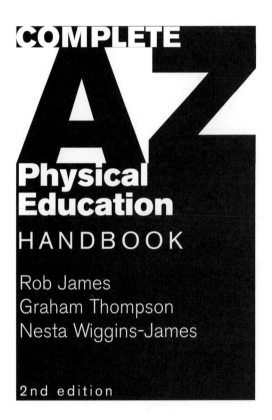

COMPLETE

A Z

Physical
Education

HANDBOOK

Rob James
Graham Thompson
Nesta Wiggins-James

2nd edition

A B C D E F G H I J K L M N O P Q R S T U V W X Y Z

Hodder & Stoughton
A MEMBER OF THE HODDER HEADLINE GROUP

British Library Cataloguing in Publication Data
A catalogue record for this title is available from The British Library

ISBN 0 340 84992 4

First published 2000
Second edition 2003

Impression number 10 9 8 7 6 5 4 3 2 1
Year 2007 2006 2005 2004 2003

Cover photograph: Max Oppenheim/Getty Images

Typeset by GreenGate Publishing Services, Tonbridge, Kent.
Printed and bound in Great Britain for Hodder and Stoughton Educational, a division of Hodder Headline plc, 338 Euston Road, London NW1 3BH, by The Bath Press Ltd.

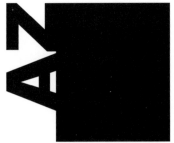

CONTENTS

A B C D E F G H I J K L M N O P Q R S T U V W X Y Z

HOW TO USE THIS BOOK

The *A–Z Physical Education Handbook* is an alphabetical glossary of terms covering all theoretical aspects of the Specifications and designed for ease of use. It does not attempt to be an exhaustive list of every term within the course, but covers the major terms that should be familiar to students. The terms are drawn from the disciplines of anatomy and physiology, psychology, sociology and history, and comparative studies.

Where possible each entry starts with a simple one-line definition and progresses to explain the term in more detail, showing how it relates to other associated areas of Physical Education. This is further reinforced with the use of practical examples where appropriate, as the application of knowledge is crucial to understanding the topics fully. Some entries do not allow for this structure, for example, those entries covering the various sporting organisations, and as a result these have been modified to outline their aims and current initiatives.

Utilising the cross-referencing system can increase your understanding of the subject areas. Within each entry any associated terms that can expand your knowledge appear in italics. The entry *flexibility*, for example, refers the reader to *cool-down*. By using this system you will gain a more complete understanding of the issues you are studying and start to develop a more synoptic approach to your study.

So while the *A–Z Handbook* is a glossary that will aid your study of Physical Education, it is important to recognise that it is not a textbook. This means that you will require further reading to complete your understanding of the topic. However, the more substantial entries will give you a sound introduction to the concepts and issues, in addition to providing a handy reference when you encounter concepts of which you are unsure.

During your course of study, the *Handbook* is essentially a book to pick up to browse through and use to complement your basic understanding as well as helping to clarify new ideas. In addition it should prove useful during revision. To help during this period three sections have been included in the appendix:

- Revision terms – have been sub-divided into key terms for each examination board for each module. These could act as a starting point for your revision and should then be expanded using the cross-referencing system.

- Examiners' terms – many candidates fail to do themselves justice in examinations, not because of a lack of knowledge but through misunderstanding of question requirements or simply not following instructions. This section outlines many key terms and describes what each means. Understanding of these terms can improve your examination technique considerably, allowing you to gain valuable extra marks.

- Synoptic assessment – it is vital that you are able to link together various theoretical aspects of the course and relate them to a particular issue or topic. This section outlines how to structure and develop synoptic answers, for both revision and the examination.

Additional sections have been included in the appendix specifically for the physiological aspects of the course to eliminate the need for excessive entries and complement your studies.

We hope that you find the *A–Z Physical Education Handbook* enjoyable to use, informative and an invaluable resource throughout your studies.

Rob James, Nesta Wiggins-James and Graham Thompson

ACKNOWLEDGEMENTS

Nesta and Rob would like to thank Ffion, Ellie, Rees and Cai for being so patient during the writing of this book.

A
B
C
D
E
F
G
H
I
J
K
L
M
N
O
P
Q
R
S
T
U
V
W
X
Y
Z

A state: see *state anxiety*

A trait: see *trait anxiety*

abduction: movement pattern involving actions away from the midline of the body or one of its body parts. It occurs in the *frontal plane,* for example at the hip joint when performing a cartwheel in gymnastics. A muscle that causes this movement is known as an *abductor.* See page 268 in the appendix for a full description of movement patterns. See also page 253.

abductor: muscle that causes the movement pattern known as *abduction* at a joint. For example, the deltoid raises the arm sideways at the shoulder joint during the preparatory phase of the discus throw. In this instance the deltoid is an abductor.

abilities are inherited, innate and generally enduring traits that an individual possesses, allowing them to complete various tasks. Certain skills require specific abilities, which can be broadly categorised into *psychomotor ability* and *gross motor ability*. The former involves the processing of information and initiation of the movement, e.g. co-ordination and reaction time; the latter involves actual movement e.g. flexibility, strength, stamina, balance and speed.

aborigines: tribe that entered *Australia* during the last Great Ice Age. Their *society* was organised, and semi-nomadic, and the spiritual world was an integral feature of their philosophy. Colonisation led to disease and death through military action, and the loss of land rights only recently being recognised and compensated for in the Native Title Act 1994. This is an example of an *ethnic group* who were affected by the *White Australia Policy*, and their fate was similar to that of the *native Americans*. They now form less than two per cent of the population.

Traditional physical activities would have a functional base, for example, *hunting* and games as preparation for battles; they also have a strong religious and *ritual* meaning. The National Aboriginal Sport Foundation is part of the *Australian Sports Commission (ASC)* and has founded the Aboriginal Sport and Recreation Programme. Aboriginal culture has seen a revival within a more liberal society, though aborigines still suffer severe discrimination.

academies of sport: training centres for the development of *elite* athletes, usually with the aim of raising the profile of sport within a country, and forming part of a national strategy in sport policy. Consequently, *national governments* are usually heavily involved in the philosophy and funding of these centres as they can help create an important *national identity*. They are based on:

- top class coaching
- world class facilities
- scientific support.

Academies and institutes of sport can be either *centralised* or *decentralised,* targeting specific sports, which may be traditional or new to the country. They often concentrate on national sports or on those with an *ethnic* identity, often utilising higher education or *local authority* facilities. These centres can either be isolated from the ethos of mass participation or allow mass sport to run parallel to it, forming the structure beneath the pinnacle (see *United Kingdom Sports Institute, Australian Institute of Sport* and *INSEP*).

acceleration: the rate of change of *velocity*. It is a *vector quantity* possessing both magnitude and direction and is integral to many sporting situations, from sprinting to the drive in golf. Acceleration is calculated using the formula:

$$\text{acceleration} = \frac{\text{change of velocity}}{\text{time}} \quad \text{or} \quad \frac{v - u}{t}$$

Newton's second law is commonly known as the law of acceleration and states:

'the acceleration of a body is proportional to the force causing it, and the acceleration takes place in the direction in which that force acts.'

More simply, the greater the force imparted the greater the resultant acceleration. This is expressed as:

$$F = ma$$

where F = force generated, m = mass of the body or object and a = acceleration.

accommodation: the process whereby different social groups live together in harmony, accepting each other's distinct identities, such as language and culture. In sociological terms it is often used to describe the mutual tolerance of different *ethnic groups* living in the same society. This is different from *assimilation*.

acetyl coenzyme A (acetyl co-A): a compound derived from *pyruvic acid* when the *aerobic energy system* is being utilised. During the process it is oxidised to release energy. Before it can be totally downgraded to release energy, acetyl co-A must combine with a four-carbon molecule called oxaloacetic acid to form *citric acid*. This compound can now enter the *Krebs cycle* to form carbon dioxide and water, and release energy for muscular contraction.

acetylcholine: transmitter substance that is released by the *central nervous system*, allowing muscles to contract. It is released when a nerve impulse reaches the *motor end plate*, and enables the impulse to cross the synaptic cleft. If sufficient acetylcholine is released the muscle fibre is said to have *action potential*, allowing the muscles to contract and movement to occur. In order to prevent continual stimulation, the acetylcholine is blocked by the enzyme cholinesterase. This allows the motor unit to prepare for new stimuli and contract again when required.

achievement motivation refers to an individual's interaction with the environment and their desire to succeed. Atkinson suggested an individual's level of *motivation* depends on a combination of personality and situational factors. People display either a *need to achieve* (nAch) or *need to avoid failure* (nAf) tendency when placed in certain situations. A situation is evaluated in terms of an individual's probability of success and the incentive value of that success, which can be expressed as:

$$(Ms - Maf) \times (Ps \times \{I - Ps\})$$

where: Ms = motive to succeed, Maf = Motive to avoid failure, Ps = Probability of success and I = Incentive value of success.

For example, the motivation level of a novice tennis player when faced with a match against a club player will depend on their perceived chance of success and whether or not they are prepared to face the challenge whatever the outcome, or merely not play in case they are seen to fail.

Critics of the theory argue it is too simplistic and that different performers perceive success in a variety of ways, depending on whether their tasks have an *outcome goal* or a *task-orientated goal*.

See also *Veroff's stages of achievement motivation*.

actin: a thin protein filament found in muscle cells. It is found in the *sarcomere* and combines with *myosin* to produce movement (see *sliding filament theory*). Each actin myofilament is composed of two proteins:

● fibrous actin – provides active sites to which the myosin cross-bridge can bind during muscle contraction

● tropomyosin and troponin molecules – aid the attachment of the myosin cross-bridge when calcium ions are released from the sarcoplasmic reticulum during nerve stimulation.

action potential: the electrical activity that is developed in a muscle or nerve cell during activity. Occurs when sufficient *acetylcholine* has been released by the central nervous system and is the stimulus for muscle contraction.

Active Australia: a national programme run by the *Australian Sports Commission* (ASC) where the focus is on participation and *Sport for All*, integrating other programmes such as *Aussie Sport* and Aussie Able into getting Australians 'up and active' at the foundation level of sport. This requires the adoption of a corporate plan by local state sport recreation departments. Active Australia identifies three main aims:

● to increase and enhance lifelong participation

● to realise the social, health and economic benefits of participation

● to develop a quality infrastructure with opportunities and services to support participation.

Its focus is entirely on sport for all rather than *excellence*.

active leisure takes place in *leisure* time and involves the individual personally participating in a physical activity (see *physical recreation*).

Activemark: an award scheme for primary schools that recognises good practice within the *physical education* provision. The higher 'gold' level can also be achieved. The Activemark and Activemark Gold awards scheme recognises and rewards primary, middle and special schools that provide young children with the opportunity to receive the benefits of physical activity. It has been developed in partnership with the British Heart Foundation (BHF) and has the theme: get active, stay active. To achieve an award a school needs to:

● offer a broad and balanced physical education programme

● provide an environment that encourages physical activities

● teach children the importance of staying active for life

● provide enhanced curricular provision through some additional opportunities for physical activity

- have an effective inclusion policy for disabled pupils.

Activemark Gold recognises all the above, plus:

- realistic in-depth physical education and physical activity development plans
- a commitment to providing a range of additional, high quality opportunities for physical activity.

A team of assessors appointed by *Sport England* reviews the schools against these rigorous criteria.

Active Sports Programme: scheme co-ordinated by *Sport England* based on four policy headings:

- active schools – forms the foundation
- active communities – looks at breaking down the barriers to participation and considers equity issues
- active sports – links participation to *excellence* such as participation in the Millennium Youth Games
- *World Class England* – operates four programmes of World Class Start, World Class Potential, World Class Performance and World Class Events.

They are meant to act as building blocks and are not necessarily linear, as shown by the illustration. They also complement the Sports Council's *participation pyramid* of foundation, participation, performance and excellence. The majority of the funding will come from the *National Lottery* and there will be a strengthening of the regional set up via *local authorities*. There will be a framework around all experiences available to potential participants such as the *National Junior Sports Programme, Sportsmark* and Coaching for Teachers.

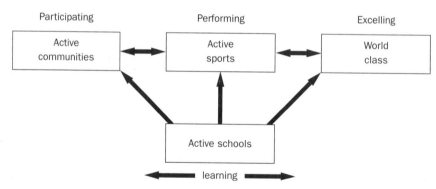

actual productivity refers to a group's or team's performance of a task. Steiner (1972) suggested that this was equal to the *potential productivity* minus the losses due to *faulty processes*. A group may contain a large number of highly skilled individuals who would be expected to perform well, but fail to do so due to *motivation* problems and poor co-ordination, the result being a poor performance, possibly displaying the *Ringlemann effect* and *social loafing*. For example, a team contains several 'flair' players who may not necessarily contribute as consistently as they should during play. The coach may decide to omit one for the good of the team, replacing them with a less skilful but harder working player, thus attempting to minimise the faulty processes so that actual productivity may equal potential productivity. See also *group productivity*.

Adam's closed loop theory suggests the performer's movement can be modified with the use of *feedback* from the various sensory *receptors*. This is an extension of the *open loop control theory* and a closing of the circuit. The concept is based on two key factors:

- the 'memory trace', allowing selection and initiation of the movement, with no actual control
- the 'perceptual trace', allowing comparison and modification against stored motor pro-grammes. The perceptual trace is developed through practice and any feedback, either during or after the performance, allows errors to be detected, compared to a reference of correctness and adjustments made.

For example, a gymnast completing a routine will constantly evaluate the movements being performed during the sequence and make adjustments as required to maintain balance, speed and control based on their knowledge of how each component should feel. The theory assumes that there is a separate memory trace for each movement pattern, which would not necessarily be accommodated by and recalled from the *long-term memory*. It also suggests practice should be accurate and variance would hinder learning, which research has refuted.

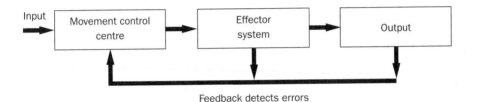

Feedback detects errors

adaptive physical education sport: an umbrella term used to encompass such areas as dance, sport, fitness and rehabilitation of individuals with impairment across the lifespan. It evolved during the 1950s, from both the medical and educational perspectives, and is a popular concept in the *United States of America*, where federal legislation in 1975 required that teaching styles, facilities and equipment should be adapted to meet the needs of both regular and special students within the mainstream *education* system. There is no compa-rable system in the United Kingdom.

adduction: movement pattern involving movement towards the midline of the body or one of its body parts. It takes place in the *frontal plane* and occurs, for example, at the hip joint, in the crossover step during the run-up phase of the javelin throw. A muscle that causes this movement is known as an *adductor*. See appendix, page 270.

adductor: muscle that causes the movement pattern known as *adduction* at a joint. For example, the pectoralis major pulls the arm across the body during the throwing action of the javelin event, and in this instance is an adductor.

adenosine diphosphate (ADP): high-energy phosphate compound consisting of adenosine and two phosphate groups attached to it. During the resynthesis of ATP, adenosine diphosphate combines with another phosphate group to form *adenosine triphos-phate (ATP)*, which can subsequently be broken down to release energy for muscular contraction.

adenosine triphosphate (ATP): form of chemical energy found in all muscle cells. The high-energy phosphate molecules are broken down to release energy for all processes, including muscle contraction, nerve transmission and digestion. An adenosine triphosphate (ATP) molecule is composed of three phosphate groups and an adenosine component and when exposed to the enzyme ATPase, a bond is broken to release a large amount of energy, leaving *adenosine diphosphate*, as shown below:

ATP $\rightarrow$ ADP + Pi + energy

The amount of ATP in the muscle cells is limited and is exhausted within a few seconds. It must therefore be constantly resynthesised in order to provide a continuous supply of energy. The resynthesis of ATP requires energy to attach a phosphate group to the adenosine diphosphate compound, as shown below:

ADP + Pi + energy $\rightarrow$ ATP

The energy used to resynthesise ATP can be derived from three sources:

1   *ATP-PC energy system* – used for high intensity power-based activities such as the 100-metre sprint

2   *lactic acid energy system* – used for medium to high intensity activities such as a 400-metre run

3   *aerobic energy system* – used for low intensity, endurance-based activities such as the marathon.

administration: management of the affairs of an organisation or institution such as sport as a whole or a sports club. It can be seen as developing from the community, for example a local sports club is surmounted by its regional, national and international counterparts. Organisations such as national *governing bodies* and *Sport England* are all concerned with administrative issues, such as:

- governing sport
- making decisions
- creating and distributing finances and resources.

adrenaline: hormone released by the adrenal gland at times of stress as well as before and during exercise. It is a pre-requisite for physical activity and forms the body's *fight or flight response*, which can affect the performer in a number of ways, as outlined below:

Effect on the body:

- increased heart rate
- constriction of blood vessels
- break down of glucose and fats
- sweat production.

Effect on performance:

- increased oxygen to the muscles – CO_2 removed
- raised *blood pressure*, increasing blood flow to muscles
- more energy released to resynthesise ATP
- prevents overheating, but can cause dehydration.

When preparing for physical activity, adrenaline can reduce activity in non-essential organs and increase activity in those organs required for the activity, namely the muscles, making it an essential ingredient during exercise.

adventurous activities: outdoor pursuit activities which take place in the *natural environment*, often in situations which are dangerous and challenging, and which may involve the *conquest* of natural obstacles or terrain. For example, rock climbing, skiing and sky diving. New activities continue to be developed, mostly as a result of technological advances, such as jet skiing and windsurfing. Many of these activities developed as a means of exploring terrain and human resources, as well through the need to *escape* from the urban to the natural environment.

Adventurous activities are not governed by rules as such, there are no winners or losers and therefore no officials. There is usually, however, a code of *etiquette* concerning safety and *conservation* of the natural environment. Recently many adventurous activities have become *sports*, involving scoring systems and officials, e.g. white water slalom racing and speed climbing.

The main challenge for the participant occurs against the elements, requiring them to differentiate between real and perceived *risk* (see *danger*). *Wilderness areas* and extreme climatic zones in the United States of America, France and Australia produce opportunities within these sports not available in the more gentle terrain and temperate climate of the United Kingdom.

advertising: paid-for communication through *mass media* such as television, newspapers or radio. Advertising and marketing have become powerful forces and sport has become a vehicle for the promotion of products and images which enable advertising companies to make profits, providing employment and income for a large number of people.

aerobic energy system: energy pathway which uses oxygen to break down *glycogen* and fat to release energy which can then be used to resynthesise *ATP*. Under aerobic conditions the glucose molecule can be totally degraded, providing an energy yield 18 times that produced in *anaerobic* conditions. The glucose molecule is broken down in special 'powerhouses' or 'factories' known as *mitochondria*, where the *Krebs cycle* and *electron transport system* take place. *Slow twitch fibres* possess a greater number of mitochondria then *fast twitch fibres* and therefore have a greater capacity to produce energy over an extended period of time. When a molecule of glucose is degraded, energy sufficient to resynthesise 38 ATP is released as follows:

- 2 during anaerobic glycolysis
- 2 during the Krebs cycle
- 34 during the electron transport system.

Because of the vast energy supply gained through aerobic metabolism, this system is used mainly in endurance-based activities where exercise is less intense and energy is required over a long period of time. This system is also responsible for supplying the energy required by the body at rest. Examples include running a marathon or time-outs during a basketball match.

aerobic fitness is the ability of the body to perform exercise over an extended period of time in the presence of oxygen. It relies upon the efficiency of the body to utilise oxygen to release *energy* that is stored in *glycogen* and *fats*. Sports performers that have high levels of aerobic fitness include marathon runners, cyclists and triathletes. In order to improve aerobic fitness athletes should undertake a period of *continuous training*. It is also known as cardiovascular fitness.

aesthetic: the quality of movement and an appreciation of art forms. Some sports, such as tennis and cricket, are won through technical superiority alone. However, *gymnastic activities* such as figure skating also award marks for artistic merit. These decisions are made by judges and will inevitably be determined to some extent by *subjective* opinions. The performer:

- experiences the aesthetic moment through his or her *kinaesthetic* flow patterns, making it subjective in character
- achieves the performance through knowing what to do and how to do it
- needs to be able to gain pleasure from executing a movement, as skillfulness alone does not ensure an aesthetic experience. This may be more easily achieved in *closed skill* situations such as gymnastics where the performer is able to focus on the inward motions with minimal interference from the sporting environment.

The spectators' experience, however, comes from outside the event and they need to bring understanding, interpretation and imagination, together with the ability to engage emotionally in the activity, in order to experience the aesthetic moment.

affective attitude: one of the components of the *triadic model*, this refers to the performer's emotional feelings towards an issue or *attitude object*, based on past experiences or values. For example, the performer may enjoy taking part in exercise, displaying a positive attitude, but may particularly dislike swimming, showing a negative attitude.

affective learning: refers to the positive attitudes and emotional components that may be required to prepare and compete effectively, e.g. etiquette, sportsmanship, confidence and focusing techniques. To maximise learning, this component should be combined with *effective learning* and *cognitive theories of learning*.

African Games (Pan): major athletics championship recognised by the International Amateur Athletic Federation, which developed from the Friendship Games of the early 1960s. They were first held in 1965 but political issues interrupted any regular meeting and the second games were held in 1973. The United Arab Republic was the most powerful nation, but the most significant successes came on the running track where *Kenya* emerged as a middle-distance running power.

African nations: the nations of Africa, which is the world's second largest continent. It is situated with the Mediterranean in the north, the Atlantic in the west and the Red Sea, the Gulf of Aden and the Indian Ocean in the east. The Sahara Desert divides the continent unequally into:

- Northern Africa – an early centre of civilisation in close contact with Europe and Western Asia, and inhabited mainly by Arabs
- Southern Africa – relatively isolated from the rest of the world until the nineteenth century and inhabited chiefly by Negro peoples. It was colonised in the eighteenth and nineteenth centuries and is now comprised mainly of independent nations.

See also African nations and sport.

African nations and sport: the states of Africa have endeavoured to modernise their political, economic and social structures to emulate those of the developed world. Sport was used early in African colonial history as a means of *socialisation* to encourage people to accept colonial rule. Western culture, including sports, was introduced by administrators, diplomats, the military, teachers and missionaries. These activities were used to celebrate Empire Day, allegiance to the Crown and to express national unity. During the Mau Mau uprising in the 1950s sport was encouraged to distract attention away from political activity and to relieve the frustration of restrictive curfews. The realisation of independence brought with it awareness within many new African governments of the political uses of sport and education in the development of *national identity*. See also *emergent cultures*.

aggression: any form of behaviour intended to injure or harm another person either verbally or physically and, within a sporting context, outside the laws of the game. All acts of aggression are viewed as anti-social, caused by biological, sociological or environmental factors:

- Biological theories suggest individuals are born with aggressive tendencies, e.g. instinct theory argues that we have developed these traits as part of the evolutionary process of survival, and aggression is either an instinctive reaction or displayed to establish control over a particular territory. Aggressive tendencies must be released for the good of the individual (known as *catharsis*). This can be in an acceptable form, e.g. sport, or as unacceptable behaviour, e.g. violence and crime.
- Sociological theories such as the *social learning theory* propose that through observation of others during the learning process, actions are copied and they are more likely to be repeated if they are reinforced and rewarded. The chance of repetition is increased if the model is of high status to the individual, e.g. if a top-class performer commits a foul but avoids punishment the observer will attempt to repeat the action given the opportunity.
- Environmental factors can lead to goals being blocked thus leading to the *frustration–aggression hypothesis*. If the performer's objective is being blocked they may become frustrated and eventually aggressive if this continues, e.g. a performer is being well marked by the opponent and eventually commits a foul because they cannot perform as desired.

Actions considered aggressive in one situation may not be in another, e.g. hitting an opponent during a hockey match compared with a punch in a boxing bout. Acceptable forms of aggression are known as assertive behaviour or channelled aggression.

aggressive cue theory suggests that although frustration will cause an increase in arousal levels, an aggressive act will only occur if a socially learnt cue is present or the environmental situation makes committing the act acceptable (Berkowitz 1993). The theory allows for some of the weaknesses of the *frustration–aggression hypothesis* as it takes into account the influence of socially learned behaviour and the situation the performer is currently experiencing. For example a basketball player who drives for a lay-up shot is constantly blocked by an opponent causing frustration, but they may only commit a foul if the coach has encouraged and tolerated this behaviour in the past.

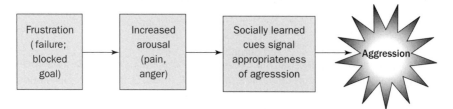

agility: motor-based component of *fitness*, involving the ability of the performer to move and change direction, and to position the body quickly and effectively while under control. For example, during a game of basketball the player has to adjust their body position whilst dribbling or driving for the basket when performing a lay-up shot, depending upon the position of defenders. It can be measured using the *Illinois agility run test*. Unfortunately training has little effect on an individual's agility as this is an innate characteristic and cannot be significantly improved.

agonist: the muscle that is directly responsible for the movement at a joint. Muscles usually work in pairs or groups to facilitate co-ordinated movement, with each performing a different function. For example, during a bicep curl exercise, when *flexion* occurs at the elbow joint the bicep brachii is responsible for the movement and is therefore the agonist. However as one muscle shortens, another lengthens and is known as the *antagonist*. In this example, the anatagonists are the triceps. Muscles work together in this way it is known as *reciprocal inhibition*. As the weight is lowered the role of each muscle is reversed and the triceps become the agonists and the biceps the antagonists. Also known as prime mover.

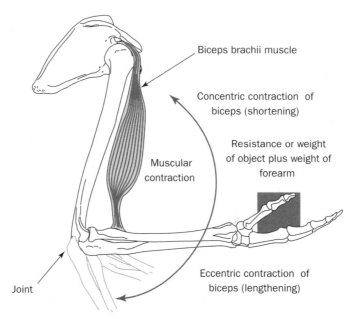

agrarian revolution: signified a dramatic movement of the population from rural areas to the towns during the *Industrial Revolution* in nineteenth-century Britain. Farming had become less important as small farms were taken over by large landowners as a result of the enclosure system and farming practices had changed with the development of machinery, reducing the need for labour. This had a large impact on people's lives and particularly on their *rural sports.*

aims can be defined as the intended purpose of a course of action achieved via objectives. For example, some of the aims of a *physical education* curriculum may include:

- to develop a range of psychomotor *skills*

- to maintain and increase physical mobility and flexibility, stamina and strength

- to develop understanding and appreciation of a range of physical activities

- to develop positive values and *attitudes* like sportsmanship, competition, necessity of abiding by the rules

- to help children acquire *self-esteem* and confidence through the acquisition of skills, knowledge and values

- to develop an understanding of the importance of exercise in maintaining a healthy lifestyle.

air resistance: a force which causes a resistance to the motion of an object or body when moving through the air. The amount of force exerted depends upon the size, weight, shape and speed of the object. The effects of air resistance are small compared with the force of gravity, for example, when using a shot putt, balls or people, but more relevant with lighter objects such as shuttlecocks. Faster moving objects have greater air resistance, which can cause deceleration, where a point is reached when the weight of the object becomes the major factor determining its flight path. Generally, the influence of air resistance is considered negligible, although it can alter the parabolic flight path of an object.

Performers often attempt to limit the effects of air resistance by using specialist equipment, which can include altering the shape of cyclists' helmets and body position as well as specialist clothing. See also *Bernouilli effect* and *Magnus effect.*

alactacid debt: the first stage of the recovery process or replenishment of the *oxygen debt.* Its function is to resynthesise *creatine phosphate* and *adenosine triphosphate (ATP)*, and to saturate myoglobin with oxygen. This is the fast stage of the *excess post-exercise oxygen consumption (EPOC)* and is accomplished by increasing the amount of oxygen entering the body, which explains why a performer experiences heavy breathing following exercise. This process usually takes 2–3 minutes and utilises up to four litres of oxygen. Once the alactacid debt has been replenished the consumed oxygen is used to remove waste products such as *lactic acid* that may have accrued and is known as the *lactacid debt.* See diagram on page 12.

alactic energy system: the first energy pathway to be utilised by the body to resynthesise *adenosine triphosphate (ATP)* without the use of oxygen. This *anaerobic* system uses stored *creatine phosphate* from the muscle cells, not for muscle contraction, but purely to rebuild ATP and maintain a constant supply of energy. A *coupled reaction* occurs very rapidly, but can only last up to ten seconds and is therefore used in activities of high intensity over a short period of time, for example high jump, shot putt and 100-metre sprint. Also known as

ATP–PC energy system. (See figure below.)

$$ATP \rightarrow ADP + Pi + energy$$

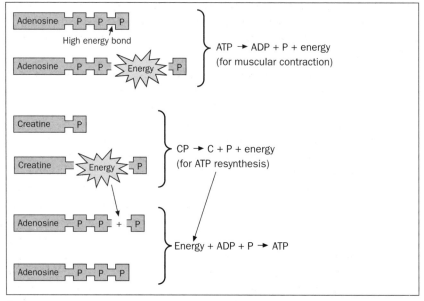

Alactic energy system

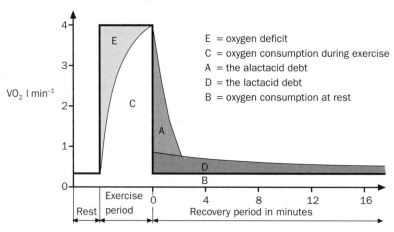

E = oxygen deficit
C = oxygen consumption during exercise
A = the alactacid debt
D = the lactacid debt
B = oxygen consumption at rest

Alactacid debt

alertness is the ability to focus on specific cues (*selective attention*) and refers to the concept of optimal *arousal* and the performer's level of awareness of the *stimuli*. If a high level of alertness can be maintained, the decision-making process can be made more effective, improving *reaction time* and performance. A defender in a game has to maintain a higher level of alertness for longer than a sprinter, and may have to be alert to more stimuli.

all or none law: this principle states that when a *motor unit* receives a stimulus of suffi-cient intensity to elicit a response, all the muscle fibres within the unit will contract at the same time and to the maximum possible extent. However, if the impulse is not of a sufficient strength to cause contraction, none of the fibres within the motor unit will contract at all. In other words single muscle fibres cannot partially contract. This does not imply that the muscle must be fully contracted or fully relaxed; the strength of contraction is determined by the number of motor units within the muscle that are contracting compared with those that are relaxing. The greater the strength required, the greater the number of motor units that contract.

Other governing factors are the availability of oxygen and other nutrients and the effects of fatigue. For example, more motor units will be recruited when sprinting than during a distance run, since greater strength and power are required at high intensity events.

alpinism: a development of the eighteenth- and nineteenth-century ideal of energetic outdoor pursuits in the natural environment. The formation of the Alpine Club in 1857 led to a trend in mountaineering amongst intellectuals and the higher social classes, which led to *exclusivity*, as they had the time and resources for such activities. It began as an extension of *tourism*, which was made more accessible by the development of the *railways*, and developed into a *competition sport*. It also had strong links with the *Romantic movement*.

altitude training: method of training based on the principle that with an increase in altitude, the partial pressure of oxygen (pO_2) in the atmosphere decreases by about a half, causing the body to adapt by increasing red blood cell mass and haemoglobin levels. It is widely used by endurance athletes to enhance their oxygen-carrying capacity. When the athletes return to sea level, these changes remain yet the atmospheric pO_2 has increased, which means that the body can transport and utilise more oxygen, giving improved endurance performance. However, there appears to be contradictory evidence concerning the benefits of altitude training and recent evidence suggests that living at altitude whilst training at sea level procures the greatest endurance performance and in doing so athletes can increase their oxygen carrying capacity of the blood by up to 150 per cent.

alveolus (pl. alveoli): small air sac found in the lungs where *gaseous exchange* occurs (see figure on page 14). The walls of the alveolus are extremely thin, composed of a single layer of epithelial cells and surrounded by an extensive *capillary* network, which allows oxygen to enter the blood stream and carbon dioxide to be removed by the process of diffusion. The effects of exercise are inconclusive, but it is thought that endurance training might improve the functioning and elasticity of the alveolar walls.

amateurism: a concept which evolved in nineteenth-century England amongst the *upper class*, who became known as *gentleman amateurs*. It is based upon the ideal that participating in sport should be for the love of it rather than for monetary gain, and the participation was deemed more important than the winning. It encompassed the belief in *fair play* and abiding by the spirit as well as the rules of the game. It originally had a *social class* distinction as it excluded the lower classes and, within a sporting context the *corinthians* were the epitome of amateurism. However, because this definition of amateurism is socially determined, it changes over a period of time.

Sports have undergone major changes in their amateur/professional status. For example, *rowing* was originally open to amateurs and professionals but the gentleman amateurs disliked being beaten by their social inferiors. This resulted in a strict amateur definition instigated by the Amateur Rowing Association called the 'exclusion clause' that effectively excluded 'all mechanics, artisans and labourers'.

Terms that have evolved to describe amateur performers who receive some form of payment include:

* shamateur – describes amateurs who receive 'under the table' payments. *Trust funds* were set up to try and combat this problem

* stamateurs – describes state-sponsored amateurs. These were common in Eastern bloc countries.

Amateurs can officially receive financial aid from *sponsorship*, trust funds and organisations such as *Sports Aid* and the *National Lottery*.

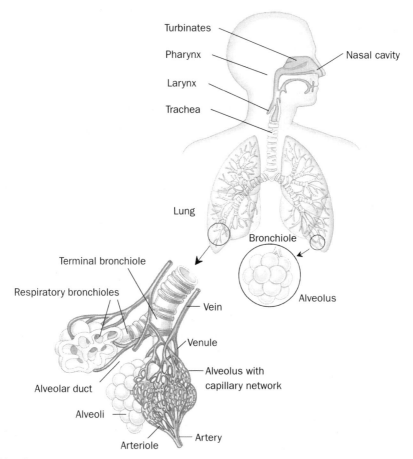

Alveolus

American dream is based on the idea that individuals are free to operate in a competitive economic environment, without class restrictions, in order to achieve individual wealth and status. It is also commonly referred to as 'rags to riches'. It presumes a single scale of success and relies on individual qualities such as initiative, resourcefulness and a material attitude towards life. It is this openness which has made the American dream attractive to many diverse cultural groups which are part of its make up. *Professional sport* in the *United States of America* has long been an avenue of *social mobility*, particularly useful for athletes from lower class backgrounds.

American football: a physical-contact and intimidating *invasion game*. It originated from the English game of *rugby football* but developed along different lines in its new culture, taking root in the *elite* colleges such as Harvard and Yale. As a result the game had *middle class* beginnings, similar to rugby, but it was not constrained by *amateurism* as English rugby was, and the win ethic, or *Lombardian ethic*, emerged alongside *professionalism*. It is also referred to as 'gridiron', which emphasises its territorial features. American football is one of the dominant *American sports.*

American sports such as *American football*, *baseball, ice hockey* and *basketball* have their own unique characteristics, but they also tend to share common elements that make them some of the most popular and dominant sports in the *USA*. They include:

- high scoring with no draws and fast play
- creation of entertainment through the *media* and *sponsorship*
- tendency to attract families rather than traditionally single-sex spectators as in the UK
- facilities that are of a high standard for both players and spectators
- operating as businesses controlled by owners, they are heavily marketed with their accompanying merchandise
- carrying of racial identity and preferences
- the *professional sport* ethos of the *Lombardian ethic* with material rewards for success reflects *capitalism*
- due to the size of the United States there is not the tradition of home and away fans as in Britain, and the crowds are therefore less partisan
- well-developed children's leagues based on the adult version
- limited *club* structure, with development of players occurring through the *inter-collegiate* system.

American summer camps: the camping movement gained acceptance after 1900 and was initiated by teachers, Scout and Guide groups. Today there are several thousand summer camps throughout the *USA*, most of which are permanent camps where children reside for up to eight weeks. The camps take children from 6 to16 years, and are responsible for their welfare. Today 'going to camp' for an extended period of time is a well-established tradition in the USA.

There has always been a tradition of sending urban children to the natural environment for holidays, and in a country where the summer holidays last three months, it is accepted for children to spend time away from their parents.

There are different types of camps:

- Private residential – these are privately owned and cater for the high-income, middle class families. They run on a profit-making policy, providing permanent residential facilities and they operate all over the country. They have a range of facilities covering various sports and crafts.
- Day camps – these can also be privately owned or run by organisations such as the *YMCA* or local towns.

- Organisational camps – these are run by Christian-based organisations like the Girl and Boy Scouts and the YMCA, though the emphasis on religion can vary.

- Camps for underprivileged children – these are operated by various social, philanthropic or religious agencies like the Salvation Army and aim to give inner-city children a break from the urban environment. These camps are heavily subsidised, with families paying little or nothing towards the cost. The facilities are more basic and the emphasis is on the recreational experience and appreciation of the environment.

- Special needs camps – these are for people with physical or mental disabilities, diabetics and people who are overweight (often termed 'fat camps').

A typical day at camp

07.15	Reveille. Short optional dip or jog.
07.45	Flag raising and personal inspection.
08.00	Breakfast, followed by clean-up of the cabin or tent.
09.30	1st activity period.
10.30	2nd activity period.
11.45	Optional general swim.
12.30	Lunch
13.30	Rest hour supervision.
14.30	1st afternoon activity period.
15.30	2nd afternoon activity period.
16.30	Free time supervision.
18.00	Dinner.
19.00	Flag lowering, followed by special evening events.
21.00	First bell – lights out for younger children.
22.00	Lights out for the seniors.

'While some routine is essential there is always something different planned to bring new experience into a busy, happy, healthy existence'

Americanisation of sports: the perceived domination of sport on a global scale by American *culture* and values as a result of the all-pervading influence of the *media* and intense *commercialism*.

amphetamines: illegal drugs taken to stimulate the *central nervous system*. In doing so they can improve alertness and increase *arousal*. Amphetamines can also improve blood flow to the muscles by increasing heart rate and through *vasodilation of arteries* supplying *skeletal muscles*. This, together with improved metabolism of *fats* gives a sense of increased *energy*. Despite these benefits, the ingestion of amphetamines can have serious side effects. As well as being addictive, they artificially increase heart rate and *blood pressure* and can cause the heart to beat irregularly (cardiac arrhythmia). Amphetamines are also a *diuretic* and can lead to *dehydration* and also suppress appetite, which can lead to *fatigue* during training if sufficient food has not been consumed.

Amphetamines can also cause athletes to become seriously ill after pushing themselves beyond their physiological limits.

AMI: see *athletic motivation inventory*

anabolic steroids: artificially produced male hormones which help to repair the body after periods of stress, for example stanozolol and testosterone. It is the main *doping agent* used in power, explosive and sprints events, which are used by performers to:

- build up their power by increasing muscle growth and lean body weight

- increase training time

- increase their recovery rate after training.

Aggression and *competitiveness* also increase, which is useful for gross body activities, however the problems caused can include liver damage and general health problems. See *doping*.

anaerobic describes the performance of work without the presence of oxygen, for example sprinting, throwing, weightlifting and rebounding in various games. The energy for such activity is provided via *anaerobic glycolysis*, but the ability to resynthesise *ATP* is quickly depleted, so this form of activity can only be sustained for short periods of time, largely due to the build up of *lactic acid*.

anaerobic capacity test measures the ability of the body to undertake exercise that is of short duration but high in intensity. It assesses the body's ability to break down glycogen to produce energy in the absence of oxygen. There are several procedures for measuring the anaerobic capacity of an individual, the most common being the *Wingate cycle test*.

Anaerobic capacity is very important in many sporting activities that require quick, powerful movements such as the 100-metre sprint or throwing events. By testing, a coach can determine whether athletes should alter their training in order to improve their anaerobic performance.

anaerobic glycolysis: see *glycolysis*

anaerobic threshold: see *onset of blood lactate accumulation (OBLA)*

analysis of activities: the analysis of a sporting activity by breaking it down into its component parts. This can be done using a hierarchy of classifications, one of which is outlined below:

- Structural – refers to the nature of the activity such as the scoring system, the *rules, role* of officials and punishments for fouls.

- Strategic – refers to the planning and decision-making aspects, with strategies devised according to the nature of the activity. For example a trampolinist prepares a sequence of movements according to the tariff of the moves and pays attention to artistic interpretation. Strategies in a game situation can often be planned in advance, such as set plays, but they will also have to be adapted according to environmental factors, such as the opposition on the day.

- Technical aspects – refer to the *skill* needed to carry out the activity effectively, and in *gymnastic* activities the athlete will attempt to produce the 'perfect' movement. (See *open skills* and *closed skills*.)

- Physical – refers to the body conditions required for a successful outcome. These can be defined in terms of strength, mobility, flexibility, *aerobic* and *anaerobic* fitness. Also, the physiques or *somatotypes* best suited to particular positions in a team can be analysed.

- Psychological – refers to the mental conditions needed for a successful outcome. This may involve a measure of *aggression* or *assertive behaviour*; concentration and ability to withstand some pain; strategic understanding and anticipation; ability to play as part of a team or individually.

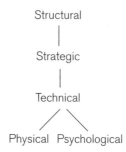

Hierarchical structure of sport analysis

ancient cultures: societies that existed during the period of history associated with slave-based production, for example Greece and Rome. These were advanced civilisations that are considered to have laid the foundations of Western civilisation, shown through their architecture, sculpture, literature, philosophy, science and *sport*. The ancient Greeks strove for physical, as well as intellectual *excellence,* and this was made possible through the use of slaves by the 'leisured class'. Many physical activities resulted from a functional need to maintain fitness for war, appeasement of the gods and the 'man of action' concept. Several *panhellenic* (all-Greek) festivals provided them with the opportunity to compete peacefully in *athletics* for their cities and individual glory. The most famous were the *Olympic Games* from which our modern Olympics are derived.

angling: an ancient practice which developed initially to provide food. By the fifteenth century it was practised in England as a *sport* and was popular with the *Tudors* in the sixteenth century. There was a clear distinction between the commercial and sporting aspects of fishing, but two main forms of recreational fishing emerged:

- coarse fishing – which generally took place in urban, often polluted, areas, and was popular with the industrial *working classes*
- game fishing – which was a more expensive pursuit enjoyed on country estates by the *gentry.*

angular motion: the branch of biomechanics concerned with rotating bodies. As with *linear motion* it is possible to analyse, identify and explain the movement of rotating bodies in terms of displacement, velocity and acceleration. For example, if a trampolinist performed a tucked-back somersault, they might have rotated through 360° in two seconds, hence their resulting angular velocity will be 180° per second. However the standard unit for angular motion is in fact radians per second (rad/s) and not degrees. There are approximately 57.3° in one radian, so the trampolinist's angular velocity would actually be 3.14 rad/s. A coach could analyse the trampolinist's angular velocity and determine whether it is necessary for them to increase or decrease the speed of rotation for effective performance.

animal sports involve animals, whether for racing*, hunting* or *baiting*. Historically, these activities took place at a variety of venues:

- *horse-racing* had its centre in Newmarket
- the *Shrove Tuesday* festival was the first major occasion for outdoor festivities and was popular for animal baiting
- *inns* and public houses often held dog and cock fights
- hunting became an *exclusive* activity as the Game Laws protected the rights of the larger landowners.

Animal sports are based on the notion that animals exist as a human resource and as such they often involve cruelty. This aspect began to be affected by an increase in moral standards and was a reflection of the *'civilising' process*, which was also being applied to other *popular recreations*. *Methodists*, *Puritans* and the more educated classes began the campaign to ban the more cruel sports such as cock throwing and bear baiting. This was due partly to a growing respect for animals but also to the belief that these sports were associated with gambling and alcohol, which encouraged the gathering of unruly sections of the community. The Society for the Prevention of Cruelty to Animals was formed in 1824 and the Cruelty to Animals Act was passed in 1835.

antagonist: a muscle that has an action opposite to that of an *agonist* (prime mover) and helps in the production of a co-ordinated movement. For example, when the bicep contracts (shortens) to cause flexion at the elbow, the tricep lengthens to enable the movement to occur.

anterior: term of direction which refers to the front of the body or body part. For example, the tibialis anterior is a muscle which exists at the front of the tibia, whilst the tibialis posterior muscle is situated at the back of the tibia underneath the calf muscles. When describing the body or movements of the body, using these terms of direction is particularly useful. Also known as ventral. See appendix, page 253.

anticipation relies on previous experience to recognise *stimuli* and *cues* that, allow the performer to process information before an event actually occurs. This often gives the performer the appearance of being highly skilled, with time to spare in their movements, e.g. an experienced batsman in cricket would watch the bowler's hand and arm action in an attempt to ascertain the type of delivery he or she could expect, thus adjusting the shot accordingly, whereas a novice batsman would watch the ball and decide what shot to play after the ball had pitched, thus having less time to react and adjust the shot if appropriate.

Anticipation can also negatively affect performance and increase *reaction time* if the initial judgement is incorrect. There are several components of anticipation:

- receptor anticipation – relies on the information gathered from the external environment, e.g. the batsman watching the actions of the bowler
- perceptual anticipation – relies on stored information in the memory, e.g. the batsman knowing what the bowler is capable of delivering
- effector anticipation – relies on knowing the feel of the movement to be performed, e.g. the timing of the shot depends on the type of delivery received.

See also spatial anticipation and temporal anticipation.

anticipatory rise: the pre-exercise response of the heart, resulting in an elevated resting heart rate. This occurs due to an increase in activity of the *sympathetic nervous system*, releasing the neurotransmitter substance *noradrenaline* and *adrenaline* from the adrenal glands.

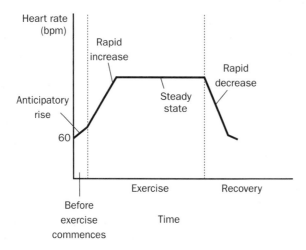

Low intensity (sub-maximal) exercise, showing the anticipatory rise

anxiety: negative emotional feelings caused by an increase in *arousal* levels when a performer is faced with a situation in which they feel threatened or fear failure. Individuals possess both *state anxiety* and *trait anxiety*. The former includes reactions that can be classed as *cognitive anxiety*, i.e. nervousness and poor concentration levels linked to the task, and *somatic anxiety*, i.e. body responses, such as sweating, nausea, increased breathing and pulse rate. The latter is due to enduring traits that dictate how the performer will react to certain situations. Anxiety can be measured using a variety of methods including observation, self-report questionnaires and biofeedback.

aorta: the major blood vessel that conducts oxygenated blood away from the heart and around the body.

apartheid can be defined as 'apartness' and refers to the system of racial segregation which operated in *South Africa* until the 1990s. In 1956 the South African Government decided to make sport a formal part of its apartheid policy which excluded non-whites from many areas, for example housing and health care. A world ban on South African sport was declared in 1964, but South Africa went to great lengths to attract world-class competition, for example in 1969 the English Rugby Union entertained a *Springbok* touring team but suffered widespread public demonstrations against its decision. The cricket and particularly rugby union administrations held out the longest in their support of South Africa.

appendicular skeleton: the part of the skeleton composed of the bones of the limbs, together with the hip and shoulder girdles that join onto the *axial skeleton*.

aquatics: see *swimming, rowing*

archery claims the oldest ancestry of any sport actively pursued today. It was originally practised for *hunting* purposes, later became important as military training and finally became a form of *recreation* . From the reigns of Henry I to Elizabeth I archery practice was compulsory for men in order to defend the realm. Regular practice was held in the church grounds and at the butts. During the *Victorian era* archery became an activity for the leisured classes and many *clubs* were established. It was considered a suitable recreation for women due to the lack of strenuous exercise involved, and the clubs' strict dress code could be adhered to. In 1861 the Grand National Archery Society was established as an official *governing body* for archery in the nineteenth century.

Argentina is South America's second largest country in the area. It covers nearly 2.8 million square kilometres or 29% of the area of Europe. There are four main physical areas; the Andes, the north, the pampas and Patagonia. The climate ranges from subtropical in the northeast to temperate in the central region to arid and semi-arid and cold in the south and along the mountains. There is a mix of ancestry and languages but the Argentines have a great sense of *nationalism*.

Having broken from colonial rule Argentina is an *emergent culture* with the idea of nationhood being consolidated through the arts, politics and sport. *Football* with its mass appeal and without the class distinctions of other sports could help unify all social groups. This is important in multi-ethnic nations. The opportunities for sporting activities are numerous: rafting, gliding, trekking, fishing, skiing, safaris and so on. Football is the national sport having been introduced by the English in the nineteenth century.

The country was under Fascist rule until Juan Peron [1946–1955] created a middle way between *capitalism* and *communism* calling it National Socialism. The future may be determined by the military regimes either in power or threatening.

aristocracy: Traditionally established as the highest *social class* whose power over society stemmed from its control of land and agricultural production. Its power was at its height in the feudal system, but became threatened by the new social group emerging as a result of the *Industrial Revolution*, namely the *middle classes*. The aristocracy or *gentry* were a wealthy, leisured class who participated in many *recreation* pursuits, such as *hunting* and *fencing*. They also acted as a *patron* to lower class individuals and many still retain this privileged status towards certain organisations.

Arnold, Thomas: the headmaster of Rugby School from 1828 until 1842, where he directed a crusade against sinful behaviour by the boys, for example bullying, lying, cheating and running wild amongst the local community. He directed his efforts through chapel sermons and close supervision of the boys' *leisure* time. He intended that the boys remain in the school grounds to reduce the incidence of poaching and trespassing, which gave the public schools a bad name in the early part of the nineteenth century. Arnold is known for his contribution to *muscular Christianity* but he valued games only for what they could contribute towards the *social control* of the boys rather than for their intrinsic benefits. Games could be catered for within the school grounds and *rules* encouraged discipline and respect.

arousal: the energised state of readiness of an individual to perform a task, motivating them to direct their behaviour in a particular manner. It can affect the performer positively or negatively, both physiologically and psychologically, depending on the individual's perception of the situation, but can be controlled to produce an effective performance. The level of arousal is controlled by the *reticular activating system,* which interprets the level of stimulation entering the body and initiates an appropriate response. The primary aim of the performer is to maintain their arousal at an optimal level suitable for the activity undertaken so that concentration and decision-making are not impaired. Arousal can be measured using a variety of methods including observation, self-report questionnaires and biofeedback. See also *inverted U theory* and *catastrophe theory*.

arterioles: small blood vessels that conduct blood from the *arteries* into the *capillary* network. They have a small diameter, which is controlled by large numbers of smooth muscle fibres. Arteries combine with pre-capillary sphincters allowing them to *vasoconstrict* and *vasodilate*, regulating the flow of blood into the capillary bed. During exercise, some arterioles constrict to divert the blood away from non-vital areas, such as the gut and kidneys, and shunt more to the working muscles, which therefore provides them with the necessary oxygen for energy production.

arterio-venous oxygen difference: the difference in oxygen content of the blood in the *arteries* and the *veins*. It is a measure of the oxygen consumed by the muscles. When at rest approximately 25 per cent of oxygen is utilised, but this rises to up to 85 per cent during periods of intense exercise. Also known as a-vO$_2$diff.

artery: high-pressure blood vessel that carries oxygen-rich blood from the heart to the muscles and other tissues. Arteries have elastic properties helping to 'cushion out 'the pulsating flow of blood from the heart. The largest artery is the *aorta*. Arteries sub-divide into *arterioles* which reduce in size the further they are from the heart. The only artery that carries blood which is low in oxygen is the *pulmonary artery*. Where an artery lies close to a bone, it is possible to measure the pulse rate, such as the radial, femoral and carotid sites. Arteries are essential in regulating *blood pressure*.

articular (hyaline) cartilage: see *cartilage*

Asian Games: an area championship of the International Amateur Athletic Federation contested by males and females from all Asian countries affiliated to the IAAF. The Games were established in New Delhi, India in 1951, but have been plagued by political controversy. Pakistan initially refused to enter due to the location and China because of the participation by Formosa. In 1962 Formosa and Israel were excluded and there was an Arab boycott of the 1966 Games in Bangkok due to the inclusion of Israel. The principal communist countries of Asia, including Cambodia, China, Indonesia, North Korea and North Vietnam, created the Games of the New Emerging Forces – GANEFO – in 1963.

The Asian Games became quadrennial from 1954, with a full Olympic programme of track and field events being held, however the general performance standards have been poor, with Japan dominating the Games.

assertive behaviour is viewed as an acceptable form of *aggression*. The actions of the performer are within the laws of the game, with no intention to harm another player, and they are goal directed. This form of behaviour is encouraged, but there is a fine line between appropriate actions that are assertive and those that become aggressive. In a sporting context, this is decided by the officials. For example, when does a sliding tackle in a football match become dangerous or when does verbal 'sledging' become unacceptable? Assertive behaviour can also be known as 'channelled aggression' or instrumental aggression.

assessment: a measure of the quality or worth of something, and also how achievement is to be evaluated. Several types of assessment are used in *physical education* such as longitudinal student profiles that contain purely *quantitative* data (e.g. *fitness tests*), and generalised teacher comments which use a mixture of *subjective* and *objective* assessments. Objective assessment involves figures such as distance thrown in the javelin, whilst subjective assessment involves to some extent personal opinions of judges, as in ice skating, though objective criteria are still applied. In physical education children need to show:

- what they know

- what they can do

- what they understand.

Examinations such as GCSE and A Level are becoming an ever-more popular way in which children choose to be assessed.

Advantages of testing	Disadvantages of testing
Gives children a clear aim, a focus for their efforts	Physical education should be about enjoyment and releasing of pressure
Motivates children to learn	Time can be wasted on testing and not teaching
Creates more teacher accountability	Children and teachers can become demotivated if testing is inappropriate or if the testing is making unfair comparisons
Recognises good teacher practice such as good organisation	
Gives status to the subject and allows comparison with other subjects	Physical activity levels can be restricted due to extra studying

assimilation: the integration of immigrant communities within the prevalent culture by adopting its values and traditions. This has tended to be the case in Britain where *ethnic groups* traditionally have been expected to adhere to the British way of life.

association football: a type of football that originated from its mob form which developed at nineteenth-century public schools, and resulted in the handling and dribbling variations of the game. The Football Association was formed in 1863 when the rules that allowed handling the ball were changed. Those who opposed this change were to form the Rugby Union in 1871.

The London football clubs dominated association football initially, but Sheffield in the north also grew in strength and formed its own association that was the forerunner of the county football associations. In 1877 these brought their own rules into line with those of the football association, and the Challenge Cup, established in 1871, was to increase the popularity of association football, leading many clubs to seek membership of the Association. Initially the Cup games were played at the Oval, attracting a crowd of 45,000 in 1893 but the venue was changed to Wembley in 1895. The major changes to the game were the:

- growing dominance of the industrial *working classes* as they received more free time

- the game became a *professional sport*.

This latter point was recognised with the formation of the Football League in 1888 that allied regular competitive fixtures with professionalism. The idea of two divisions came about when the second division emerged in the 1892–3 season and the third in 1920–1.

associationist theories imply that *learning* is based on the performer developing a relationship between a *stimulus* and a response (the *stimulus–response bond*). The *environment* can be manipulated, often by the coach, to produce a certain action or behaviour which is strengthened through regular practice, e.g. a batsman may be trained to recognise a ball bowled in a certain manner (stimulus) and play the correct shot (response). Also known as stimulus–response theories or conditioning theories.

Conditioning theories are generally divided into two categories, *classical conditioning* and *operant conditioning*. See also *drive reduction theory*.

associative phase of learning: involves the performer physically implementing the motor programme learned during the *cognitive phase of learning*. *Fitts and Posner's stages of learning theory* suggests this is the intermediate phase. The skill learned is refined and gross errors eliminated through repeated practice, developing an effective and consistent technique. As *kinaesthetic* awareness of the movement develops, the performer is able to provide internal *feedback* to supplement any external information. The timescale before progressing to the *autonomous stage of learning* may vary depending on the level of ability, complexity of the task, type of practice and quality of feedback.

atherosclerosis: a progressive disease characterised by the laying down of fatty deposits (atheroma) in the *arteries*. It is a condition associated with *cardiovascular disease* and *obesity*.

athletic activities: these include the categories of races, field athletics and weightlifting, and all test the explosive or sustained power of the athlete. The winner of the 100 metres is the person who reaches the tape first. All race events, whatever the form of locomotion, are decided in this way: the high jumper clears the bar, the thrower achieves the furthest distance. This relies on *quantitative* and *objective* methods of assessment where scientific criteria are applied. Advances in the level of technology used have allowed extremely fine units of measurement to be applied. In order to be fair the athletes adhere to strict *rules* and may take it in turns.

athletic motivation inventory (AMI) was a questionnaire developed by Ogilvie and Tutko (1966) to measure *personality* traits and categorise athletes. The questionnaire was considered to be of limited use, as it was not validated and proved to be unreliable.

athleticism: physical endeavour with moral integrity. It became a cult in the latter part of the nineteenth century, with its foundations in the English *public schools*. These schools took seriously their *role* of producing gentlemen with qualities of honour, integrity, courage and leadership. Athleticism could only be developed by instilling a strong moral code and was considered to enhance:

- physical qualities, such as the value and enjoyment of a healthy lifestyle, the correction of the temptation to over-study and the ability to learn to cope with winning and losing in a competitive society

- moral qualities, such as working as part of a team, conforming and respecting authority

- spiritual links of godliness with manliness, which has been called *'muscular Christianity'*

Athleticism was promoted through competitive events, beginning with school house matches and eventually inter-school fixtures. Though masters initially had little to do with athletic activities they eventually became involved as *blues* and coaches.

Though developed in a small number of schools in England, the expansion of athleticism was rapid through the activities of the *old boys/girls*, the *codification* in the universities and subsequent club developments. Industrialists, clerics and teachers spread it across the UK whilst diplomats and army officers spread it across the *British Empire.* The passion for athletic activities gradually overrode its moral basis and athletic activity became valued as an end in itself dominating the *elite* education system to the detriment (many believe) of academic standards. Prestige through winning was so important that schools, which purported the *amateur* ideal, employed professional coaches!

athletics: sporting events that developed historically from a functional need, such as throwing events from *hunting* and war, from rural pursuits, e.g. hurdling and pole vaulting from clearing obstacles such as ditches. Race walking or *pedestrianism* developed in *Stuart* and Georgian times when young men were sent ahead of the *gentry* carriage to warn the innkeeper of their imminent arrival. Wagers were placed and the gentry acted as *patrons.*

Athletics was originally *professional* and became a commercial activity, but it was tainted with corruption and bribery was rife to 'fix' races. This was to be its downfall, and it was later that the *amateur* ethos from the *public schools* took over with administrative organisations such as the Amateur Athletic Association. Athletics in the UK denotes activities such as running, jumping and throwing events. In the *USA* these activities are referred to as track and field and the term 'athletics' refers to other physical sporting activities.

atom: an atom is built from negatively charged electrons, positively charged protons, and neutrons, which have no charge. The atomic number of an atom is the number of protons it possesses, for example, hydrogen, with one proton has the atomic number 1.

atria: the top two chambers of the heart which receive blood returning from the organs of the body. The right atrium receives blood returning from the muscles and other organs of the body via the venae cavae, whilst the left atrium receives blood rich in oxygen returning from the lungs via the pulmonary vein.

ATP: see *adenosine triphosphate*

ATP–PC energy system: see *alactic energy system*

atrioventricular node (AV node): mass of conducting cells located in the right atrial wall, forming part of the conducting system of the heart. The AV node acts as a distributor and passes the *action potential* to the atrioventricular bundle (bundle of His), which is a mass of conducting fibres that together with the branching Purkinje fibres spread the excitation throughout the ventricles. There is a delay of about 0.1 seconds from the time when the AV node receives stimulation to when it distributes the action potential throughout the ventricles. This is crucial to allow completion of atrial contraction and ensures that all the blood enters the ventricles before ventricular contraction. An electrocardiogram trace shows the relationship between electrical activity of the heart and the different stages of the cardiac cycle. See diagram on page 26.

attainment targets are set out in the *National Curriculum* for many subjects, including *physical education*. Attainment targets require children to 'demonstrate the knowledge, skills and understanding involved in areas of activity encompassing *athletic activities,* dance, *games, gymnastic activities,* outdoor and *adventurous activities* and *swimming.*

There are eight levels showing a gradation of difficulty with 'exceptional performance' criteria for the most gifted.

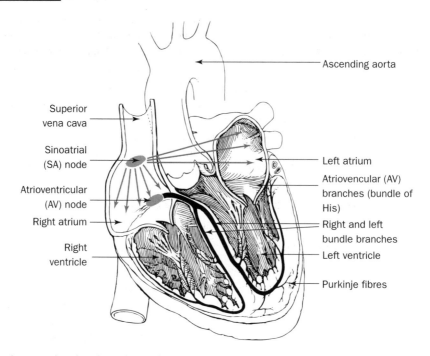

The heart – showing the atrioventricular node

attention: the ability to focus on cues appearing in the *display* and identify those which are relevant. Attention capabilities may vary depending on the age, experience and *arousal* level of the individual and on the nature of the task. Various forms of the concept of attention have been proposed, including *selective attention*, and *attentional* or *perceptual narrowing* linked to arousal. Capacity theories suggest that two or more tasks can be completed simultaneously, provided the total attentional capacity is not exceeded, with each task having a different attention requirement. For example an experienced performer may be able to control the ball, look for opponents and team mates and assess numerous options at the same time, whereas a novice may devote much of their attentional capacity to control and not be able to focus on the other factors. Nideffer suggested individuals are either 'effective' or 'ineffective attenders'. The former are able to process information externally, e.g. position of players, and internally, e.g. analytical thoughts, allowing them to switch their focus of attention quickly without missing important cues. The latter experience difficulty concentrating, become confused and miss the relevant cues. As a result certain sports or positions may be better suited to different individuals. For example, an effective attender may perform better at team sports compared with an ineffective attender, who may perform more consistently at individual activities or in a position requiring limited decision-making.

attentional or perceptual narrowing links arousal levels directly to the individual's ability to focus on relevant *cues* and *stimuli* (see *cue-utilisation theory*). If the performer reaches their optimal arousal level, they will identify the appropriate cues, but over-arousal will hinder the process. As perceptual narrowing continues, vital cues will be missed, (see *attentional wastage*), leading to a decrease in performance. For example, a basketball player may not detect a team mate in an open shooting position or may fail to see a defender closing down their space as they move in to shoot.

attentional wastage occurs when the performer's concentration is misdirected to cues that are irrelevant, causing a decrease in performance. For example, during a game of netball, the player may listen to shouts from the crowd rather than focus on the position of players on court. This may be eliminated by developing the performer's *selective attention*.

attitude: a relatively stable belief or view on a specific *attitude object*. A person's attitudes are developed through past experiences, *significant others*, the media or any other interaction with the social environment. Their attitude may be positive, negative or neutral. For example a person may swim regularly and enjoy the benefits, creating a positive attitude; a friend may have fallen into water without being able to swim, creating fear and a negative attitude; someone who has neither had the opportunity to swim nor had a bad experience may have a neutral attitude.

The *triadic model* proposes that attitudes have three components:

*   cognitive – beliefs and thoughts, e.g. benefits of swimming
*   affective – emotions and feelings, e.g. enjoyment of swimming
*   behavioural – actions, e.g. swimming regularly.

However, an individual's attitude and behaviour may not always be predictable, e.g. they may think swimming is beneficial and fun but do not always make the time to participate. If this is the case, or a negative attitude needs to be altered by eradicating *stereotyping* and *prejudices*, the most commonly used methods are *persuasive communication* and *cognitive dissonance*.

See also *attitude tests*.

attitude object: the focus of an individual's *attitude*, which may be an object, an event, an activity, a person or an idea. Such predispositions can be general or specific, e.g. a person may have a positive attitude towards sport, but a negative attitude towards swimming.

attitude tests: methods used to assess the opinions and feelings of an individual, which are used to describe their attitude. A variety of methods can be used, the most common of which are:

*   observation of body language and behaviour
*   physiological tests e.g. heart rate and *galvanic skin response*
*   *questionnaires* or interviews e.g. *Likert, Thurston* and *Osgood scales.*

Testing for attitude can be difficult, due to the problems of *reliability* and *validity* of procedures. It may also prove difficult for an individual to express their attitude when faced with questions in a written form.

attribution: the perceived reasons for the success or failure of an event or pattern of behaviour. A team may infer they lost because of a lucky goal by the opposing team or a poor refereeing decision. The correct use of attributions are vital to ensure performers' motivation levels are maintained (see *attribution theory*). (See figure on page 28.)

attribution retraining involves the coach or teacher developing and changing an individual's perception of failure, allowing them to deal with it effectively and improve future performances, avoiding *learned helplessness*. For example, a talented swimmer may not believe they have the ability to succeed, but if taught a slight variation in their technique will produce considerable improvement and they will persevere with the task. *Goal setting* is vital in this process, especially the use of *outcome* or task goals rather than *performance goals*.

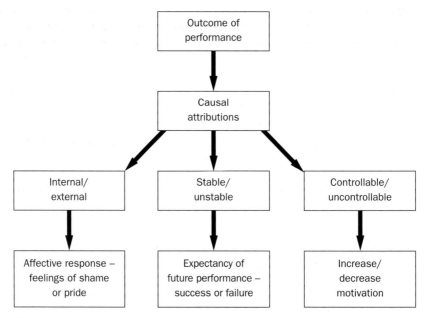

attribution

attribution theory suggests that the reasons perceived by an individual or team for the outcome of their actions can affect their levels of motivation in future performances. Attributions help to explain success and failure, ensuring motivation levels remain high. Weiner proposed four categories of attribution: ability, effort, task difficulty and luck, which are divided into two dimensions, as shown below:

	Locus of causality:	
	INTERNAL	**EXTERNAL**
Locus of stability:		
STABLE	Ability	Task difficulty
UNSTABLE	Effort	Luck

Roberts and Pascuzzi suggested a more sport-specific adaptation of the model:

	Locus of causality:	
	INTERNAL	**EXTERNAL**
Locus of stability:		
STABLE	Ability	Coaching
UNSTABLE	Effort	Luck
	Psychological factors	Task difficulty
	Practice	Team work
		Officials

Generally, to gain feelings of satisfaction, success is attributed to internal factors (see *self-serving bias*) and failure to external factors. To maintain motivation using the 'locus of stability', success is based on stable factors and failure on unstable factors.

audience: those people watching, who can have a positive (*social facilitation*) or negative (*social inhibition*) effect on performance. The presence of others tends to increase *arousal*, with the dominant response being the result (see *drive theory*), e.g. during a hockey match a novice will tend to make more mistakes, while the experienced player will usually display their skills effectively. Audiences cause a distraction for the performer, creating *evaluation apprehension*, which is further increased if it includes *significant others*. This can also affect experts, creating feelings of fear of failure, worry, embarrassment, etc., possibly explaining one reason why they do not always perform to their potential.

auditory system (audition): the *sensory system* concerned with gaining information from outside the body through hearing; a form of *exteroceptor*. It allows the performer to process *stimuli* from the *environment* without actually seeing them, e.g. the sound of the gun to start a race, the call from a team mate or the noise of the racket string when playing a shot.

augmented feedback: see *feedback*

Aussie Rules football dates back to 1858 when two men, Harrison and Wills, decided to design a purely Australian game. The game shows influences from *cricket* (oval pitch), Gaelic football (played by Irish troops) and the English game of *rugby football*. It is a physical-contact, *invasion-game*. The size of the pitch is not set but has minimum and maximum dimensions, and is possibly one reason why the sport has not been easy to transfer to other countries.

Aussie Sport: a national sporting initiative in *Australia,* committed to the development of young people through sport. The *Australian Sports Commission* (ASC) and the state depart-ments of sport and education work closely together in order to foster positive community relationships and to ensure a co-ordinated approach to junior sport in their area. Aussie Sport is about:

- supporting quality teaching and *coaching*
- promoting and developing quality sport for young people
- making sport more accessible, easier to play and enjoyable
- fostering greater community involvement in junior sport.

Various programmes are tailored to suit different needs, including:

- Sportstart – aimed at working with young children through informal *play* activities and playshop courses to help parents understand their children's play habits.
- Sportit – designed for primary school children to learn basic motor *skills* used in major sports. The Modified Sport Programme is a way of reducing adult sport programmes. An example is Netta Netball.
- Sport – Everyone's Game – aims to reach all groups within society and particularly those with lower active participation ratios. Examples include The Active Girl's Campaign and Willing and Able.

Aussie Sport also runs leadership programmes for secondary school children which can be compared with the British *Central Council of Physical Recreation (The British Sports Trust)* Sports Leader Awards.

Australia is made up of six states, namely Victoria, New South Wales, Queensland, Tasmania, South Australia and Western Australia, and two territories, Northern Territory and the Australian Capital Territory. It is a large country with a relatively small population concentrated in urban areas, particularly in the coastal cities. There is a tropical climate in the north and a temperate climate in the south. The Pacific coasts receive the most rainfall whilst the interior is very dry. The problems of geography and demography make travel expensive and often limit competition opportunities in sport, so major international games are very significant to Australians.

The states retain their own parliament and governor, whilst legislative power is held by the *Federal* parliament based in Canberra, and political power rests with the prime minister who heads the government. *Aborigines* were the indigenous population but European settlers arrived in 1788 and Australia's links with Britain began. It is still a member of the Commonwealth of Nations. It became a popular country for immigration of the World War II resulting in a diverse multicultural society.

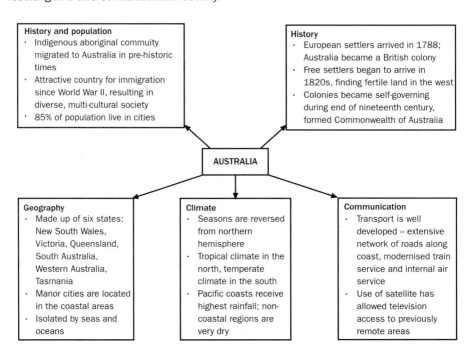

Australian Athlete Scholarship scheme: similar to *Sports Aid* in the United Kingdom, but it receives federal money and has a larger budget. The primary aim is to give direct financial aid to *elite* athletes who will have been nominated by their national sporting bodies, which are similar to *governing bodies* in Britain.

Australian Council for Health, Physical Education and Recreation (ACPHER) deals with issues such as the amount of time devoted to *physical education* in schools and the training of teachers.

Australian Institute of Sport (AIS): based in Canberra, and established in 1980. It cost $100 million to construct and possesses a sophisticated sports science and *sports medicine* support service which, with the development of *coaching*, form its basic functions. The Federal government pays approximately 95 per cent of the money and athletes receive *scholarships* to cover expenses. Other community groups, similar to the British Centres of

Excellence, can also use the facilities but they are mainly for the *elite* who reserve most of the bookings and who can afford the high fees. Out-reach centres exist in major cities as a form of *decentralisation,* in recognition of the size of the country, and national academies have developed as a consequence in Canberra, Brisbane, Adelaide, Melbourne and Sydney, each specialising in particular sports.

Australian Sports Commission (ASC): based in Canberra, the ASC has two main functions:

- to increase sport participation by Australians through programmes such as *Aussie Sport*
- to increase *excellence.*

Australian Sports System: located within the Department of the Environment, Sport and the Territories (DEST) under the programme of Sport and Recreation. The overall objective of the programme as stated by DEST is 'to contribute to the quality of life of all Australians by promoting and facilitating opportunities for participation in *sport* and *recreation* activities, encouraging sporting *excellence*, reducing harm associated with the use of *doping* in sport, and examining the economic and social impact of the sport and recreation industry'.

This is achieved through:

- funding at the *elite* level where financial support is provided by the government
- The *Australian Institute of Sport* and the *Australian Sports Commission* supply the national sports organisations with funding and services
- state organisations fulfil a similar role at state level.

Local government is involved in supporting regional and local sports organisations by providing services and facilities in which to participate.

autocratic or authoritarian leader: this type of leader tells the group what actions to take, with very little or no input from the members of the group in terms of decision-making. They are generally not concerned with inter-personal relationships within the group and are task orientated. Research by Lewin (1935) suggested a group under this form of leadership worked hard when the leader was present, but became aggressive and independent when left alone. This is useful when the task needs to be completed quickly, is complex or is dangerous. See also *democratic leader* and *laissez-faire leader.*

autogenic training involves the performer imagining they are in familiar surroundings where they feel comfortable and able to relax. For example, an athlete may imagine they are lying on a beach in the sun, which initiates feelings of warmth, tranquillity and comfort. This technique is similar to that of *progressive relaxation* and *self-directed relaxation.*

autonomic (or involuntary) nervous system: part of the nervous system controlling parts of the body not under conscious control, such as cardiovascular functioning (including heart rate and blood pressure) and respiration rate. The autonomic nervous system has two divisions, the *parasympathetic nervous system* and the *sympathetic nervous system*. The former controls bodily functions during normal resting conditions, whilst the latter controls the individual's reaction to situations of stress or emergency, or indeed during exercise. The effect of the sympathetic system upon the heart is to increase heart rate whilst the parasympathetic system returns the heart rate to its normal resting level.

autonomous stage of learning: reached when the performer demonstrates the ability to complete skilled actions with increased efficiency, accuracy and speed involving little conscious control. *Fitts and Posner's stages of learning theory* suggests this is the final stage of learning. The information processing time is reduced and distractions have less effect on performance. The performer has the ability to analyse their own actions, allowing external feedback to be used to develop finer points of technique, strategies and tactics. In order to maintain their performance at this phase, practice must continue. (See *associative phase of learning*.)

autonomy: the freedom of individuals and organisations to act in certain circumstances. Many sports organisations are deemed to be autonomous, that is, they can act independently of the government in power. An example of this would be the Sports Council (now *Sport England*) which was given a Royal Charter in 1972, leaving it free from political control.

The states in *Australia* and the *USA* also have a degree of autonomy within the wider federal system. For example, they could develop different education systems and may have different laws. 'States righters' are groups who are constantly defending the rights of the states.

a-vO$_2$ diff: see *arterio-venous oxygen difference*

axial skeleton: structure that provides the main area of support for the body and includes the cranium, vertebral column and the rib cage. It provides sites of attachment for the limbs of the *appendicular skeleton*.

What other subjects are you studying?

A–Zs cover 18 different subjects. See the inside back cover for a list of all the titles in the series and how to order.

Baccalaureat: school certificate for higher education entrance in *France* which includes a compulsory *physical education* section. The especially gifted child can also take an optional sporting activity to add to their overall mark. The aim is to broaden children's educational experiences and as such is being recognised as good practice by education authorities in the United Kingdom where there are numerous suggestions for transplanting the idea to this country. A disadvantage, however, is that the physical education lesson in France can be narrow and inflexible, as it is geared towards pupils passing the exam.

baggataway is the name for the earliest game of *lacrosse*, invented by the Native American Indians. The game had a religious significance and was also played as a means of training tribal warriors. Matches lasted for two or three days, with the goals marked by trees, some 460 metres apart.

baiting involved a bull or bear being tied up and terriers set at it. The aim was that the dogs hang on to the bull or bear without being dislodged; the dogs would fail if they were tossed away. The activity was first recorded in the reign of Henry II and wagering took place over the individual dogs. The need for powerful jaws was important and this is how bulldogs got their name. Bear gardens were popular in the sixteenth century under the *Tudors* and there was one located behind the Globe Theatre. This sport was banned in 1835 with the Prevention of Cruelty to Animals Act.

balance: the maintenance of the centre of mass over the base of support. This can occur when the body is static such as in a handstand or whilst the body is moving such as in the performance of a cartwheel.

ball and socket joint: see *synovial joint*

barbarian schools: nine established gentry *public schools* namely Eton, Rugby, Winchester, Shrewsbury, St Paul's, Merchant Taylor, Harrow, Charterhouse and Westminster. They maintained the *gentry* tradition and remained exclusive. The emergence of the *middle classes* saw the development of the *proprietary colleges*, which were direct copies of the gentry schools.

Baron Pierre de Coubertin: Frenchman who revived the ancient *Olympic Games* in 1896. This resulted from him visiting England in the nineteenth century and being impressed with the English *public school* notion of *athleticism*. De Coubertin wished to draw countries together in healthy competition, free from political issues, with the aim of keeping the importance of winning in perspective. He also viewed it as a way of reviving French *nationalism*. He elected the first members of the *International Olympic Committee* hoping they would continue the spirit of the Games he had created.

baroreceptors: nerve cells capable of responding to changes in *blood pressure*, which are found in the walls of the atria of the heart, venae cavae and aortic arch. When stimulated the baroreceptors will reduce blood pressure through *vasodilation* of blood vessels. This works in conjunction with the *parasympathetic nervous system* to reduce heart rate and therefore blood flow following exercise.

Barr sex tests: this test requires a sample of cells to be scraped from the inside of a woman's cheek to determine the presence of 'Barr Bodies' (sex chromatin). If the count drops below a minimum percentage, the athlete is disqualified. Some believe this to be a form of *discrimination* against women in the world of sport, as men do not have to undergo a similar test.

baseball: an *innings game*, which is thought to have evolved from the game of rounders. It began as a *working class* sport and developed in inner cities in the *USA*, and as such it has similar roots to football in England. The game shares the characteristics of all the dominant *American sports*. The rules were written around 1845 and the New York Knickerbockers are generally considered to be the first organised team. It developed from a polite amateur game into a commercialised pastime, controlled by promoters, played by professionals in urban areas where there was a need for a mass of people to be entertained. Major and minor leagues developed as did *Little League* and Babe Ruth Leagues for youngsters.

basketball: a fluid, individualistic type of *invasion game*, created by James Naismith in 1891, through his work with the American *Young Men's Christian Association* (YMCA). The aim was to channel young men's energies and develop their moral character through a game based on skill rather than strength in order to give an equal opportunity to each player. The YMCA and US servicemen spread the game across the world. The International Amateur Basketball Federation was established in 1932 and it became an Olympic sport in 1936. The professional National Basketball Association in America achieved major league status in 1949. It is now accepted as one of the most popular spectator sports in the world and has become a symbol of black identity and black social power.

Basque province: a region in *France* around the Western Pyrenees. Its *rural sports* include pelota, bull fighting and boules. It has survived rapid cultural changes, like other *ethnic* sports, and possesses a distinct language and way of life which has been allowed to co-exist within the wider culture. This is a form of *accommodation.*

bathing machines were used at the seaside for people to change their clothing. Either a man or a horse then pulled them to the water's edge for people to modestly slip into the sea. They made their first appearance in Scarborough in 1753 reflecting the growing popularity of sea bathing and were replaced by bathing tents or huts at the turn of the twentieth century.

behaviourist theories of learning: see *associationist theories*

Bem sex role inventory: measures the 'masculine' and 'feminine' traits of our *personality* which are not linked simply to our biological sex. The original test consisted of 60 characteristics, completed on a 1–7 rating scale, of which 20 are typically feminine (e.g. loyal, gentle), 20 typically male (seek challenge, aggressive) and 20 neutral. These have been reduced to 30 items. The results indicate if we are masculine (low feminine; high masculine scores), feminine (high feminine; low masculine scores), androgynous (high feminine; high masculine scores) or undifferentiated (low feminine; low masculine scores). Research suggested those who succeed in sport have been found to possess higher masculine or androgynous traits.

Bergman Osterberg was appointed Lady Superintendent of *Physical Education* in 1881 for the London School Board. She brought with her from Sweden a belief in *Swedish gymnastics* with its focus on health and posture allied with a diet of English *games* such as *hockey, cricket* and *lacrosse.* She established the first teacher training college in 1885 at Broadhurst Gardens, later moving to Dartford Heath in 1895.

Bernouilli effect: concept which uses fluid dynamics (air and water) to explain why projectiles and aeroplanes can remain in flight. An aerofoil, for example the wing of an aeroplane, is shaped so that air flowing over the top of it must travel further than that flowing underneath, and this air must therefore increase in velocity in order to reach the back of the wing at the same time as the air on the bottom. As velocity increases, pressure decreases. A pressure differential exists between the upper and lower surfaces and a lift force results from high to low pressure which keeps the plane in flight. This is the Bernouilli effect.

The Bernouilli effect also explains how projectiles such as the javelin and discus remain in flight. By changing the shape of a projectile the size of the lift force can be altered.

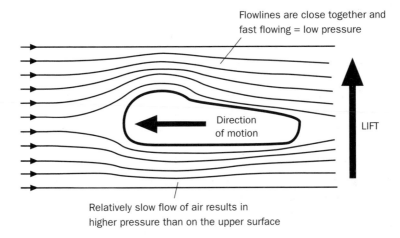

Flowlines are close together and fast flowing = low pressure

Direction of motion

LIFT

Relatively slow flow of air results in higher pressure than on the upper surface

Best Value: central government's agenda for modernising *local authorities* focuses on the need to make changes to the ways local authorities:

- communicate with local people
- structure and organise themselves
- seek and deliver services.

Best Value is the way local government measures, manages and improves performance. Best Value can apply to a service or a department.

Sport is one of these services. Best Value impacts on *Sport England's* work as local authorities constitute one of its most important partnerships. The main aim of Best Value is to improve the cost and quality of local services.

The document 'The Value of Sport' responds to the challenge and demonstrates that sport can make a difference to people's lives and to communities in which they live. It emphasises that for every pound spent on sport there are multiple returns in improved health, reduced crime, neighbourhood regeneration and improved employment opportunities.

beta blockers: *drugs* such as atenolol and oxprenolol which can be used by sport performers to steady nerves, and are useful for activities requiring fine skills such as shooting. They reduce the heart rate and blood pressure to relax nerves and stop trembling. The side effects are low blood pressure, slow heart rate and tiredness.

beta oxidation: the first step of fatty acid oxidation, whereby fatty acids are broken down to acetic acid before being converted to *acetyl co-A* and entering the *Krebs cycle*. Beta oxidation is used when performing low-intensity aerobic exercise such as jogging or cycling since more energy can be acquired from fat than glycogen and exercise can be performed for a longer period of time. However fatty acid oxidation must occur in conjunction with *glycolysis*.

Big Time programmes: sport programmes for the American collegiate system. Huge incentives can distract athletes from academic work and are characterised by *commercialism*, poor rights for athletes and distorted views of gender and race. These are high profile sports with *scholarships* and entertainment values.

bilateral transfer: see *transfer of learning*

bioelectric impedance: test to measure *body composition*. The performer has an electrical current passed through their body and the resistance is recorded. The higher the reading, the higher the level of body fat, as fat does not conduct the current effectively. This test is particularly important for assessing the percentage of body fat of an athlete.

biofeedback: measurement of the body's muscular reaction to *stress* using objective techniques to help control stress levels. The performer is made aware of the physiological responses occurring and employs suitable techniques to calm themselves. The effectiveness of this can be viewed immediately and accurately. Eventually the performer can recognise the physiological changes taking place without the aid of the machinery and implement the stress management techniques they have learnt during competition. Commonly used methods are:

● galvanic skin response – measures the skin's electrical conductivity when sweating. If tense, more sweat is produced to remove the heat generated by the muscles

● electromyography (EMG) – measures muscle tension via a series of electrodes taped to the skin, emitting a louder sound when tension is high

● skin temperature – thermometers attached to the skin measure the temperature, which is lower during times of stress.

The disadvantages of these methods include the interference with performance of being 'wired-up', increased arousal due to being evaluated, and the difficulty of using them in actual competitive situations.

biomechanics: branch of sport science that uses mathematics and *Newton's laws of motion* to explain movement. Central to the study of biomechanics is a grounding in human anatomy and a sound understanding of Newton's laws and how to apply them to human movement. An understanding of biomechanics is essential for a coach in order to optimise an individual's performance and adjust their technique. For example, a sprinter can improve their starting technique if they understand how to exert forces in the most efficient way.

Bisham Abbey National Sports Centre: see *National Sports Centres*

blocked practice involves the performer completing a set number of practices of one skill before progressing to the next skill. There is minimal interference from other activities to hinder learning, allowing full concentration on the specified skill. For example, a golfer will hit a set number of shots with one club during a practice session before moving onto a new club. Although this method improves performance at the time, it can have limited effect in terms of long-term learning as the golfer may not be able to reproduce the shots on the actual course. As a result the use of random practice may be more effective.

blood doping: the removal and reinfusion of a person's blood to improve the *aerobic* capacity by increasing the numbers of red blood cells, and thus increasing the blood's oxygen carrying capacity. There is a danger of increasing the viscosity of the blood and 'overcrowding' the capillaries, thus blocking them, which can lead to heart failure. See also *doping*.

blood pressure: the force exerted by the blood against the walls of the blood vessels. It is measured using a sphygmomanometer and is usually expressed as:

$$\frac{\text{systolic pressure}}{\text{diastolic pressure}}$$

and recorded as millimetres of mercury (mm Hg). Systolic pressure refers to the pressure experienced when the heart pumps blood out into the *arteries*, and diastolic pressure to the pressure in the arteries when the heart is relaxing and filling with blood. During exercise the blood pressure changes are dependent upon the type and intensity of exercise being performed. During rhythmic, aerobic exercise the blood pressure may not alter significantly, but when periods of high intensity exercise are undertaken, such as weightlifting, the systolic and diastolic pressure rise significantly.

blood sports involve the infliction of pain or death on animals for the purpose of entertainment. They were very popular in Britain up to the end of the nineteenth century and were characterised by:

- physical violence
- gambling
- enjoyment of the infliction of pain
- their popularity in rural and urban areas amongst both the *working class* and the *gentry*.

They were popular for a variety of reasons including:

- the excitement generated, particularly as there was limited other entertainment
- the incentive of winning money was attractive
- they were cheap and accessible
- the general *culture* was violent so the concern for the welfare of animals was not of paramount importance.

Blood sports were banned in 1840 when the new era of evangelical and humanitarian concern resulted in a general civilising of society and *urbanisation* stimulated new concepts of *recreation*.

blue: term used at Oxford and Cambridge universities where sport performers were awarded a 'colour' for representing the team in their annual derby fixture. In the nineteenth century, 'blues' often returned to the public schools as teachers to assist in the coaching of sporting activities. An old Rugbeian, Robert Collis, described the receiving of a 'blue' as being regarded as 'a more desirable achievement than becoming a Member of Parliament. The social position it confers lasts for many years, for to be an 'old blue' is to have an assured status for life'.

BMI: see *body mass index*

Board of Education: the government department set up to deal with the implementation of compulsory *state education* in the nineteenth century, following the Forster Education Act 1870 (see *Education Acts*). The medical division was established in 1908 in order to oversee the physical welfare of children and it was responsible for devising the *Syllabuses of Physical Training* from 1909 to 1933. The schools under their control were known as 'board schools' or 'elementary schools'.

body composition: the chemical composition of the body; typically the relative amounts of fat mass and fat-free mass (which includes non-fat tissues such as bone, muscle and connective tissues). It is usually measured via skin-fold tests or *bioelectric impedance*. The relative amounts of fat and fat-free mass required for different activities differ depending upon the type of activity concerned. For example, activities that require strength and muscular endurance, such as rowing, would benefit from an increased amount of fat-free mass (muscle), whilst endurance athletes would not benefit from increased muscle mass, since this represents a greater load to carry over longer distances.

body mass index (BMI): the body mass (weight in kg) divided by the height of the individual squared:

$$\frac{m}{h^2}$$

It is often used as an indicator of obesity. It is assumed that the higher the BMI, the greater the level of 'adiposity' or fat. Critical values of BMI are 27.8 for males and 27.3 for females, and scores above these figures assume obesity.

Boer War: war that took place in South Africa between 1899 and 1902. The reasons for the failure of the British army were considered to be the lack of fitness, discipline and poor general health of the *working classes* and these factors were blamed for the heavy loss of life. *Swedish gymnastics* was criticised as not being effective enough in improving the fitness of the working classes sufficiently for the hardships of war. Following the Boer War in 1902, Colonel Fox of the War Office initiated the *model course*.

Bohr effect: a lowering of the blood pH level due to increased levels of CO_2 which causes oxygen to be released more readily from *haemoglobin*. This results in the oxygen–haemoglobin dissociation curve shifting to the right (see figure below).

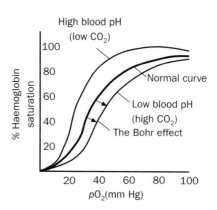

Book of Sports: a declaration by James I to his subjects in 1618 concerning lawful sports. It was aimed at protecting the people's right to *recreation,* which was under threat from the *Puritans* who were intent on prohibiting the recreational pursuits of the commoners on Sundays and other holy days. James I encouraged acceptable recreations following the church service, including dancing, leaping and vaulting. He also encouraged the May games, Whitsun ales and morris dances. Charles I reaffirmed the Book of Sports in 1663.

Bosman case: case brought about by the Belgian footballer, Jean Marc Bosman. The European Court of Justice recognised in this case that there was no reason why professional sports people should not enjoy the benefits of the single market and in particular the free movement of workers. This has resulted in national competitions being open to players throughout Europe and has revitalised major European leagues. The new legislation also abolished transfer fees if a player was out of contract.

bowls: a very popular sport in the sixteenth century, encouraged by growth in the importance of the *inn,* providing recreation for both the local community as well as travellers on the road. Bowling greens followed on from the alleys, and were found suitable for private use in homes that had lawns. Bowling was prohibited in James I's *Book of Sports* in the seventeenth century as it usually took place in alehouses and was accompanied by too much drinking.

boxing: an ancient sport enjoyed in Ancient Egypt, Greece and Rome. *Pugilism* (meaning bare fist) was introduced to the *Olympic Games* in 686BC and the sport was used in Roman times for gladiatorial *combat.*

Boxing was revived in England towards the end of the seventeenth century with the first organised bare-knuckle fight taking place in 1681. There were initially very few rules and even kicking was allowed. However, boxing was one of the first sports to have a code of rules, and London aristocrats, London publicans and patrons arranged early national championships. Two key figures helped shape the sport: James Figg, who opened an Academy of Boxing and Jack Broughton, known as the 'father of boxing', who added respectability to the sport that led to the London Prize Ring Rules being drawn up in 1838. These rules later became known as the 'Marquis of Queensbury Rules'. *Working class* boxers often received *patronage* from the *upper classes* and became folk heroes.

boycott: the refusal of a faction to participate in a sporting event in order to deliver a political message, usually the rejection of a political regime. The Soviet Union boycott of the Los Angeles *Olympic Games* in 1984 had a large impact on the event. Some countries such as the *United States of America* and the old Soviet Union, can refuse to allow their athletes to enter a competition, whereas others, such as the United Kingdom can only advise athletes, as the sporting system is relatively free from political control.

Boy's Brigade: founded in Glasgow in 1883 by William Alexander Smith. The aim was to revive interest in organised religion through the provision of military-style training and uniforms. Sporting activities played an important part in countering the attraction of less socially acceptable forms of behaviour. This was part of a wider movement during the nineteenth century to promote *rational recreation* with *middle class* values to inner city working class youth. Sport in this instance was used as a vehicle of *social control* and Christian recruitment, but was popular amongst the working class youth who had very little alternative recreation provision. Smith believed that 'by associating Christianity with all that was most noble and manly in a boy's sight, we would be going a long way to disabuse his mind of the idea that there is anything effeminate or weak about Christianity'. (See also *Youth Movements*.)

bradycardia literally means 'slow heart'. In exercise physiology, the term is used to denote a resting heart rate of below 60 beats per minute. It occurs largely as a result of long-term endurance training and the accompanying enlargement (*hypertrophy*) of the heart. Essentially a larger heart can pump more blood around the body per beat and therefore the heart does not need to beat as often per minute whilst at rest.

bread and circuses: a theory which suggests that the mass of a population can be kept relatively content through having basic needs and entertainment provided. A cynical viewpoint may be that sporting activities can be used by governments to divert attention from social problems by channelling people's energies into a more socially acceptable form.

Brighton Declaration on Women and Sport: this occurred in May 1984 when sport policy and decision makers at both national and international level met. It was organised by the British Sports Council (now *Sport England*) and supported by the *British Olympic Association*, with 82 countries taking part. Based on discussions the following points were developed:

- *equal opportunities* should be developed through policies and programmes
- facilities should take into account the needs of women
- *physical education* programmes need to take into account the needs of girls
- *elite* women should receive similar encouragement in terms of competitive opportunities, rewards, incentives and recognition as their male counterparts
- research and information should reflect women's involvement.

British Academy of Sport: see *United Kingdom Sports Institute*

British Empire: a term used to describe the colonisation of many other countries by Britain. British imperialists believed they had a duty to spread their forms of government, religion and *culture,* including their sporting activities, to those nations they considered less advanced or civilised. Numerous groups of people were involved, such as soldiers, administrators, missionaries, engineers and businessmen. Occasionally, a sport was imported to Britain from a member country of the British Empire, for example British soldiers imported polo, with the first match played in England in 1871.

British International Sports Committee is the combination of the Sports Council (see *Sport England*), the *British Olympic Association* and the *Central Council of Physical Recreation*. It was intended to be the beginnings of a more co-ordinated approach towards national and international sporting matters.

British Olympic Association (BOA): a non-governmental organisation whose function is to:

- encourage interest in the *Olympic Games*
- foster the ideals of the Olympic movement
- organise and co-ordinate British participation
- assist the governing bodies in their preparation for competitions
- advise on public relations with the press

- provide a forum for consultation among governing bodies
- organise an Olympic day
- raise funds through the British Olympic Appeal.

British Paralympic Association: the organisation responsible for selecting, preparing, entering, funding and managing British teams which compete at the *Paralympic Games* and Paralympic Winter Games. It was created following the Seoul Games in South Korea, as a more permanent structure was required. Its specific tasks are:

- to create the best possible environment for the Games
- to develop competitive standards through increased training opportunities via facilities and trained staff
- to raise sufficient funds to finance Britain's participation at international events
- to establish a clear policy framework for the ongoing tasks of the organisation and to represent Britain at international meetings and conferences.

The BPA liaises with the National Disability Sport Organisations, the Sport Foundation, the International Paralympic Association, the *British Olympic Association, Sport England* and *Disability Sport England*.

Its main focus is on *excellence* rather than *grass roots* development.

British Sports Association for the Disabled: see *Disability Sport England*

British Sports Trust is the charitable arm of the *Central Council of Physical Recreation*. It was set up in 1989 to help in the development of sporting volunteers and leaders. This is significant as *volunteers* in the United Kingdom run most governing bodies and their clubs. The Trust trains people from all walks of life to be leaders in their community, by developing the skills of leadership such as communication skills, planning and organisation and the ability to motivate others. In 1998 43,000 people were trained, mainly between the ages of 14 and 25 via the Sports Leader Awards.

broken time payments: payments made to compensate *working class* players for loss of earnings whilst playing sports such as soccer and rugby football. This tended to lead to *professionalism* in some sports and was looked down upon by the *gentleman amateurs*.

Brundage Avery: President of the *International Olympic Committee* from 1952 to 1972. The impact of Brundage on the Olympic movement was enormous. He had to see the *Olympic Games* through many turbulent years including the controversies over the state-sponsored amateurs of the Soviet Union; the expulsion of *South Africa* in 1972; the *IOC*'s recognition of Taiwan, as The Republic of China isolating the People's Republic of China until 1984. He tried to steer sport clear of politics and his philosophy was:

- the Olympic Games should remain amateur
- the Olympic movement should not embrace commercialism
- women's role in the Olympics should be reduced
- the Olympic Games should not seek a global impact
- South Africa should not be excluded.

However, on one point he did accede, the need for television to boost the coffers by advertising the Olympic movement and as a result 'rule 49' came into being. Any televised coverage of the Olympic Games exceeding three minutes of news briefs aired three times a day would have to be bought. He was therefore much more popular with conservatives than those with more liberal viewpoints.

BSRI: see *Bem sex role inventory*

buffering: a system in the body which reduces the effect of a decrease in blood pH. It occurs as a result of a combination of two chemicals, an acid and the salt of an acid, which maintains the pH balance of the blood. During exercise this system is used to resist changes in pH due to *lactic acid* build up.

burnout: the progressive loss of energy and enthusiasm for an activity due to continuous high levels of *stress* created by that activity. Often the performer experiences physiological and psychological exhaustion as well as a reduction in their performance levels. For example a talented young athlete may devote their spare time for several years to developing their performance. However they either stop participating before fulfilling their potential, becoming disillusioned and fatigued with the effort of training and competing at a consistently high level, or still compete but at a significantly lower level than previously.

bursae: small sacs of *synovial fluid* located at friction points, usually around joints. Their function during exercise is to lubricate joints and ease joint movement, for example the prepatellar bursa of the knee joint allows flexion and extension to occur. Bursae enable people to perform all actions used in sport where stress is imposed upon the body such as running, jumping, kicking and throwing.

Butler Education Act: see *Education Acts*

Do you know we also have A–Zs for:

- Biology
- Geography
- Travel and Leisure
- Health and Social Care?

Ask for them in your local bookshop or see the inside back cover for ordering details.

camps: places where specialist groups such as the Scouts or school groups erect tents, cabins or other temporary structures for their own use. See also *American summer camps*; *colonie de vacance*.

cancellous bone lies beneath and inside *compact bone* with a honeycomb or trabecular appearance. This criss-cross matrix of bony plates is developed along lines of stress on the bones and is constantly reorganised in response to the altering lines of stress. For example the lines of stress alters when an infant starts to walk as opposed to crawl. Exercise can strengthen bones by laying down new bony plates. Also known as spongy bone.

capillary: microscopic blood vessel that connects arterioles and venules. Capillaries are found near most cells in the body, but particularly those that require more oxygen and nutrients, such as the muscles, liver and kidneys. The capillary wall consists of a single layer of endothelial cells which permits the exchange of nutrients and waste between the blood and tissues. This is aided by the very small diameter of the vessel which squeezes the blood cell out of shape, increasing the surface area which can pick up oxygen. Aerobic training can cause an increase in the number of capillaries surrounding each fibre (up to 15 per cent), allowing a greater exchange of gases, waste and nutrients between the blood and the working muscles.

capitalism: an *economic system* based on free trade and private ownership of the means of production, property and capital. The focus on maximising profits has, some would argue, led to the development of the 'good life' whilst others would claim that the single scale of success, namely monetary values, can alienate many within a population. The *United States of America* is a typical example of a capitalist society.

Professional sport in particular shares some of the characteristics of capitalism, having a heavy competitive emphasis on winning, and offering rewards that are mostly materialistic.

carbohydrate: an organic compound containing carbon, hydrogen and oxygen. The hydrogen and oxygen atoms are usually found in a two-to-one ratio, for example glucose has the formula $C_6H_{12}O_6$. Carbohydrates (which are stored in the liver and kidneys) are vital to sports performers, as they are the body's most readily available source of energy. They are also essential for the efficient functioning of the nervous system and the metabolism of fat. Ideally an athlete's diet should consist of approximately 60 per cent carbohydrate, which can be found in bread, pasta, rice and potatoes. Some performers seek to manipulate the stores within the body through *glycogen loading*.

carbo-loading: see *glycogen loading*

cardiac cycle: the sequence of events that takes place during one complete heart beat. This includes the filling of the heart during the diastolic phase, and the emptying of the heart into the arterial system during the systolic phase. Each cycle lasts approximately 0.8 seconds and occurs on average 72 times per minute. Through *cardiac hypertrophy* athletes can reduce the amount of times this occurs per minute largely due to an extended diastolic phase. There are four stages to each heart beat:

1   atrial diastole

2   ventricular diastole

3   atrial systole

4   ventricular systole.

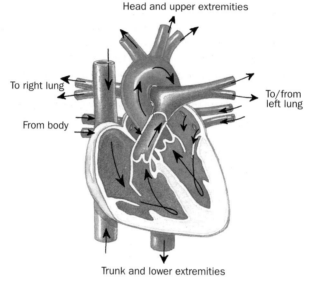

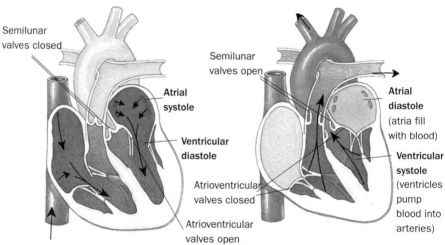

cardiac hypertrophy: the enlargement of the heart due to the effects of training. Like skeletal muscle, cardiac tissue adapts as a result of training and cardiac hypertrophy is characterised by a larger ventricular wall and a thicker *myocardium*. Endurance athletes tend to display larger ventricular cavities, whilst those following high-resistance or strength training regimes display thicker ventricular walls. Cardiac hypertrophy is usually accompanied by a decrease in resting heart rate known as *bradycardia*.

cardiac output (Q): the volume of blood pumped from one ventricle of the heart in one minute. It is equal to the product of *stroke volume* and heart rate:

$$Q = \text{stroke volume} \times \text{heart rate}$$

During periods of exercise the cardiac output needs to increase to meet the demands of the body and can rise from approximately five litres per minute up to 40 litres per minute. A performer who follows a structured training programme often experiences *cardiac hypertrophy*, which is the enlargement of the heart which in turn increases cardiac output during exercise.

cardiovascular diseases: disorders of the heart and circulatory system commonly associated with risk factors including smoking, obesity, hypertension (high blood pressure) and lack of exercise. The figure below shows their long-term pattern of development. The benefits of exercise in the prevention of such diseases are well documented. Any health-related exercise programme should involve some form of continuous or aerobic activity which exercises large muscle groups and is performed at low intensity (approximately 50 per cent of MHR – maximum heart rate). Non-weight-bearing or partial weight-bearing activities such as swimming or cycling are ideal but brisk walking or light jogging would also be very appropriate.

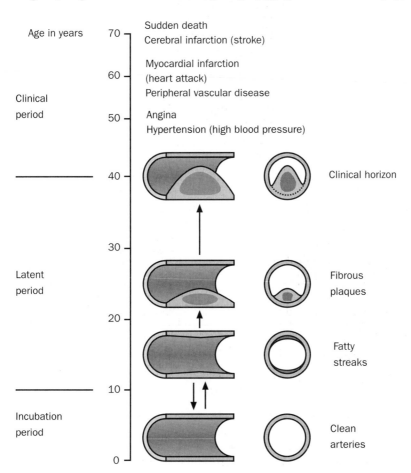

cartilage: firm, resilient connective tissue, consisting of cells (chondrocytes) which exist in small spaces (lacunae) within a matrix. Cartilage is 'avascular', meaning that it does not have a blood supply and receives nutrition via diffusion from the *capillary* network outside the tissue. All bones begin as cartilage in the developing foetus, and it gradually develops into solid bone. There are three basic types of cartilage:

- Hyaline/articular cartilage – found in joints at the articulation between two bones. It protects the bone tissue from wear and tear, reducing friction between the moving bones. Exercise can cause a thickening of hyaline cartilage.

- White fibrocartilage – a much tougher tissue and is found in areas of the body where high amounts of stress are imposed. For example, the semi-lunar discs of the knee joint and the intervertebral discs of the vertebral column are composed of fibrocartilage, acting as a shock absorber, particularly during exercise.

- Yellow elastic cartilage – a much more pliable tissue, which offers structure to some body parts such as the ears and the nose.

cartilaginous joint: joint where the bones are linked by tough, fibrous *cartilage* and no *synovial fluid* is present. The joints are stable and possess large shock-absorbing properties, allowing only a small amount of movement. For example the intervertebral discs between the lumber vertebrae enable flexion, extension and lateral flexion of the trunk.

catastrophe theory suggests that an increase in *cognitive state anxiety* will improve performance at low levels of physiological arousal, but will have a negative effect on performance at high levels of physiological arousal – a catastrophe. Hardy and Frazey (1987) modified the inverted 'U' theory, using physiological arousal as a variable factor rather than *somatic anxiety*. For example, during training a badminton player will have low levels of arousal and complete shots successfully, but in a competition they may become over-aroused causing a dramatic reduction in performance, including loss of concentration, ineffective decisions and poor execution of shots. The player must take time to recover from this position and return to an optimum level of arousal or their performance may continue to deteriorate.

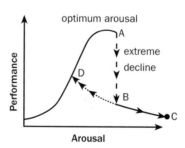

Point A – over-arousal – threshold of catastrophe

Point B – arousal level after catastrophe

Point C – continued deterioration of performance

Point D – recovery of arousal levels and gradual return to optimum arousal

catharsis: the release of *aggression* in a positive manner, causing a reduction in levels of frustration. Instinct theory suggests this can be achieved through participation in, or observation of, physical activity. For example, an individual may become frustrated at work but after completing a run when they return home feel calmer. However, rather than having a cathartic effect, *social learning theory* suggests observation of some aggressive acts can lead to repetition of those actions.

Cattell's 16 personality factors questionnaire measures 16 personality *traits* of an individual, each scored on a 1–10 scale. Developed from the *Eysenck personality inventory*, Cattell acknowledged personality was dynamic, depending on motivational, emotional and situational factors.

centering: breathing technique used to control levels of tension before or during competition. It involves the performer relaxing the chest and shoulder muscles, then focusing on the movement of the abdominal muscles whilst taking slow, deep breaths. The technique is beneficial as it can redirect *attention*, can be performed anywhere and if practiced can be completed quickly and privately.

Central Council of Physical Recreation (CCPR): established in 1935 and is the independent voice for sport in the United Kingdom.

- It promotes and protects the interests of its members – the governing bodies of sport.
- It represents the interests of anyone who plays sport, at any level in numerous activities.
- Most governing bodies and their clubs are run by volunteers, who are now supported by the *British Sports Trust*.

The CCPR liaises across a wide range of sporting activities and has divided them into six divisions:

- games and sports
- outdoor pursuits
- major spectator sports
- water recreation
- movement and dance
- interested organisations.

The CCPR advises the government and its agencies, for example the *Department of Culture, Media and Sport* and the Department for Education and Employment on the best possible policies for sport. It is involved in issues ranging from *physical education* in schools, the sale of playing fields through to sponsorship matters and broadcasting rights. It is financed from five main sources:

- subscriptions and donations
- industry and commerce
- *sponsorship*
- sales of publications and research finding
- contractual support from *Sport England*.

central nervous system: consists of the brain and spinal cord and is responsible for the co-ordination and control of the nervous system. Messages are sent to all regions of the body, including the *autonomic nervous system*, which controls the heart rate of the performer.

centralised means to draw under central control – the central government directs policy across a country. State legislation co-ordinates and supports policies, such as an education curriculum. *France* is an example of a centralised political system. Although the United Kingdom is not centralised, the *National Curriculum* brought in after the 1988 Education Reform Act (see *Education Acts*) was a move towards more centralisation of control over the *education* system.

Advantages of centralisation	Disadvantages of centralisation
Provides uniformity of experience	Can be rigid and inflexible
Is a co-ordinated system	May not cater for different local needs
Funded by the government	Can be difficult to monitor the system effectively, particularly in large countries
	Can reduce the initiative of individuals

centrality: theory highlighted by Grusky that can be seen in a game such as *baseball* where black people tend to occupy the outfield positions despite the fact that there used to be a very successful black baseball league. It was when white owners moved in that the status of black players began to change. They believed that the more central positions required skills such as strategic thinking, decision-making and closer social interaction and that therefore these positions were more suitable for white players. In other words, the *dominant culture* has determined the access and opportunities available, and challenging these ideological factors takes time.

centre of gravity: the point at which all weight tends to be concentrated, signifying that the object or body is balanced in all directions. The centre of gravity may be fixed, such as in a shot putt, or may move, as in humans when limbs change position. Knowledge of this can allow performers to optimise their techniques and maximise their efficiency of movement. For example, the centre of gravity of a high jumper when employing the Fosbury flop technique actually passes underneath the bar. An individual will remain balanced if the centre of gravity remains over the base of support, for example during a handstand.

centres of excellence: high-class sporting facilities which are intended primarily for developing *elite* performers but which can also be used by other sporting groups. They tend to specialise in a few areas and athletes come to them for training and support. They usually have excellent facilities, high-class coaches, financial support with sport science and medical support. A prime example would be the *National Sport Centres*.

cervical vertebrae: the top seven bones of the vertebral column, which support the weight of the head by enabling muscle attachment through the spinous process. The top two vertebrae, the atlas and axis, enable the head to move up and down and side to side respectively. (See appendix, pages 257–259.)

chaining: see *progressive part method practice*

Champion Coaching: part of the *National Junior Sports Programme* launched by the Sports Council (now *Sport England*) and the *Youth Sports Trust* in 1996. Its aim is to provide good quality coaching for talented young sportspeople and improve the standards of the coaches themselves through links with *Sport Coach UK*.

channelled aggression: see *assertive behaviour*

character building: often referred to as a desirable outcome from participation in sporting activities. This was a widely held belief in the nineteenth century in relation to *athleticism*. Some examples of desirable character values were:

* *leadership* and response to leadership

* *co-operation*

* courage and bravery

* commitment to a team

* self-discipline and loyalty.

cheerleading: primarily a female role in today's American sports system. It is a cosmetic role which many believe perpetuates a stereotype of *femininity* with its emphasis on physical appearance combined with a spectator role in sport. Cheerleaders stand on the sidelines and provide entertainment for their team and their fans, provide support for the men and fill in the breaks during the games. Selection to be a cheerleader is considered a sign of popularity and acceptance.

Chelladuri's multi-dimensional model of leadership suggests the characteristics of the situation, the leader and the group members must be considered before adopting a particular leadership style. The three types of leader behaviour which affect the outcome are:

* required behaviour – depending on the situation and task

* actual behaviour – leader's action in a situation

* preferred behaviour – what the group wants depending on its skills and goals.

The effectiveness of the leader is determined by the performance of the group and its own levels of satisfaction.

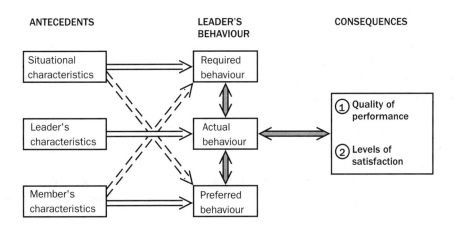

For example, a novice basketball team is about to play its first competitive game. The situational characteristics are to have fun and enjoy the game with no pressure to win.

Therefore the required behaviour is to help the players use their skills in a team situation. The members of the team are inexperienced and youthful players, so the preferred behaviour would need to provide support and encouragement to implement their skills. If the leader's actual behaviour does this, the team will enjoy the game and perform well in the match. However as the team become older, more experienced and skilful a different approach needs to be taken if the performance is to be effective and enjoyed.

chemoreceptors: sensory cells which monitor the level of acidity of the blood. Any increase in the blood acidity (decrease in blood pH) resulting from increased carbon dioxide and *lactic acid* production will cause an increase in heart rate and ventilation rates. Chemoreceptors are sited in the aortic arch and in the carotid arteries. When exercise commences, the muscles produce carbon dioxide as a result of the break down of *glycogen*. Chemoreceptors detect this increase in carbon dioxide production and causes the heart to beat faster, which has two significant effects:

● increased oxygen supply to the working muscles

● disposal of carbon dioxide via the lungs.

children's sports programmes: are usually copies of adult sports programmes. *Little League* baseball is an example of a well-organised sports programme for children. They are usually characterised by:

● selection

● competition

● leagues and tournaments

● modified playing areas.

Children's sports programmes are generally taken very seriously. Success is valued highly, and they are thought to be useful avenues of *socialisation*. However several problems are associated with them, including:

● a reduction in the spontaneity and creativity of children

● they do not require the children to make their own decisions

● rule-making is externally imposed and enforced

● some of the enjoyment from sport can be lost.

choice reaction time: time taken to respond when presented with a variety of *stimuli* each with a different response. As the number of stimuli increases so does the *reaction time* (see *Hick's law*). Within a game of rugby, if a player can perform a wide range of skills, such as passing, dummying, side-stepping and kicking, their opponent will take longer to respond as they are unsure of which action will be executed. The reaction time may also be influenced by the *stimulus–response compatibility*.

chunking: technique to increase the capacity of the *short-term memory*, by organising pieces of information together into new units or 'chunks'. For example a free kick in a game of football will be remembered by a single number or word rather than a series of separate moves.

Church: building designed for public forms of worship, especially Christian worship. The clergy (church 'employees') are distinguished from the laity (others). It has been an institutionalised form of political and social control.

In early medieval England, pagan customs began to be taken over by the Church and as such were given new religious meanings. 'Holy days' were put aside for feasting which is how the word 'holiday' emerged. In many countries, towns and villages had their own special festivals and saint days, which celebrated the death of a saint. Easter is the most important feast of the Christian church and was a time for feasting and fun. Recreations took place within a wide social pattern, and activities included *mob football, wrestling, animal sports* and *bowls*.

After the civil war (1646) Oliver Cromwell was made Lord Protector of the Commonwealth. He allied parliamentary rule with a puritan lifestyle. Puritanism particularly objected to:

- practising sport on a Sunday
- gambling
- inflicting cruelty on animals
- idleness, drinking and profanity generally associates with public houses.

As many of the traditional pastimes took place after church on a Sunday they came under fierce attack from the Puritans.

In the eighteenth century the *Methodists* continued in the same vein as the Puritans believing the violence associated with them was against Christian principles. This was also the time when a more disciplined workforce was required to work in the large factories and mills.

The Victorian era (nineteenth century) brought a climate of suppressing vice and encouraging religion and virtue. However, church attendance began to decline and in an effort to restore some control over the working classes the Church began in various ways to encourage *rational recreation* through a movement that became known as *muscular christianity* and *youth movements* such as the *Boy's Brigade* and the Church Lads Brigade. These movements were used to help instil religious, moral and militaristic values and to make the church a more attractive place as congregations were dwindling and hence control of the population.

circuit training: a method of training commonly used to improve strength, endurance, mobility and aerobic endurance. It consists of performing a series of exercises set out so that different muscle groups are worked at consecutive stations. The great benefit of circuit training is that it can allow large numbers of performers to participate, yet be easily adapted to meet the needs of individuals. Exercises can be made activity- or game-specific. Typically circuit training is used as a general pre-season conditioning session, or to maintain fitness during the competition period. See figure on page 52.

circumduction: movement pattern which is a combination of flexion, extension, abduction and adduction. It occurs at *synovial joints* where a circle can be described by the body part. True circumduction can only really occur at ball and socket joints of the shoulder and hip. For example, circumduction or at least part-circumduction occurs at the shoulder when performing a serve in tennis. (See appendix, page 271.)

citric acid: an intermediary product of the breakdown of glucose, produced when *acetyl co-A* combines with oxaloacetic acid. In doing so the resulting citric acid molecule can be totally degraded via the *Krebs cycle* and *electron transport system*, producing a great deal of energy under aerobic conditions. This method of energy production is vital to the performance of endurance-based activities and can be improved through training.

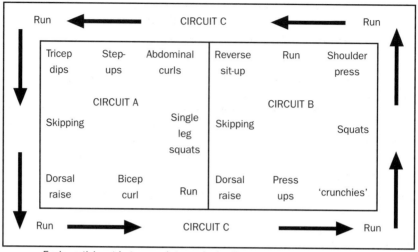

Each participant is to complete each circuit.

Circuit A = 8 exercises x 30 secs = 4 mins
Circuit B = 8 exercises x 30 secs = 4 mins
Circuit C = Run around outside = 4 mins
Repeat 2 or 3 times

Circuit training

civilising process: an analysis of the evolution of human manners and the way in which changes in social structures affect an individual's *personality*, in particular how they behave towards others. Many aspects of human social behaviour from table manners to the types of sport practised, have undergone centuries of change, increasingly requiring individuals to practise self-restraint in social situations. This process began amongst the *upper classes* and slowly filtered down through the lower social classes. Codes of behaviour and etiquette became the norm and violence, which had once been a normal part of life, was controlled so that behaviour that was acceptable at one time would now be considered a form of *deviancy*.

Clarendon Commission: a government report in 1864, requiring the Commission to 'inquire into the revenues and management of certain colleges and schools and the studies pursued and the instruction given there'. The 'certain schools' referred to were the *barbarian schools*. When the report was issued it stressed the educational importance and value of organised games for boys as agents of *character building*.

classical conditioning involves the replacement of an existing *stimulus–response bond* with a new response. Ivan Pavlov put forward his findings based on experiments with dogs and their digestive patterns in the early 1900s. He observed that dogs would salivate (unconditional response or UCR) in anticipation of the food being served (unconditional stimulus or UCS). By modifying the environment, i.e. ringing a bell (conditioned stimulus or CS) and providing food (unconditional stimulus or UCS), the dogs would still salivate (unconditional response or UCR). Over time and through repetition, the signal of the bell (conditional stimulus or CS) produced salivation (conditional response or CR) even if no food was produced.

Before conditioning	CS (bell)	→	No response
	UCS (food)	→	UCR (salivation)
During conditioning	CS + UCS	→	UCR
After conditioning	CS (bell)	→	CR (salivation)

The practical application for skill learning may include the coach giving commands at a certain time to ensure the action is completed at the correct moment, e.g. a high jumper immediately after take-off is given the instruction 'hips' to encourage them to move into the correct layout position, which will be remembered and repeated. The use of commands for 'drill' training or some aspects of relaxation are further examples of its use. However the theory does not encourage the performer to understand their actions and is of limited use when teaching complex skills.

classification: an attempt to group sports competitors to enable fair competition. This was done by gender where separate competitions developed for men and women, and by weight in sports such as boxing. It is now used to include individuals with disabilities. Two types of classification have been and are used:

- Medical classification – developed in the 1940s and dominant into the 1990s. It was based on the level of spinal cord lesion. It was designed to enable individuals with similar severity of impairment to compete against one another. It was used for wheelchair and amputee athletes. Many other disability sport federations adopted this system resulting in a multiple classification system.

- Functional classification – an integrated classification system, which places emphasis on sport performance by disability groupings rather than by specific disability. This has enabled disability sport to move on from its original rehabilitation base to *elite, competition sport*. Wheelchair basketball was the first sport at the *Paralympic Games* to experiment with this system in 1992 at the Barcelona Games. This new system demands that the athletes be evaluated on what they can and cannot do in a particular sport.

Functional classification versus medical classification:

- The goal of medical classification is to enable each competitor, regardless of impairment, to compete in a fair manner with others of similar ability/disability. This causes problems of administration and logistics in dealing with numerous classes for competition.

- Functional classification provides for athletic competition based upon ability, not disability. This has the tendency to eliminate the most severely affected athletes from elite competition.

classification of activities: activities can be divided into four distinct areas:

- *conditioning* activities
- competitive games and sports, see *competition sport*
- outdoor adventure activities, see *adventurous activities*
- *aesthetic,* movement or *gymnastic activities.*

See also *analysis of activities.*

closed loop control: form of *motor control* that involves the use of *feedback* to detect errors and make adjustments if required. This may occur on two levels, either sub-consciously or consciously. See also *Adam's closed loop theory*.

closed skill: skill performed in a stable, unchanging, predictable environment, which allows the performer knowledge of what is required and when. It is usually a *self-paced skill* and may be practised until the *autonomous stage of learning* is reached, e.g. gymnastic movements, athletic throwing events and weightlifting. However some closed skills can be performed in an 'open' environment, where the position of other players may have to be considered, such as a service in a racket game or taking a penalty shot (see also *open skill)*.

closed societies: societies in which there is little *social mobility* and individuals occupy rigid roles with virtually no opportunities to improve their social status. An example would be the Indian caste system.

clubs: groups or associations of people with common aims or interests. Sports clubs were first established in nineteenth-century England where sport was first rationalised, setting the precedent for the rest of the world. Many sports clubs are fee-paying, private institutions, usually voluntary in nature, which are affiliated to the appropriate national *governing body* for that sport. For example a football club is affiliated to the Football Association. Most sports clubs have sections for youth development, coaching, veterans and social committees. In Britain the tradition is to have single-sport clubs whereas in other countries, such as *France* there are multi-sport clubs. In the *United States of America* there is not a strong tradition of *grass roots* development of clubs apart from the country clubs, which often operate an *exclusivity* policy.

coaching involves the instruction or training of an athlete by a qualified and experienced person. Coaches are expected to hold qualifications and have knowledge of:

- sport-specific techniques and tactics
- performance-related topics, e.g. fitness, nutrition and mental preparation
- *ethics*, philosophy and codes of practice
- management and vocational skills, e.g. planning, time and money
- teaching and coaching methodology with effective communication skills
- application to the practical coaching situation.

Coaches can be voluntary and unpaid, which is the cohort that makes up the majority of coaches in the United Kingdom, or they can coach as a full-time career. *Sport Coach UK* works with the governing body to raise the standards of coaching in this country. (See *roles*.)

coactors: individuals completing the same task as the performer, but who are not in direct competition with them. This can lead to the 'coaction effect', where the performer may be influenced by their presence, leading to *social facilitation*. For example, when training with others, a high jumper may be aware of others observing and possibly evaluating their actions, which can have a beneficial or detrimental effect on performance.

coccyx: four fused bones, which form the base of the vertebral column. Its function is to act as a *process* for muscle attachment. See appendix, page 259.

codification: the systematic organisation of laws or *rules* into one recognised system or code. Codification of most sports occurred in nineteenth-century England when the foundations of modern sport were being laid. The nineteenth-century *public schools* and universities brought together the local and regional variations of traditional games and devised nationally recognised codes in order that fixtures could be played further afield to common rules.

cognition: an individual's thoughts, *attitudes* or beliefs about their behaviour and surroundings. They may be consistent, creating positive feelings (consonance) or inconsistent and in conflict with each other causing tension (dissonance). Cognitions are altered to change a person's attitude utilising the *cognitive dissonance theory*.

cognitive anxiety: performers' thoughts and worries concerning their perceived lack of ability to complete the task successfully caused by *stress*. The athlete often experiences feelings of nervousness, apprehension and may have difficulty concentrating before and during competition.

cognitive attitude: one of the components of the *triadic model* and refers to the performer's attitude towards an issue or *attitude object*, based on past experiences or values. For example the performer may believe swimming is good for them and helps to keep them fit.

cognitive control: see *meditation*

cognitive dissonance theory: method of changing an *attitude* by creating feelings of psychological discomfort with conflicting *cognitions* within the performer. Festinger (1957) suggested the individual must experience opposing beliefs (dissonance), and to return to a consistent state one must become dominant. For example, an individual knows swimming is beneficial to health, but does not enjoy participating as they think it is boring, so they do not take part. To create dissonance the person may be encouraged to attend a group where the emphasis is on fun and enjoyment or linked to a new activity such as water polo. A positive attitude towards swimming may then be created. Other methods that may be employed include the use of *role models*, provision of new information and reduction in the importance of the cognitions held. See also *persuasive communication*.

cognitive phase of learning: involves the performer gaining an understanding and creating a mental picture of the required action to form an *executive motor programme*. *Fitts and Posner's stages of learning theory* suggests this is the initial stage. Information is provided by the coach in the form of demonstrations, video footage, pictures, posters or verbal instruction. The performer receives extrinsic *feedback* from the coach, directing them towards specific *cues*, as they have yet to develop a full understanding of the movement requirements. The length of the phase is generally short as performers quickly retain or dismiss actions when appropriate.

cognitive re-appraisal: method of managing *stress* by redefining the nature of the situation or the expected outcome. For example, a netball player may believe or expect to always complete the game without a single mistake and therefore worry about not achieving their aim. To overcome this anxiety, they could be encouraged to accept that mistakes are inevitable, be provided with performance feedback and negotiate personal short- and long-term goals.

cognitive skills: these include the performer's mental ability to solve problems, plan and make decisions, as well as their understanding of the nature of their sport. For example, tactics will be developed prior to a game, based on knowledge of the team's strength and those of the opposition. Their effectiveness will be evaluated and modified if required.

cognitive state anxiety: performers' temporary thoughts concerning their ability to complete a specific task successfully. Recent research has shown it can be positive or negative. The athlete will often experience feelings of nervousness and apprehension, and have difficulty concentrating before and/or during competition. For example, before the start of a race or in the closing moments of a tennis match.

cognitive theories of learning suggest an individual learns through thinking about and understanding what is required, rather than developing a series of responses to various stimuli (see *associationist theories*). The problem is solved as a whole, using previous knowledge and *perception*; no trial and error learning occurs. For example, a basketball player possesses the required skills to play the game but is not as effective as they could be in the game situation. The coach explains the concepts of offence and defence clearly to the player and they then understand their role within the game, and how to deploy their skills for the benefit of the team rather than just themselves. Similarly if the player is presented with a variety of situations in training, this knowledge can be used later in the game to overcome a new problem which they may encounter. This is also known as *insight learning* or *Gestalt theory*.

cohesion: the dynamic process and tendency of a group of individuals to stay together and combine their efforts in order to achieve a common task, objective or goal. Cohesiveness depends on many variable factors, including the situation, member characteristics, levels of *motivation*, *leadership style* and success. It is suggested that the more cohesive a group the better the performance, but this is not always the case and can depend on two aspects of group cohesion:

- task cohesion – how well the group works together to complete the task, e.g. winning the match
- social cohesion – how well the group interacts and supports each other.

Each aspect can be independent of the other, but task cohesion is more important than social cohesion to the successful completion of the goal. For example, a football team may win most of their games but do not socialise particularly well, while a rival team get on well together but do not actually win many games. However some conflict may produce positive results as new ideas are developed, or rivalry can motivate individuals to perform better.

collegiate: a term used in the USA, meaning relating to college or high school.

colonialism: the policy and practice of a power in extending control over weaker peoples or areas. Examples include the 13 colonies that became the *United States of America* or the colonies of the *British Empire*. (See also *emergent cultures*.) Many former colonial states have become or are now in the process of becoming *emergent cultures*.

colonie de vacance: outdoor summer camp in *France*. These camps were set up as part of a structured programme in order to take children away from the inner cities. It was intended that the children should learn to appreciate the *natural environment* as part of the concept 'le plein air'. They are aimed at low income, disadvantaged groups and the costs are subsidised by the state. They have permanent facilities set in attractive areas with professional and temporary staff.

combat: to be in conflict with individuals or groups. It implies a struggle, and in a sporting context, it involves one person beating an opponent. Examples of activities would be judo or *wrestling* where stylised moves are tested.

command-style teaching: teaching style in which the teacher adopts an authoritarian manner, making all the decisions with no input from the group. All learners experience the same actions, have little social interaction and have no decisions to make. It ensures the objectives are clear, routines are established and control is maintained. It is useful when instructing large groups of beginners, or when time is limited and safety is vital. However it does not encourage the learner to take responsibility for their learning, is of limited use for the development of *open skills* and makes it difficult for the teacher to provide individual *feedback*. Also see *Mosston and Ashworth's spectrum of teaching styles.*

commercialism: an emphasis on the principles of commerce with a focus on profit. As 'spectator sports' emerged, their entertainment value was exploited by individuals who saw the opportunity to organise regular sporting events. Promoters and agents emerged, and commercialism became an integral part of sport. Countries with a market economy (see *economic systems*) were initially more open to this kind of approach as they had the environment to create profitable enterprises.

The conditions required and characteristics for commercialism can be seen in the illustration below.

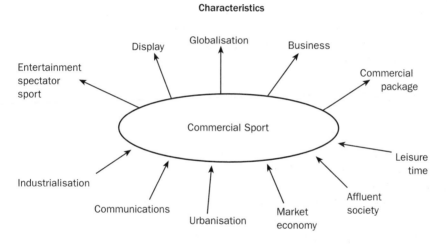

Characteristics

Conditions required

Advantages to sport	Disadvantages to sport
Provides revenue for sports events.	Uneven development across sports
Provides revenue for athletes training.	Revenue goes to already popular sports and stars
Provides income in professional sport.	Withdrawal of money can lead to events crashing
Can help stimulate grass roots activity.	Political considerations can become important
Can help raise standards.	Tensions between the sport and sponsor
Can help in the development and innovation of sport	

Commonwealth Games: originally called the British Empire Games, this is the next most important multi-sport competition after the *Olympic Games.* They involve approximately 65 countries with a range of 25 sports. They maintain a strong British influence as a result of the colonisation of these countries by Britain earlier in their history. They concentrate on *amateur* sports and are held every four years.

communism: an *economic system* based on the abolition of private ownership, and with an emphasis on state control and collective responsibility. Social class barriers are supposedly broken down. Athletes are subsidised by the state in order to excel and promote the superiority of communism as a political system.

Community Sports Leader Awards (CSLA): run by the *British Sports Trust* as part of its Leadership in the Community Programme. The CSLA is a preliminary Sports Leader Award and is an effective qualification in promoting the concept of leadership roles in sport for young people over the age of 16. It enables people to assist in the voluntary activities of a *club* or youth organisation, and to lead groups in sporting or recreational activities. This scheme operates within schools, colleges and community groups, being recognised by the *Duke of Edinburgh Award Scheme* at gold level.

compact bone: hard surface layer of all bones and the cylindrical shaft or *diaphysis* of long bones. Its function is to protect the bones from external forces or blows and allows weight-bearing to occur. The compact bone is surrounded by the *periosteum* for protection and allows attachment for tendons. Also known as hard bone.

competition sport has as its primary aim to determine who is the best in a particular sporting activity given equal circumstances. For example, athletes are matched within categories of level of ability, such as *club*, county or national standard; by age, weight and often gender. They adhere to the same standardised *rules* and their *skill* level, physical and mental fitness are the main criteria of winning.

Competitive sport enables participants to compete at levels appropriate to their ability. They can compete at three levels:

- Recreational competition – a friendly and informal level of competition. The result has no significance to anyone else and although rules are adhered to no officials are likely to be present. This represents the *grass roots* end of the continuum and involves many people.

- Representative competition – a more formalised level of competition, administered by officials, and the participants may represent a club, district or town. The competition may be organised into leagues or tournaments where the result can affect later progression. A sense of obligation to do well is present.

- *Elite* competition – occurs at the highest level such as county, national and international. The demands on the performer are considerable, physically, mentally and emotionally, often involving the additional pressure of national pride. Very few participants actually reach these levels.

competitive state anxiety inventory: form of self-report *questionnaire* measuring cognitive worry, *somatic anxiety* and self-confidence in a sporting situation. It is used to assess an individual's *state anxiety* and their corresponding behaviour patterns. The test is commonly referred to as *CSAI-2*. See also *competitive trait anxiety*.

competitive trait anxiety: the tendency of a performer to see competitive situations as threatening and to respond with feelings of apprehension or tension. An individual with a high *trait anxiety* is more likely to experience a high *state anxiety* when faced with a stressful situation, such as competition, where they feel others may be evaluating their performance (*evaluation apprehension*). For example, a gymnast who tends to worry generally will perceive the next competition as highly threatening. They may experience high levels of *cognitive state anxiety* and *somatic anxiety* which could hinder their performance. Competitors' anxiety levels can be measured using the *SCAT* and *CSAI-2* tests.

	HARDLY EVER	SOMETIMES	OFTEN
1 Before I compete I worry about not performing well.	a	b	c
2 When I compete I worry about making mistakes.	a	b	c
3 Before I compete I am calm.	a	b	c
4 I get nervous waiting to start a game.	a	b	c

competitiveness: aiming to achieve what another person is aiming to achieve at the same time. It induces an element of *conflict*. There are advantages and disadvantages to competitive sport.

Advantages of competitiveness	Disadvantages of competitiveness
Children have natural competitive instinct and as they are more motivated to practice, enjoyment of sport increases	Continued feelings of failure can cause stress and anxiety
	The need to win can encourage unsporting behaviour
Can raise self-esteem and ability to cope with failure and success	

complex skill: a skill that involves the performer having to think about it, consciously control it and make decisions about its execution. For example, a player preparing to make a tackle must assess the position, speed and angle of the attacker, options they may have and the position of team mates before deciding on the appropriate technique to use. Initially, when learning the skill, it may be broken down into *subroutines* for the performer to gain a fuller understanding and mastery of the task.

compulsory competitive tendering (CCT): situations in which private companies must tender for any work to be carried out. Following the Local Government Act 1988, ranges of *local authority* services were tendered, including the management of leisure services. It was an attempt to create a more competitive environment in order to reduce costs. CCT is part of *Best Value* schemes.

Advantages of compulsory competitive tendering	Disadvantages of compulsory competitive tendering
Reduce costs	Sport is no longer seen as a social service
Free local authorities from day-to-day running problems	The *Central Council of Physical Recreation* felt it was a serious threat to the traditional provision of sports facilities

concentric muscle contraction involves a muscle shortening whilst contracting. It is a form of *isotonic muscle contraction* and occurs, for example, in the bicep during the upward phase of a bicep curl or in the tricep during the upward phase of a push-up. In this case *actin* filaments within a *sarcomere* are pulled closer together. See also *eccentric muscle contraction*.

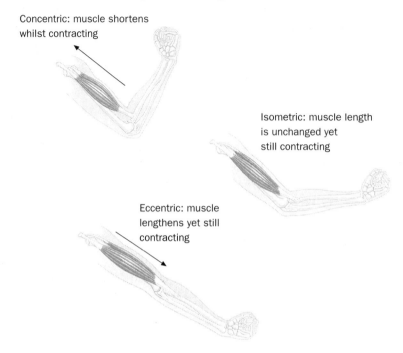

Concentric: muscle shortens whilst contracting

Isometric: muscle length is unchanged yet still contracting

Eccentric: muscle lengthens yet still contracting

Concepts of physical activity: see *play, leisure, recreation, physical education, outdoor recreation* and *sport.*

Conconi test: used to measure the *onset of blood lactate accumulation (OBLA)* or *anaerobic threshold*. It involves monitoring the heart rate of the athlete as the intensity of exercise increases up to maximal effort. Initially the heart rate will increase proportionally to intensity, but a point arrives at which the heart rate is no longer rising even though the intensity continues to rise. This point is known as the heart deflection point.

conditioning activities are designed primarily to improve the physical and mental condition of the performer. Examples of such activities are aerobics, *circuit training* and *weight training*. A programme of work is set and should be followed on a regular basis if it is to have the desired effect. Some participants will use it for the general conditioning effect whilst others will use it to achieve fitness for a particular sport. Some conditioning activities have developed into *competition sports* in their own right, for example weightlifting and aerobics.

conditioning theories: see *associationist theories*

conflict theory: a sociological theory opposed to *functionalist theory*. This theory does not view society as a stable system. Instead it is believed that society is made up of an ever-changing set of relationships affected by economic differences. As such society is bound by inequalities as some sections of society will have more power and control of resources than others. It is based on the ideas of Karl Marx and is used mainly to explain events in countries with *market economies*. It is based on the idea that workers with little control over their working lives will constantly seek entertainment and excitement. They can be coerced into their choices through consumerism and mass entertainment spectacles. *Sport* is a popular form of entertainment, incorporates sales and merchandising as well as ideological assumptions such as achievement-orientated behaviour, obedience and discipline. This theory tends to include a more cynical view of sport and focuses on the need for change.

conquest: a means of overcoming an obstacle, such as a mountain or a feeling e.g. fear, and usually involves some force, be it physical or mental. It suggests control and power over another object. In sport, it is a term used mostly in the context of outdoor and *adventurous activities*.

conservation: the protection of the *natural environment* through the planning and careful management of natural resources. Outdoor *adventurous* activities are growth sports and are providing some problems regarding conservation which need to be addressed. The areas in which they take place are often country parks, nature reserves, green belt areas, Areas of Outstanding Natural Beauty (AONB) and *National Parks*. Some of the problems caused are:

- erosion of land and rivers
- pollution caused by motor sports
- disturbance of wildlife and local residents.

Rather than simply banning these sports, organisations such as the *Countryside Commission*, the National Parks authorities and the sports *governing bodies* need to liaise in order to plan ways in which these activities can be enjoyed with minimum damage to the environment.

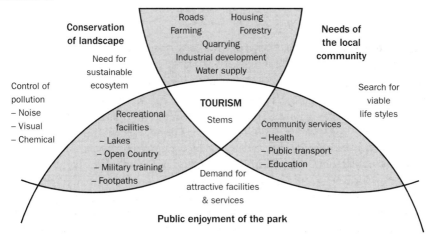

contingency theory of leadership: leadership theory that proposes that the effectiveness of a leader is dependent on (contingent on) a combination of personality *traits* and the situation. Fiedler (1967) identified two types of *leadership styles*:

- task centred/task-orientated leader – concentrates on completing the task, setting goals, getting the job done and performance
- relationship centred/person-orientated leader – concentrates on developing interpersonal relationships within the group.

The effectiveness of each style depends on the 'favourableness' of the situation, which is dependent on:

- the relationship between the leader and the group
- the leader's position of power and authority
- the task structure.

The task-orientated style would be more effective in highly favourable or highly unfavourable conditions, whereas a person-orientated style would be better employed in moderately favourable conditions.

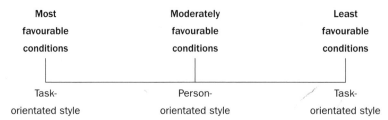

For example, the situation would be favourable if the coach of a team had an excellent relationship with the group and was respected by them, had the clear objective of winning the league and was well-resourced in terms of facilities. By comparison, another team had a poor relationship with its coach, poor facilities and no clear objectives for the group. For both of these scenarios a task-oriented style of leadership could be used. However, a third rival team has reasonable a relationship with its coach, limited facilities and a mid-table position in the league. In this instance a person-oriented style may be the most appropriate to use.

continuous feedback: see *feedback*

continuous skill has no clear beginning and end; the completion of one movement becomes the start of the next. This type of skill is placed on the same *continuum* as a *serial skill* and a *discrete skill*. Examples include swimming, cycling and running actions.

continuous training: method of training performed for a long period of time at low intensity. Continuous training involves the performance of rhythmic exercise, using large muscle groups at a steady state for up to two hours. It is designed to improve endurance performance and is widely used in distance running, swimming and cycling. The intensity of the training should be between 60 and 70 per cent of *maximum heart rate*, as outlined in the *Karvonen principle*. Continuous training is also recommended for health-related reasons, since the intensity of the exercise is fairly low yet benefits the cardiovascular system. It can therefore be used as part of a programme to avoid *cardiovascular diseases* and *obesity*.

continuum: an imaginary line placed between two extremes. It is used to classify items or subjects between extremities depending on how closely they match set criteria. For example, skills are often classified in this manner (see *open* and *closed skills*).

contract to compete: the hallmark of participation in sporting activities. It implies that each performer has entered into an unwritten contract whereby they are committed to:

- competing under the *rules* of the sport
- playing as well as they can

- allowing others the same opportunity to demonstrate their *skill* and effort
- voluntarily accepting and understanding the need for codes of behaviour such as *sportsmanship* and *etiquette*.

The contract can be broken when:

- these rules are broken, e.g. a foul
- when equal opportunity is denied to others, e.g. not trying your best to win or the use of performance-enhancing drugs.

contractility: the capacity of cells to generate a force to shorten or contract for movement. Muscle fibres exhibit a high degree of contractility and in doing so enable people to perform a whole host of movements seen in the sporting arena.

cool-down: period of light, continuous activity following exercise during which time heart rate remains elevated. The purpose is to keep metabolic activity high and *capillaries* dilated, so that oxygen can be flushed through the muscle tissue, removing and oxidising any *lactic acid* that may have accumulated. This prevents pooling of blood in the veins which can cause dizziness if exercise is stopped abruptly. The final part of a cool-down period should involve a period of mobility exercises, which can also facilitate and improve flexibility. Also known as warm-down.

co-operation: working with others to achieve the same end. Some *cultures* are co-operative in nature, such as *primitive cultures* where the group or collective effort often means the difference between survival and death.

Even within competitive team games there is an element of co-operation as the teams agree on the fixture and to abide by the *rules*, and the team members work together to achieve a victory.

co-ordination: a skill-related component of fitness, involving the interaction of the motor and nervous systems. It is simply the ability to perform motor tasks accurately. Co-ordination is essential for most sporting tasks to be completed successfully. The performer needs to be able to combine effectively the use of various limbs to maintain balance and execute skills such as dribbling, passing, dodging and kicking.

Cori cycle: a series of chemical reactions in which the *lactic acid* produced from the breakdown of muscle glycogen is converted to blood glucose in the liver.

corinthian: the epitome of the *amateur* ideal of a sportsman. Consistent with St. Paul's letter to the Corinthians that 'not everyone can win but those that do should do so according to the rules and spirit of the time'. The corinthians were drawn from the elite of Victorian society and followed this code during games. For example, the Corinthian Casuals, founded in 1882, would withdraw their goalkeeper on the awarding of a penalty to the opposing side, on the principle they should accept the consequences of a foul.

Cornish hurling is a traditional game of *football* played in Cornwall. In Richard Carew's 'Survey of Cornwall' 1603 he gives a detailed description of a game of football or hurling as it was called in Cornwall, which reveals complex rules and strategies (for the time) for deceiving the opposition. In the east of Cornwall 'hurling to goales' involved teams of 15, 20, or 30 in which each player paired himself with another from the opposing team and attempted to block his advance, as in American football today.

'The hurlers are bound to the observation of many lawes as that they must hurle man to man, and not two set upon one man at once; the Hurler against the ball must not butt, nor handfast under the girdle; that he who hath the ball, must butt only in the other brest'. There was even an offside rule 'that he must deal no foreball, viz he may not throw it to any of his mates, standing nearer the goale than himself'.

Cotswold Games: an annual sports event, which included activities for the *gentry* and the peasantry. It suffered under the *Puritan* regime but was revived by Robert Dover who, following the Restoration in the seventeenth century, wished for a return to the 'merrie England' concept where all social classes enjoyed recreational pursuits together. They later became known as the *Dover Games*.

Coubertin, Baron Pierre de: see *Baron Pierre de Coubertin*

Council of Europe: established in 1949, the Council of Europe focuses on cultural, sporting, educational and environmental issues; for example the use of *drugs* in sport, the economic effects on sports investments, football *hooligans* and developing support for the *Paralympics*.

counter culture: a subsection of *society* which develops different values, behaviour, ideas and beliefs which are often in conflict with those of the *dominant culture*. Counter cultures can emerge from a common interest, and from social experiences, and they are often associated with alternative cultures. In sport, some groups are attempting to make sport less competitive. This is a counter culture which conflicts with the dominant idea that major force in sport is competition.

The dominant concept in American sport is the *Lombardian ethic*, where winning is considered the only important thing. Therefore 'Eco-sport' is a counter culture movement which takes a more anti-competitive viewpoint and sees the process rather than the outcome as the important thing. The New Games Foundation aims to change the way people play by creating informal situations, emphasising group effort rather than group reward. See the figure below.

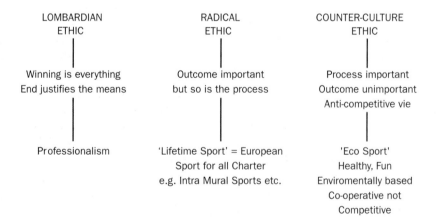

Countryside Commission: public body with a wide range of responsibilities in England and Wales, and was formed under the National Parks and Access to the Countryside Act 1968. It has various functions including:

- selection and designation of *National Parks*, Areas of Outstanding Natural Beauty (AONB) and country parks
- establishment of long-distance footpaths and bridleways
- provision of information services about the countryside
- advice on the use of the countryside for open air *recreation* balanced by a concern for the *natural environment*
- carrying out research and experimental projects
- giving grants and loans to non-public bodies.

coupled reaction: a two-part chemical reaction, involving the production of energy in the first stage, which is used in the second stage for resynthesis of *adenosine triphosphate (ATP)*.

$$PC \rightarrow Pi + C + energy$$
$$energy + ADP + Pi \rightarrow ATP$$

coursing: a field sport where dogs or hounds are matched against one another in pairs, for the hunting of hares by sight. Hare coursing dates back to 1500BC in the Valley of the Nile and was introduced to Britain in approximately 500BC. Its original function was to obtain food for human survival but the competitive element was introduced during the reign of Elizabeth I, becoming a popular social event in rural England in the nineteenth century. Hares were flushed out of cover and the 'slipper' – the official responsible for the releasing of the dogs simultaneously – unleashed two greyhounds. The *gentry* rode on horseback and private ground was often crossed by the lower classes on foot. In the 1920s circuit tracks were built, in which greyhounds trailed an artificial hare on the track to test the speed and agility of the dogs. *Gambling* was a popular aspect of this activity.

courtly refers to something which is deemed suitable for a royal court, meaning refined in manner.

creatine monohydrate supplementation is a legal *ergogenic aid*, which is used to boost levels of *phosphocreatine* in the body and therefore improve the ATP-PC *energy system*. Some studies have shown creatine supplementation to boost maximal *strength* and lean tissue mass and for such it is widely used by a variety of athletes from sprinters through to weight lifters. As with most *ergogenic aids* that are ingested, there does appear to be a few side effects, the main ones being water retention and muscle cramps.

creatine phosphate: high-energy phosphate molecule found in muscle. During periods of high-intensity exercise which is short in duration, creatine phosphate is used to resynthesise *ATP* under anaerobic conditions. Sprint *interval training*, *strength training* and, more recently, creatine supplementation by athletes can increase the amount of work performed under such conditions and speeds up recovery following exercise.

cricket: one of the oldest-established games, played from the outset by both the aristocrats and the commoners. The game reflected the feudal structure of the village and each *social class* had particular *roles* assigned to them to signify their status. The game took place in the summer season when light was at a premium allowing workers time to participate. Due to its non-violent nature, the early *rules* and gentlemanliness ensured a level of respectful behaviour. The term 'gentleman versus players' distinguished the amateurs from the professionals. The Duke of Richmond drew up the first rules in 1727 and the Marylebone

Cricket Club (MCC) emerged as an organisational force comparatively early in the game's development. (See the figure below.)

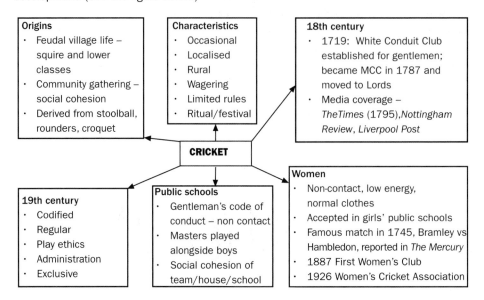

Origins	Characteristics	18th century
• Feudal village life – squire and lower classes • Community gathering – social cohesion • Derived from stoolball, rounders, croquet	• Occasional • Localised • Rural • Wagering • Limited rules • Ritual/festival	• 1719: White Conduit Club established for gentlemen; became MCC in 1787 and moved to Lords • Media coverage – TheTimes (1795),Nottingham Review, Liverpool Post

CRICKET

19th century	Public schools	Women
• Codified • Regular • Play ethics • Administration • Exclusive	• Gentleman's code of conduct – non contact • Masters played alongside boys • Social cohesion of team/house/school	• Non-contact, low energy, normal clothes • Accepted in girls' public schools • Famous match in 1745, Bramley vs Hambledon, reported in The Mercury • 1887 First Women's Club • 1926 Women's Cricket Association

critical theory is about power in social relations and about action and political involvement in order to bring about equity, fairness and openness. In relation to sport, it recognises that people who are involved in sports use their power and resources to build up cultural practices. It recognises that conflict and harmony between different groups can co-exist through negotiation, compromise and coercion. Therefore sport will change as society changes and will at the same time exert its own considerable influence. This sociological theory attempts to help understand the complexity and diversity of societies without the limitations imposed by theories such as *functionalist* and *conflict theories*.

cruciate ligaments: located in the knee joint, these ligaments prevent anterio-posterior movement. Together with the lateral and medial collateral ligaments they co-operate in order to maintain the stability of the joint. Injuries to these ligaments are common in contact sports such as football and rugby but can also occur as a result of twisting in sports such as basketball. See the figure on page 67.

Crystal Palace: see *National Sports Centres*

CSAI-2 questionnaire: see *competitive state anxiety inventory*

cue: a part of a *stimulus* that allows the performer to discriminate between it and another stimulus, or a particular aspect of the stimulus that can guide behaviour. For example, in the *cue-utilisation theory*, the coach may tell a basketball player learning how to perform a lay-up shot to focus on the square around the basket when aiming their shot.

cue-utilisation theory involves the use of relevant *cues* to focus the performer's *attention* as *arousal* levels increase in order to complete the task successfully. This involves *perceptual narrowing:* If, however, this continues as arousal increases, the performer may actually begin to miss vital cues and signals, leading to a reduction in their performance level. For example, a golfer may be playing the final holes of a close match. They usually direct their thoughts to several checks before completing the stroke, but as the pressure increases they neglect to complete their normal routine, missing key points. As a result the shot is poor leading to a further increase in arousal levels.

culture denotes the way of life of a *society*, encompassing its language, customs, dress, the symbols and artefacts. These are passed down through the generations with whatever modifications any single generation wishes to make. Cultures can evolve gradually, or occasionally change almost overnight. Individuals undergo the *socialisation* process, learning the cultural *values* of their society and institutions, and social structures are founded to achieve specific aims for that culture. Examples of different cultures are:

- *emergent*
- *primitive*
- *ancient*
- modern. (See *Western* and *Eastern European sport.*)

culture and sport: physical and sporting activities have different functions in different cultures. For example:

- *primitive* cultures – functional, where sporting activities are developed for survival, e.g. to learn how to hunt for food, defence and religious or *ritual* meanings
- *emergent* cultures – functional, survival, *integration* of peoples, *nationalism,* labour and defence
- *ancient* cultures – functional, religious and *recreation* for leisured class
- modern Western cultures – *socialisation* for adult *roles, commercialism, recreation* and *excellence.*

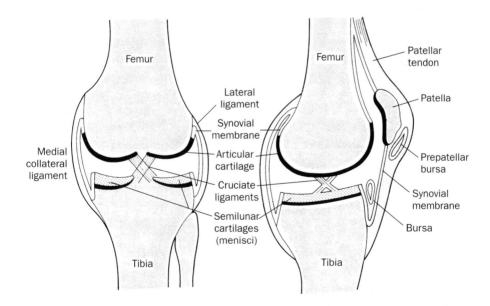

Cruciate ligaments

cycling: an activity that reflected the technological advances and social changes in the nineteenth century. Bicycles could be mass-produced and were appealing initially to the *middle classes* who required a mode of transport different from the horse. The lower classes had to await the development of the second-hand trade. The popularity of the bicycle grew because of the growing freedom of *gentry* ladies, the opportunity now available to escape to the countryside, the increase in clubs and various technological advances. Some of the early models were the Hobby horse (1818); the Boneshaker (1868); the Penny Farthing (1870–90); the National Royal Tricycle (1884) and the Rover Safety (1885).

Do you need revision help and advice?

Go to pages 274–287 for a range of revision appendices that include plenty of exam advice and tips.

danger: the state of being vulnerable to injury. In the sporting arena this risk is heightened in outdoor and *adventurous activities.* Subjective danger is that which is under the control of the individual such as choice of safe and appropriate equipment, and choice of route; however there is no such control over objective danger such as an avalanche.

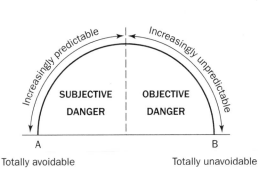

In the context of mountaineering, for example, beginners will work at the left end of the base line AB.

Experienced climbers will work from the right end of the base line.

dead space: air remaining in any area of the respiratory passages which is not involved in *gaseous exchange* between the blood and *alveoli.*

decentralised: the dispersal of power away from the centre towards outlying areas. It is a system of government or administration that is organised into smaller units with more *autonomy.* Examples include *local authorities* in Britain and the individual states in the *United States of America.* The government in power provides guidelines that can be interpreted according to regional needs, including the type of education system. For example, *physical education* in the United Kingdom traditionally had a decentralised system within which teachers devised their own syllabus. However, the advent of the *National Curriculum* brought a more centralising influence.

Advantages of a decentralised system	Disadvantages of a decentralised system
It is more flexible	Not a uniform experience nationally
It can cater for regional needs	It can be difficult to co-ordinate policy
Individual initiative can flourish	The quality of provision can be dependent on individual initiative

decision-making: involves the performer combining information gathered from the present environment and past experiences in order to initiate a response. *Cues* gathered from the *display* are analysed and a *motor programme* formed. The faster the process, the quicker the *reaction time* therefore the better the chance of success. For example, a badminton player must evaluate the position of the opponent; the speed and direction of the shuttle-cock; their own skills and the chance of success. This information is then used to decide which shot it is appropriate to play. Also known as the *translatory mechanism*.

dehydration results from the loss of body fluids. Dehydration largely occurs during athletic performance as a result of the sweating that accompanies increased body temperature. As exercise intensity increases so does the rate at which we metabolise our food fuels. This produces heat, which in turn leads to sweating in an attempt to cool the body and maintain body temperature. Even fluid losses of as little as 2% of body weight can cause an impairment to endurance performance by 10–20%. Fluid loss reduces blood plasma volume, which decreases blood flow to the muscles, increases blood viscosity (thickness) and causes heart rate to increase.

In order to maintain optimal performance, rehydration is essential. Many endurance athletes will require drinks of a *carbohydrate* solution of 4–6% of body weight during exercise in order to boost blood glucose and stave off dehydration. A level of dehydration equal to 5% of body weight has been shown to reduce performance by 70%.

delayed onset of muscle soreness (DOMS): characterised by tender and painful muscles often experienced in the days following heavy and unaccustomed exercise. The explanation of this soreness is quite simple and results from the damage to muscle fibres and connective tissue surrounding the fibres. The soreness is usually temporary and goes within a couple of days as the muscle fibres repair themselves. DOMS is most likely to occur following *eccentric muscle contraction* and can result from *weight training*, *plyometrics* or even walking down steep hills.

democracy: a system of government that involves some form of election of the government by the people. Democracy is given a high value ideologically. *Capitalism* is believed to require a democratic society in order to succeed. This is the opposite of a one-party state.

democratic leader: a leader who encourages the *group* to discuss ideas and become involved in the decision-making process, but who will make the final decision themselves and oversee the completion of the task. The leader is generally more informal and relaxed within the group when compared with an *autocratic leader* but has considerably more input than a *laissez-faire leader*. Research by Lewin (1935) suggested the group led by a democratic leader continued to work and co-operate if the leader was not present. This type of leader works well with more experienced or individual performers.

demonstration: an explanation, display or illustration showing how to complete a task correctly. It is a form of *visual guidance* that is especially useful during the *cognitive phase of learning*. To be effective the demonstration must be clear, accurate and relevant. The action is more likely to be repeated if the model is of high status or respected (see *social learning theory*). For example, to teach a young gymnast how to execute a front somersault, the coach must ensure they watch a skilled performer, so they can create a mental image of the movement requirements. Often the use of *verbal guidance*, directing the novice to technical *cues*, can enhance the effectiveness of the demonstration.

Department for Culture, Media and Sport (DCMS): the governmental 'home' of sport, providing funding for *UK Sport* and various other sports councils. It is the government department responsible for government policy on sport and recreation and the *National Lottery,* as well as other cultural sectors such as broadcasting and films. It is headed by a Secretary of State, assisted by various Parliamentary Undersecretaries of State, one of which represents sport. A Sports Cabinet under the chairmanship of the Secretary of State for Culture, Media and Sport was introduced in 1999 to work alongside UK Sport and to bring together ministers with responsibility for sport in the four home countries.

The Department promotes its policies for the range of sectors that can be broadly defined as 'culture'.

In relation to sport this can be translated as:

- *Sport for All*, aiming to widen access to sport and recreation to the masses
- achieving *excellence* in national and international competition
- the Youth Sports Unit which promotes the importance of *physical education* and sport for young people in conjunction with the Department for Education and Employment (DfEE), and which also has responsibility for children's play, via education and training
- supporting major international events, e.g. attracting the 2003 World Athletics Championships. The Department supports the relevant organisations in terms of bidding for and staging the events
- sport as part of the overall social inclusion policy and neighbourhood regeneration work.

Sport is funded via the UK Sports Council (which is also the National Lottery distributor, see *lottery fund*) and Sport England which in turn provides grants to governing bodies as well as advice and support to schools, local government and sports clubs.

Department of National Heritage: the *Minister for Sport* is located within this structure, which was founded in 1992. The creation of this Department, within the *Department for Culture, Media and Sport*, gave advantages to sport by locating it firmly within a wider cultural and leisure brief and giving it a voice at cabinet level. However, sport has to compete with other areas such as the arts, broadcasting, films, *tourism* and heritage.

detraining: see *reversibility*

developing cultures: see *emergent cultures*

deviancy: behaviour that goes against the society's general *norms* and *values*. This can include behaviour that goes against the law and is therefore criminally deviant, for example burglary, or against the moral values of the society but which is not criminally deviant, for example promiscuity. Deviancies can be relative according to the balance of power in society. The *dominant culture* usually decides on what is lawful and morally right and this can isolate other subsections of society who, should they form contradictory values, could be classed as *subcultures*. There are two categories of deviancy:

- Negative deviancy – in sporting situations this can include violations such as deliberately fouling another player or taking performance-enhancing *drugs*.
- Positive deviancy – athletes are often encouraged to behave in ways that would be unacceptable in other spheres of life. This can be classed as overconformity or positive

deviancy. Examples would be where athletes are encouraged to train obsessively; participate when injured and sacrifice other aspects of their life for the sport.

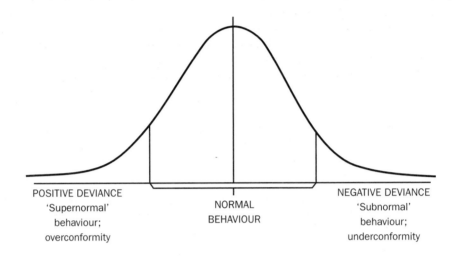

POSITIVE DEVIANCE	NORMAL	NEGATIVE DEVIANCE
'Supernormal'	BEHAVIOUR	'Subnormal'
behaviour;		behaviour;
overconformity		underconformity

Deviancy

diaphysis: the shaft of a *long bone*.

diastole: the filling of the chambers of the heart with blood when relaxing. It forms part of the *cardiac cycle*.

disability sport: a term used to describe the participation in sport of disabled people. 'Disabled' in this context covers people with a physical, sensory or mental impairment. The term 'disability' is used when impairment adversely affects performance. Other terms used are handicapped sport, sports for the disabled, adaptive sport, wheelchair sport and deaf sport. Competitive sports have either been designed specifically for the disabled, such as goalball for the blind, or have been modified, such as volleyball, and wheelchair basketball and tennis. (See also *integration* and *inclusiveness*.)

Disability Sport England (formerly *British Sports Association for the Disabled*) promotes sport for disabled athletes. Its aims are wide-ranging and include:

- to provide opportunities for disabled people to participate in *sport*
- to promote the benefits of sport and *physical recreation* to disabled people
- to support organisations in providing sporting opportunities for disabled people
- to educate and make people aware of the sporting abilities of disabled people
- to enhance the image, awareness and understanding of disability sport
- to encourage disabled people to play an active role in the development of their sport.

With more than 50,000 members Disability Sport England aims to make a healthy lifestyle and participation in sport a reality from the *grass roots* through to *Paralympic* medal winners.

discovery teaching style: style of teaching in which the teacher guides the learner to find the correct movement pattern by providing information, clues or asking questions when appropriate. It is an open-ended and creative approach to learning when compared with the *command teaching style*. It is useful for the creation of dance or gymnastic routines and during some outdoor activities. Advantages of this style include a greater understanding of the task by the performer due to increased *decision-making*, along with a subsequent improvement in their self-confidence and *motivation* towards the task. However this method is time-consuming as well as being difficult to use with large groups, as the teacher has to adapt for individual needs, *abilities* and progress. Also see *Mosston and Ashworth's spectrum of teaching styles*.

discrete skill has a well-defined beginning and end, which is usually completed quickly. It is a specific skill with an action that can be repeated. This type of skill is placed on the same *continuum* as a *serial skill* and a *continuous skill*. Examples include a dive, passing, catching, kicking and hitting.

discrimination: making a distinction or giving unfair treatment, especially because of *prejudice*. It occurs when opportunities available to one social group are not available to all and when a prejudicial attitude is acted upon. It includes:

- overt discrimination – for example, laws which form part of the structure of a society, e.g. the former system of *apartheid* or a membership clause of a private sports club. This can be officially wiped out by changing the laws

- covert discrimination – hidden or less obvious, for example people's *attitudes* and beliefs, which can be very hard to dislodge.

When subordinate groups in society are discriminated against their opportunities are limited, including opportunities of *social mobility*. Discrimination can also be affected by whether a system is 'open', as in a true *egalitarian* society, or 'closed' such as the Indian caste system. Groups that can be discriminated against include *women,* the disabled, lower class and *ethnic groups.*

Numerous factors can lead to discrimination in sport:

- finance – the cost of joining a sport club
- time – longer hours of employment; women with careers/family
- location – number and type of facilities available
- education – philosophy and facilities available
- information – poor *media* coverage of gender and type of sports
- cultural factors – for example, *stereotyping, social class* or religious beliefs may hinder participation
- access – transport and opportunity.

display (psychology): the physical environment surrounding the performer. It contains various *stimuli* or *cues* which are used during *information processing*, from which the performer has to select those which are relevant at the time (see *perception*). For example, during a game of netball the display would contain the position of team mates, opposition, umpires, spectators, location of the individual themselves on court as well as the speed and direction of the ball. Also known as the *environment*.

display (socio-cultural): something exhibited or performed for others. This is a term used to denote a moment when a sporting activity has moved along the continuum from play, to where the intention is more exhibitionist. Performing for others and providing a spectacle are central to this idea.

Play  Display

dispositional theory: see *trait theory*

dissonance occurs when a performer has two or more thoughts (*cognitions*) of conflicting views which cause feelings of psychological discomfort. When an individual experiences these feelings the need to restore harmony or consonance is paramount, as suggested by the *cognitive dissonance theory*.

distributed practice: type of practice in which the performer completes a set number of practices followed by a rest or recovery period, before progressing to the next set of tasks. This practice is useful with novices or less experienced performers and when the task is of a gross, complex or dangerous nature. It allows for variation and the effects of fatigue and can therefore raise motivation levels. For example, when coaching a school rugby team, the coach may develop a variety of skills within one session, allowing a recovery period after a block of strenuous skills for the players to focus their attention on a less physically demanding activity. An experienced performer may use the rest period for *mental practice*. The inclusion of recovery periods has proved to produce better results generally when compared with *massed practice*.

diuretics: drugs used to reduce the weight of athletes by increasing the flow of urine. Examples are hydrochlorothiazide and chlorthalidone, which are particularly beneficial in sports such as horse racing and boxing. The side effects are muscle cramps, dehydration and possibly kidney failure. See also *doping*.

Doggett's Coat and Badge: the oldest sculling race in the world held on the River Thames, instituted by Thomas Doggett in 1715. Crews race for an orange livery with a silver badge, hence the title 'Doggett's Coat and Badge'.

dominant culture: the particular set of ideas, viewpoints and beliefs which are values present in a society. It will ultimately serve the interests of the *ruling class* who will have imposed them through social structures such as the *mass media*, *education* systems and the law. If these values are radically undermined then social order will deteriorate and *sub-cultures* can emerge, which develop different ideas and values. It is mainly the case now in the Western world that a plurality of ideas and viewpoints can coexist within one society.

dominant learnt response: see *drive theory*

DOMS: see *delayed onset of muscle soreness*

doping: illegal methods of enhancing performance, which have been used since athletes in ancient Greece and Rome took substances to improve their athletic abilities. However, drug use in modern sport has become regular and systematised. Research shows it is more than a peripheral problem and operates at both *amateur* and *professional* level, among male and female athletes and across a wide variety of sports. Factors that led to an increase in the use of drugs include advances in biology and medicine; the use of drugs in World War II and the development and availability of testosterone, steroids and growth hormones in the 1950s. Drugs allow athletes to control and alter their bodies, though if used unwisely can lead to a loss of control. (See figure below.)

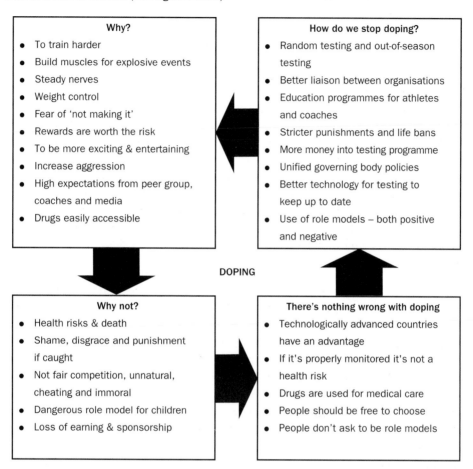

doping agents: a term used to denote any illegal drug such as cannabis or a narcotic. The *International Olympic Committee* defines doping agents as:

'the administration of or use by a competing athlete of any substance foreign to the body or any physiological substance taken in abnormal quantity or taken by abnormal route of entry into the body with the sole intention of increasing in an artificial and unfair manner his/her performance in competition'. See table on page 76.

dorsiflexion: movement pattern involving the decrease in angle at the ankle. The foot is raised upwards towards the tibia (shin bone) in the median (*saggital*) plane. For example, dorsiflexion occurs at the ankle during the 'kick' phase of the breaststroke and during the preparatory phase of a basketball jump shot as the player squats down before jumping into the air. (See appendix, page 269.)

Dover Games: see *Cotswold Games*

Doping agents

Types of drugs used	Reasons for use	Side effects	Which sports
Anabolic steroids – artificially produced male hormones e.g. nandrolone testosterone	Promote muscle growth Increase lean body weight Ability to train harder with less fatigue Repair body after stress Increased aggression	Liver damage Heart disease Acne Excessive aggression Females: Male features Irregular periods	Power and explosive events e.g. weightlifting, athletics, swimming
Narcotic analgesics – pain killers e.g. morphine, methadone	Reduce amount of pain Mask injury Increase pain limit	Highly addictive Increase initial injury Breathing problems Nausea and vomiting	All sports
Stimulants – stimulate the body mentally and physically e.g. amphetamine, ephedrine	Reduce tiredness Increase alertness Increase competitive Increase aggression	Rise in blood pressure Rise in body temperature increased heart beat Loss of appetite Addiction Death	Cycling Boxing
Beta blockers – can be used medically e.g antenolol, propanalol	Steady nerves Stop trembling	Low blood pressure Slow heart rate Tiredness	Shooting Archery Snooker Diving
Diuretics – remove fluid from the body e.g. triamterene bendrofluazide	Lose weight quickly Increase rate of passing urine	Dehydration Faintness Dizziness Muscle cramps	Horse racing Boxing
Peptide hormones – Naturally occurring e.g. erythropoietin/HCG Synthetic analogues e.g. EPO	Stimulate growth of naturally occurring steroids Build muscle Mend tissue Increase oxygen transport	Muscle wasting Abnormal growth of hands and feet EPO increases red cells in blood Clotting Stroke	Similar to steroids
Blood doping – Injection of blood to increase number of blood cells	Gives body more energy to work	Allergic reactions Hepatitis or AIDS Overload circulatory system Blood clots	Running Cycling Marathons Skiing

draft system: the pro draft system exists in the sports of *basketball* and *American football*. The strength of the *Big Time* inter-collegiate sport programmes in the *United States* ensures a steady influx of talented players into the professional sport scene. The draft is ranked and basically the lowest placed professional club has the first choice.

drill: see *military drill*

drive: the performer's energised state or level of *motivation* that is directed towards achieving a specific goal. The greater the need to succeed, the greater the drive. For example, an athlete with the ability to win a medal at the next *Olympic Games* may have a greater drive to train and alter their lifestyle compared with a person who jogs twice a week for reasons of personal fitness. Similarly, a novice tennis player's drive may be to learn how to serve consistently. The performers will remain motivated until they feel they have succeeded or reached their optimal level, as suggested by the *drive reduction theory*. When these objectives have been met new challenges need to be found.

drive reduction theory suggests that learning will occur due to the performer's desire to complete the task and only by achieving the goal will their *drive* be satisfied. When the task becomes habitual or a *skill* and the *S-R bond* strengthened, a new challenge needs to be set to motivate the performer to continue their development. For example, once a young tennis player learns to execute a basic forehand drive successfully, the coach will start to develop the power and accuracy of the shot before progressing to the more advanced topspin drive.

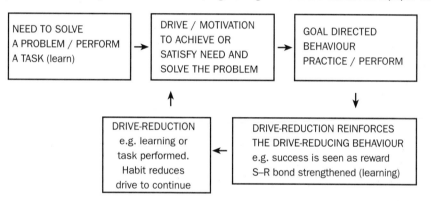

drive theory suggests that there is a linear relationship between *arousal* and performance. Later research adapted the theory, proposing that the performer's dominant learnt response would be more evident as their arousal level increased. This is often expressed as:

$$P = f(H \times D)$$

where P = performance, f = function, H = habit or dominant response and D = drive. As arousal increases, if the performer is highly skilled the performance will be of a high quality, whereas a novice will display their dominant habit: an incorrect technique. For example, a young basketball player during training has learnt the technique of a lay-up shot and is able to execute the skill reasonably well in practice. During a game situation, the pressure increases and the new skill that is not yet fully learnt is unsuccessful. However an experienced player's lay-up would be executed properly. Critics question the theory, as it does not explain the reasons why performers in the *autonomous stage of learning* often fail to complete skills in situations of high arousal. (See figure on page 78.)

dropout: the issue of dropout is closely related to *burnout*. One of the problems of highly organised sport programmes is that they expose children to intensely serious sport experiences. Dropping out of sport need not always be seen as a problem but as a natural shift in children's interests. However, should a child drop out due to negative experiences then this is viewed as a problem as a negative *attitude* has formed. Research suggests that negative experiences are often associated with situations where competitive abilities and competitive outcomes are heavily emphasised.

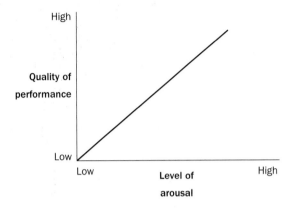

Drive theory

drug abuse: see *doping*

drug testing: process to ascertain if an athlete has been utilising an illegal substance to enhance performance. Various factors influence the effectiveness of such tests, such as the competitive calendar; the training regime; the type of activity involved and the technological capacity of the testing equipment. Decisions about the level and timing of testing are made by *UK Sport* in consultation with the *governing body* of sport. Testing at competitions is generally accepted as an effective method of deterring the use of *stimulants*, *beta blockers* and *diuretics*. See also *drug testing procedure*.

drug testing procedure: the procedure followed for *drug testing*. Athletes can be tested for drugs at any time, either on the day of competition or during training, and either very short or no notice is given. The procedure to be followed is outlined below:

1   athletes are notified in writing by an Independent Sampling Officer (ISO) that they have been selected for a drug test

2   a urine sample is given under supervision at the Doping Control Station

3   a pair of pre-sealed bottles A and B are chosen by the athlete and they are asked whether any medication has been taken

4   the sample is analysed at an accredited laboratory

5   if sample A is found to be clean sample B is destroyed and the negative result reported

6   if traces of a banned substance are found the governing body and the athlete are informed

7   sample B is then analysed

8   if sample B is found positive a decision is taken to suspend or ban the athlete

9   every athlete has the right to appeal.

dual use: the use of school facilities by the local community. This policy began in the 1970s when local *education authorities* were attempting a more efficient use of sporting facilities.

Advantages	Disadvantages
Maximise use of local sporting and recreational facilities	Time constraints; the local community cannot use during the school day
Increase revenue	Wear and tear of facilities; maintenance problems
Local and accessible facilities	Responsibility for the facilities is unclear
	School image may not be attractive to adults

Duke of Edinburgh Award Scheme: scheme that involves young people of between 14 and 20 years making positive use of their *leisure* time by encouraging them to commit themselves to numerous, challenging activities in order to develop their personal and social skills. Established in 1956, with bronze, silver and gold awards that are recognised and valued nationally.

dysfunction occurs when a part of the social structure does not contribute positively to the maintenance of society, resulting in disharmony and conflict. Behaviour or certain forms of organisation can upset the balance of the *social order*. This is closely related to *functionalist theory* but attempts to counter the problems associated with it, namely that everything in society is motivated by the need to allow that society to function effectively. In relation to sport, dysfunctional elements could be hooligans or when athletes are not co-operating within the sporting experience.

Do you need help with the synoptic element of your Physical Education course?

Go to page 274 for tips and advice.

Eastern European sport: from the end of World War II until the mid-1980s, East European sport was organised on a *centralised* approach, ideologically orientated, was state run and used as propaganda.

East German model: this became widely known as the 'East German machine' and was developed by the former German Democratic Republic in order to use sport as a vehicle for political propaganda. This system was similar to the old Soviet system (*Eastern European sport*) in their early sport *talent identification* schemes and specialised coaching methods using scientific knowledge. Problems associated with the system are now widely known and reported, particularly institutionalised drug use. However, their more positive legacy has been the adoption by many modern cultures of the *academies of sport* idea.

eccentric muscle contraction: involves the lengthening of the muscle during movement. It is a form of isotonic muscle contraction. It occurs, for example, in the bicep when lowering a weight during a bicep curl, or in the triceps during the downward phase of a press-up. The actin filaments are slowly moved away from the centre of the sarcomere. See also concentric muscle contraction.

economic systems: a term that stems from the control of material resources. Economic systems are often dependent on political ideologies. There are several forms, including:

* Market economy – which allows market forces to determine the allocation of resources. Factors of production are determined by supply and demand. This type of system allows freedom of choice and can efficiently allocate resources leading to economic growth. However, it leads to inequality of income and those with most money usually hold the most power.

* Socialism – system that involves collective ownership of the means of production and a major role for the state in the provision of services. In its extreme form of *communism* it dominated the centrally planned economies of Eastern Europe until 1989. China, North Korea and Cuba are still mainly governed in this way.

* Mixed economy – one that combines a market economy with some centrally planned or state-run enterprises. Governments are able to regulate the workings of the market through legislation. For example, the United Kingdom has a mixed economy.

* Transitional economy – occurs in countries which had centrally planned economies but which are now allowing market forces to operate at least in some parts of the economy. Many East European countries are in transition.

Centrally planned economy	Mixed economy	Market economy
Production organised and run by the state	Some production state-run, e.g. large-scale, 'essential' services	Production market-driven
Labour force directed and paid by the state	State and private firms compete for factors of production and customers	Wages determined by the market
Prices of goods and services controlled		Prices determined by supply and demand

economics of sport: this area of research focuses on issues such as performers salaries and their productivity, transfer of players, structure and operation of sporting leagues, sport products, inequality of resource distribution regarding racial and sex issues.

The sports industry produces vast amounts of income for governments, who also provide sport with grants. The size of the grants given to sport by different governments will often depend on their philosophy or ideology towards the place of sport in their society.

To some extent the sport industry is different to other industries in that sport organisations have to collaborate with each other to produce the product, for example a football match. In other industries companies cannot collude with each other. In the USA baseball receives special exemption from the governments anti-monopoly legislation. Sporting leagues are cartels where movement in and out is strictly controlled.

In the United Kingdom professional football clubs have floated on the stock exchange. They invest in new stadia and television revenues continue to expand and cause controversy over the amount of control the media should then wield.

education: the process of acquiring knowledge and skills in both a formal and informal manner. It is viewed as a life-long process but formal structures such as an education system play a major part, particularly during childhood and adolescence. In other cultures, such as primitive cultures, these more formal structures may not operate and education of the community takes place through their social groups (see also *public schools* and *state education*).

Education Acts: government legislation introduced with the specific aim of raising the standard of the education of children. They have been modified depending on the needs of society at the time and include:

Forster Education Act (1870) – was a great milestone in social welfare, as it created a system of state education whereas previously the education of the poor had been a parish responsibility. There was a developing initiative to build more schools and the Act was a result of some radical changes in social thinking by philanthropists and social reformers. The main points of the Act were as follows:

- England and Wales divided into 2500 school districts
- the Churches were to decide if new schools were to be built
- school boards had to be elected to finance schools from the rates
- a small fee was required initially, to be paid by the family but the very poor could receive free education

- the school age was not less than five years but no more than 13
- in terms of physical activity, military or Swedish *drill* was permitted.

The Butler Education Act (1944) – planned to reform education in Britain as it was a major social reform, aiming to ensure equal opportunity for all. Its main provisions were:

- there were to be 146 local *education authorities* rather than 300
- school-leaving age was raised to 15
- grammar school entry was to be free following a pass at the 11plus examination; other children to attend a secondary modern
- secondary grammar, technical and modern schools aimed to provide the most appropriate education based on the 11plus examination but this also proved to be a *social class* distinction
- local education authorities were to provide recreational facilities
- *physical education* teachers were to be given the same status as other teachers.

Education Reform Act (1988) – the Act was a far-reaching one, affecting *physical education* within the wider education system. A Conservative government seeking more control was challenging the traditionally *decentralised* system of education, which necessitated cutting the powers of *local authorities*. The following reforms were introduced:

- a *national curriculum* for children of school age in the state school system
- Statutory Attainment Targets were to provide guidelines on standards and secure some accountability
- *Local Management of Schools (LMS)*, where schools were given control of their own budgets
- some schools chose to opt out of *local authority* control and valued the status of being grant maintained. They received money directly from the government. Initial funding was generous but further changes have retracted this situation.

education authorities are committees with county councils and metropolitan district councils. The *Butler Education Act (1944)* made it mandatory for them to provide recreational facilities within schools. In the 1970s and 1980s local authorities helped the education authorities by providing money and these facilities became known as *dual use* and *joint provision* facilities.

Education Reform Act (1988): see *Education Acts*

Edwardian period: term given to the period between 1901–18, following the Victorian era. During this a time there was a heavy emphasis on improving the provision for the urban population, with increased *leisure* time for the *working classes,* better transport and improved communications. The suffragettes were fighting campaigns for equal rights for women, as were the trade unions for the workers. In terms of sport, the upper and middle classes were removing themselves even further from the working classes and the increase in exclusive sports clubs continued; particular examples were *golf* and *tennis*. Social factors enabled sport to become a major entertainment market with football the most popular. The northern *professionals* were beginning to threaten the southern *amateur* hold and the minimum professional wage was set in 1904 at £4 a week. The 1908 *Olympic Games* were held in London, although public interest was not great, but other activities such as horse racing, cricket and rugby league were popular.

Public schools continued their sporting traditions but the state schools now followed the *Forster Education Act* providing the working class children with the experiences of *military drill* and *Swedish gymnastics*. The *Syllabuses of Physical Training* were introduced by the *Board of Education* with games and recreative activities taking over from drill.

effective learning refers to the development of a performer's *motor programmes* and their execution. For example, the skills of catching, throwing, jumping and kicking. To maximise learning, effective learning should be combined with *affective learning* and the *cognitive theories of learning*.

effector mechanism: component of the *information-processing* model, which transfers the decision that has been made to the muscular system via motor nerves. For example, after a batsman decides which shot they wish to play based on the bowler's delivery, the effector mechanism starts the movement.

egalitarian: the philosophy of the equality of mankind and the desirability of political, social and economic equality. This has led to an emphasis on equity issues in sport such as creating more fairness of accessibility to sport participation.

ejection fraction: the percentage of blood that the heart pumps from the left ventricle with each contraction. It is calculated by dividing the *stroke volume* by the volume of blood in the ventricle following the diastolic (filling) phase of the *cardiac cycle*, and multiplying by 100. The heart of a trained athlete can contract more forcibly and can therefore eject more blood per beat. It therefore has a higher ejection faction.

elasticity: property of skeletal muscle which enables it to return to its original shape following contraction or extension. This enables repeated contractions to take place, such as when running or cycling.

electron transport chain: series of oxidation and reduction reactions in the breakdown (catabolism) of glucose. It forms the final stage of the *aerobic energy system* and occurs in the cristae of the *mitochondria*. It releases energy which can then be used to resynthesise *adenosine triphosphate (ATP)*. Hydrogen ions released in the *Krebs cycle* are oxidised in the electron transport chain to form water, whilst the electrons pass through a series of reactions and can generate large amounts of energy.

eligibility rules: rules that aim to set a 'level playing field' in sport so that all competitors, in theory, have an equal chance of succeeding. Such rules are needed to prevent cheating; competitors are sometimes tempted to cheat because of the attractiveness of financial rewards in modern sport.

There are eligibility rules that determine whether an athlete or sport is deemed to meet the requirements for entry to the *Olympic Games*; these rules can cover, for example, *amateur status*, age, gender, nationality and skill level.

elite: the most talented sports people or the most educationally gifted. The term suggests that only a minority can achieve the highest standards and usually determines unequal access to resources – facilities, personnel and funding. It is therefore an exclusive situation at the apex of the *participation pyramid* and it is suggested that the wider the base of participation the greater chance of producing elite athletes. In international competition the elite athletes are often considered to be ambassadors for their country.

emergent cultures means countries coming into being or notice. Some countries such as those in Africa, Latin America and South East Asia can be referred to as developing countries, or as less economically developed countries (LEDC). They do not necessarily come under the *communist* or *capitalist* systems but they were in the main colonised by the wealthier countries in the West. These countries face common social and sporting problems:

- their economies were land based, yet they are experiencing a shift towards an industrial economy
- an increase in urban populations led to a less active society
- their sport infrastructure could not initially match that of the West in terms of organisation and facilities
- Western sport tends to be more specialised, requiring more resources
- *discrimination* under colonial rule usually excluded native participation in sport at a high level. Independence helped to produce the democratisation of sport where the masses can experience activities previously enjoyed by the governing class.

New independent governments face the dilemma of either providing scarce resources for the masses or funding elite athletes who could compete on the world stage, which would in turn provide prestige, international recognition and potential financial gain – all factors difficult for governments to ignore. Appropriate selection of activities is needed if they are to realise their aims. This will be based on the resources available and the traditions of the population.

emergent leader: a leader who gains a position of authority by emerging from within a group, with the support of the members, based on their personal expertise, skill and knowledge. For example, the members of a local football team could vote amongst themselves to decide who they wished to be captain. This type of leader is in contrast to a *prescribed leader*, which is chosen externally.

emotions: a state of *arousal* experienced by a performer, which can be pleasurable, or unpleasurable depending on their perception of the situation. If the latter situation occurs the body makes physiological adjustments, as suggested by the *General Adaptation Syndrome*, in an attempt to return to a state of equilibrium. Emotions include joy, sadness, apprehension and excitement, all of which tend to be reactions to specific situations or experiences.

endocardium: the innermost layer of the heart composed of a single layer of epithelial cells. It enables the blood to flow more easily through the heart's chambers by preventing friction.

endorsements: where athletes display companies' names on their equipment, clothing and vehicles. This is known as endorsing a product. The performers are contracted to declare publicly their approval of a product or service. David Beckham of Manchester United endorses Adidas products, but his team mate, Ryan Giggs, endorses Reebok goods. Sports stars in the 1990s have emerged as personality advertising and are used as a 'big sell'.

endothermic reactions are those chemical reactions that occur (in the body, for example) that require *energy*. The resynthesis of *adenosine diphosphate (ADP)* into *adenosine triphosphate (ATP)* requires energy and is therefore endothermic. Thus:

$$ADP + P_i + energy \longrightarrow ATP$$

endowed schools: schools with a regular income, controlled by trustees.

energy: the capacity of the body to perform work. In terms of physical activity, energy and work can be used interchangeably and energy expenditure can be calculated by:

energy (work) = force × distance moved

This is measured in joules (which can be defined as the work done when a force of one newton (N) acts over a distance of one metre (m). By multiplying the subject's body weight (in kilograms) by ten we can determine the force in newtons. To calculate the energy expended by a 90 kg person walking over 100 m we would perform the following calculation:

energy (work) = 90 × 10 × 100 = 90 000 joules

Energy expenditure is mainly of concern when following a weight control programme, where we might need to analyse energy input from food and energy expenditure through exercise.

energy systems: the process of energy production in the body for muscular contraction that occurs when chemical energy is transformed into mechanical energy. Chemical energy exists in the muscle cell in the form of *adenosine triphosphate (ATP)*, a high energy phosphate molecule which when broken down releases the energy stored within its bonds. The energy can then be used to initiate muscle contraction and therefore movement.

The stores of ATP are limited in the body and the aim of the energy systems is to resynthesise or rebuild ATP, so that energy can be continually provided. There are three energy systems used for resynthesis of ATP, each operating depending upon the duration and intensity of the exercise that is to be undertaken:

1   *alactic energy system* or ATP-PC system – the first of the systems is the immediate source of energy, used in activities that are of short duration but high in intensity, such as a 100-metre sprint

2   *lactic acid energy system* or *glycolysis* – the second of the systems is used in activities or periods of exercise that are of fairly high intensity, such as a 400-metre run or whilst running up hills in cross country

3   *aerobic energy system* – the third system is the most efficient, since oxygen is available and is predominantly used in activities that are of long duration and low intensity, such as a marathon run.

The three energy systems

	Alactic (immediate)	Lactic acid (anaerobic glycolytic)	Aerobic (oxidative)
Substrate(s)	ATP, PC	glycogen or glucose	glycogen or glucose, fat, protein
Relative rate of ATP production	very fast	fast	slower
Duration at maximal pace	0–10 sec	0–180 sec	>3 min
Limiting factors	PC depletion	lactic acid accumulation	glycogen depletion
Examples of activities	power/weight lifting short sprints jumping, throwing	longer sprints middle-distance field games	endurance events marathon running field games

Essentially all of the energy systems are always functioning, even at rest. It is the relative contributions that each system makes in providing energy that varies. We can therefore view the energy systems as operating along a continuum.

environment: see *display (psychology)*

enzyme: a biological catalyst that is a protein found in the body used to speed up chemical reactions, especially the processes of energy release. Endurance training can improve the activity of oxidative (*aerobic*) enzymes, which work on breaking down our food fuel to release the energy stored within. In doing so the body's ability to utilise *glycogen* and fat as a fuel is increased which promotes a greater amount of available energy and an improved performance. Under *anaerobic* conditions the enzymes responsible for the breaking down of phosphocreatine (creatine kinase and phosphofructokinase) and our glycolytic enzymes respond positively to anaerobic training, e.g. sprint interval training and strength training.

EPI: see *Eysenck's personality inventory (EPI)*

epicardium: see *pericardium*

equal opportunity: the principle and practice of providing all people with the same chance to succeed irrespective of their sex, age, gender, physical ability or religious group. In the descriptive sense human beings patently do not possess the same amount of physical, mental or moral qualities. In the prescriptive sense, however, people ought to treat each other with equal respect, dignity and consideration. During the twentieth century there has been a growing democratisation of education, the workplace and sport in order to reduce the amount of *discrimination* felt by some sections of the population.

ergogenic aid: a substance or object that is used to enhance athletic performance. These can range from simple nasal strips (designed to improve oxygen intake) through to performance enhancing drugs (such as *human growth hormone*). Ergogenic aids generally fall into one of four categories:

- **pharmacological e.g.** *amphetamines/caffeine*
- **hormonal e.g.** *anabolic steroids/human growth hormone*
- **physiological e.g.** *blood doping/recombinant erythropoietin*
- **nutritional e.g.** *creatine supplementation/glycogen loading*.

Performers turn to these ergogenic aids in the hope of gaining a winning edge. Whilst many ergogenic aids remain legal, others are illegal and instead of enhancing performance can actually impair it, sometimes with fatal consequences.

erythopoietin (EPO): a naturally occurring hormone produced by the kidneys which stimulates red cell production. Increases of erythopoietin are very beneficial to the athlete since they increase the blood's oxygen-carrying capacity. This can occur naturally through *altitude training*, but since the introduction of a synthetic version it has become the cheater's choice of drug.

Although it has proven benefits, such as increases in haemoglobin content, fatigue index and *maximum oxygen uptake* (VO_2 max), EPO has a fatal side. In the early 1990s several Dutch cyclists died as a result of injecting EPO. It is not known how many red blood cells the drug produces when injected and it is thought that increased viscosity of the blood can lead to clotting and heart failure.

escape: to get away from or break free. With industrialisation in the eighteenth and nineteenth centuries, the movement of people from rural areas to the towns, poor working and living conditions led to the need for those people to get away and experience the *natural environment.* Numerous activities have been associated with the idea of escape, such as *cycling* and *rambling.*

Eskimo: see *Inuit*

esteem: to have great respect or high regard for. Talented athletes who reach the pinnacle of their sport are awarded honour and prestige that raises their social status. Such athletes may also become *role models* to younger people and their own *self-esteem* is also raised by a sense of achievement.

ethics: derived from the Greek word 'ethike', meaning science of morals or character. Ethics can be the moral principles or set of moral values held by an individual or group. It raises issues that have a moral dimension, such as debates over *doping* in sport and *gamesmanship* versus *sportsmanship*.

Ideal	Real
MOTIVES	
good bad	
Excellent play	Win at all costs
INTENTIONS	
good bad	
Sportsmanship – good game strategy	Gamesmanship – deceitful strategy
ACTION	
right wrong	
Purpose – establish dominance through excellence	Purpose – take out of game, do physical, emotional, mental harm

ethnic groups have racial, religious, linguistic and/or certain other traits in common. The social group usually sees itself as a distinct unit and attempts to preserve its identity through maintaining traditions and customs. Where a group forms a minority in the population this need can be heightened. In 1990s surveys suggested only 5.5 per cent of the British population described themselves as belonging to an ethnic group.

ethnic sports: see *Highland Games, Lakeland Sports, Wrestling, Cornish hurling*

etiquette: the customs or rules governing behaviour regarded as correct or acceptable in social or official life. Often a conventional but unwritten code of behaviour is followed by members of a social group. An example in sport may be shaking hands before a match (see sportsmanship).

European Charter on Sport for All: legislation requiring governments to promote sport as an important factor in human development. They should encourage and enable every individual to participate in sport, notably all young people – who should receive *physical education* and acquire basic sports skills. Participation should also take place in a safe and healthy environment

In co-operation with the appropriate sporting organisations governments should:

- ensure that everyone with ability and interest should be able to reach their own levels of personal achievement or publicly recognised levels of *excellence*

- protect and develop the ethical and moral basis of sport, protecting sports and sports people from exploitation for political, commercial and financial gain, including *doping*.

European sport: in 1988 the European Commission identified sport as performing five functions within society:

- educational
- social
- cultural
- recreational
- public health.

The Commission's main role is to consult with sports organisations across Europe to plan for sport development and identify potential problems. Europe can be seen as having two distinct identities – *Eastern Europe* and *Western Europe*. However, the structure tends to include the elements outlined below:

- there is a *grass roots* approach, which is different from the approach in the United States of America, which has a more professional base, linked to business

- *national identity* is important – the Amsterdam Declaration states 'sport represents and strengthens national or regional identity by giving people a sense of belonging to a group, uniting players and spectators'. International competition remains an important element in countries demonstrating their culture and nationhood. This is again different from the United States where there is less need for inter-state competitions

- traditionally modern sport has its roots in Europe where the birth of industrialisation occurred, and it has a set place within our societies

- European Union regulations can be applied to sporting matters, such as the *Bosman* ruling and the decision to phase out from 2001 all forms of tobacco *sponsorship* and *advertising*, except on premises where cigarettes are sold.

eustress: form of positive *stress* that performers actively seek to test their *abilities* to the limit. It can enhance performance by focusing *attention* and heightening the emotions felt. If the individual successfully completes the task in situations involving danger or high expectation, it can lead to high levels of *intrinsic motivation* and self-satisfaction. For example, many *adventurous activities* can initiate this response, as do performances in front of *significant others*.

evaluation apprehension: form of *anxiety* caused when an individual perceives their performance is being judged by an *audience*. Cottrell (1968) suggested *social facilitation* occurs in the presence of others, but higher and detrimental *arousal* was caused if the performer felt others were assessing their actions. For example, an athlete may execute techniques in training correctly, but in competition may worry about what the spectators think of their performance. The result may be a deterioration in performance.

evangelism: the practice of spreading the Christian gospel. It emphasises personal conversion and faith for salvation. In the nineteenth century the evangelists restricted the recreations of the working classes believing their *popular recreations* to be sinful and associated with gambling and alcohol.

eversion: movement pattern which takes place at the ankle characterised by turning the sole of the foot laterally outwards. For example, during the breaststroke 'kick' action in swimming, the foot is everted to increase the contact of the foot with the water. (See appendix.)

excellence: a special ability beyond the norm, to which many aspire but few go on to achieve. For our purposes we mean the superior, *elite* athletes at both *amateur* and *professional* level who reach the pinnacle of performance in their chosen sport. Excellence usually suggests a specialism in one or a few activities and is judged against national and international standards. For example, the developers of excellence in sport are usually *Sport England*, the national *governing bodies*, *Sport Coach UK*, the *British Olympic Association* and *local authorities*. The pursuit of excellence in sport is encouraged for a variety of reasons including:

- sport can bring about change in peoples' lifestyles which have become increasingly sedentary and controlled
- curiosity about individual and human potential often means sport is called 'the last frontier'
- sport can provide alternative employment with the added attraction of high social status if high-level success is achieved
- it can give individuals a high sense of *self-esteem,* a feeling of quality or worth in their lives
- sporting success can boost national pride and morale and accrue economic benefits
- mass populations can be entertained in socially accepted activities
- the base of the *participation pyramid* can be increased by others wishing to participate in sport.

However the problems with attempting to develop excellence include:

- it is elitist – it only serves the interests of a few
- costly resources are required for a minority of sport participants
- over-specialisation and obsession with a physical activity can occur which may have damaging physiological and psychological effects
- the moral value of sport can be lost due to the 'win at all costs' attitude that is likely to be exacerbated when the stakes are higher.

See the diagram on page 90.

excess post-exercise oxygen consumption (EPOC): the amount of oxygen consumed during recovery above that which normally would have been consumed at rest in the same period of time. This is commonly referred to as the *oxygen debt* and will accrue whenever the body has undertaken some form of exercise anaerobically, at quite intense levels of exercise lasting up to three minutes, or when the *anaerobic threshold* has been exceeded. The EPOC consists of two components: the *alactacid debt* (fast component) and the *lactacid debt* (slow component). (See the figure on page 91.)

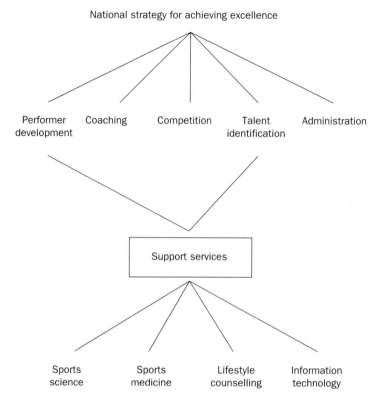

National strategy for achieving excellence

Performer development   Coaching   Competition   Talent identification   Administration

Support services

Sports science   Sports medicine   Lifestyle counselling   Information technology

Excellence

exclusion: a shorthand label for what can happen when individuals or areas suffer a combination of linked problems such as unemployment, poor skills, low incomes, poor housing, high crime environments, bad health and family breakdowns.

In the most intensive study of exclusion Europe-wide, it is seen that unemployment and low income lead to exclusion from a fair share of social 'goods' and capital in the form of recognition, income and work. Combinations of aspects of exclusion can be said to lead to double deprivation, for example, being elderly and from an ethnic minority. If exclusion is prolonged in youth it can have lasting effects in terms of playing recreationally, socialising and competing to achieve. The opportunity to realise sporting potential is significantly influenced by an individual's social background.

Governments now regard sport and recreation as having wider benefits to society, particularly in helping people feel included and important in their own communities. See also *inclusiveness*.

exclusivity: belonging to or serving a privileged minority. An example is a private school or private sports *club*. Access is denied to others who may not meet the criteria and this can involve *discrimination*.

executive motor programme: this organises a series of *subroutines* into the correct sequence to perform a movement, adapting it to changes in the environment. Motor programmes are based on a hierarchical structure, involving movements that are autonomous

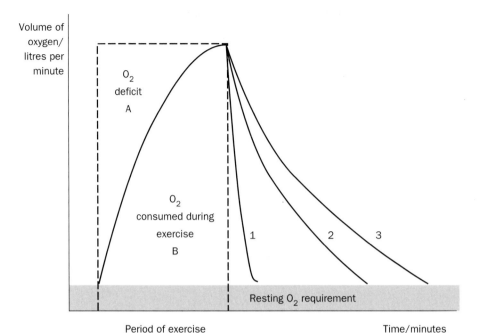

$$A+B = \text{Total oxygen demand during}$$
$$\text{period of exercise in excess of}$$
$$\text{that required at rest.}$$

$$1 = \text{Fast component or alactic EPOC}$$
$$2 = \text{Lactic acid EPOC}$$
$$3 = \text{Non-oxygen deficit EPOC}$$
$$2+3 = \text{Slow component}$$
$$1+2+3 = \text{EPOC or 'oxygen debt'}$$

Excess post-exercise oxygen consumption (EPOC) (see page 89)

at the lower level with more complex subroutines at the peak. As the performer becomes more skilled, the existing executive motor programme is relegated and superseded by a new programme. For example, a tennis player will initially develop the skill of hitting the ball by learning the stance, grip, swing and follow-through. When the *autonomous stage of learning* is reached, these form part of the new programme, which may include drive, smash, volley and lob. These in turn may become forehand shots and so on. These well-learnt programmes are often considered to be under *open loop control*, while the actions that need some sort of evaluation are under *closed loop control*. However, some of the limitations of these theories were answered by the *schema theory*.

exhaustion: final stage of the *general adaptation syndrome*, when the body begins to fail to cope with the effects of *stress*. The performer starts to develop various physiological disorders, which can include heart disease, high blood pressure and the inability to fight infection.

exothermic reactions are those chemical reactions that give off *energy*. For example, the breakdown of adenosine triphosphate (ATP) releases energy for muscular contraction.

$$ATP \longrightarrow ADP + P_i + energy$$

expectations: generally accepted codes of behaviour and roles within a group or society that are actively promoted. They are used as part of the *socialisation* process. Positive expectations from a coach or teacher can motivate the performer to fulfil those expectations. For example, a coach may encourage *assertive behaviour* during the game situation of all players, rather than acts of *aggression*, which may lead to fouls and penalties. Expectations can also be negative when they are informed by *stereotypes* and *prejudices*.

experiential learning involves the performer learning by doing. Gallway (1977) suggests the individual should be allowed to discover movement patterns, experience the consequences and subsequently modify the action to cope with the situation. Learning is based on the use of *internal feedback*, making the performer responsible for the understanding of the action and developing *kinaesthesis*. For example, a football player is given the task of shooting from different positions. During the practice session they develop a 'feel' for how hard to kick the ball for the shot to be effective.

expiration: breathing out or the process by which air is forced out of the lungs into the atmosphere. At rest, this is usually a passive process involving a relaxation of the inspiratory muscles (external intercostal muscles and the diaphragm) and elastic recoil of lung tissue. During exercise, expiration becomes a more active process, which involves the internal intercostal muscles speeding up the process by pulling rib cage down. In addition skeletal muscles such as the latissimus dorsi and the abdominal muscles assist the action.

expiratory reserve volume (ERV): the maximum volume of air that can be expelled from the lungs after a normal expiration, which for an average adult male is approximately 1500 cm³. During exercise the expiratory reserve volume decreases to enable an increase in the performer's *tidal volume*. (See appendix, page 273.)

extension: movement pattern involving an increase in angle of articulating bones. For example in performing a press-up, the angle between the humerus and ulna increases causing extension at the elbow. A muscle which causes extension is known as an *extensor*, which in the case of a push-up, is the tricep brachii. Extreme extension, usually at an angle of greater than 180°, is known as hyperextension. (See appendix, page 268.)

extensor: a muscle which causes *extension*. For example, the quadriceps femoris causes extension of the lower leg at the knee joint when kicking a football.

external feedback: see *feedback*

externally paced skill involves the performer reacting to the changing environmental conditions. They have little control over when the movement has to be executed. These types of skill are placed on the same *continuum* as *self-paced skills* and are often examples of *open skills*. Examples include receiving a pass during a game of hockey, white water rafting or batting in a game of cricket.

exteroceptors gather information from outside the body. They allow the performer to detect *stimuli* from the *display* by means of vision, touch, hearing, smell and taste. Other components of the *sensory system* include proprioceptors and introceptors.

extra-curricular sport: taking place outside the normal school timetable. The main focus is on improving performance standards rather than the educational process that is the main emphasis in the *physical education* lesson. It is viewed as an opportunity for children to extend their interest or ability in physical activities. The changes in society and education in the last 20 years have affected such opportunities with a reduction in emphasis on the sporting *elite*. Factors affecting extra-curricular activities have been:

- the teachers' strikes in the early 1980s which diminished teacher goodwill
- financial cuts felt in terms of transport
- the *Local Management of Schools* enabled schools to boost their funds by selling off playing fields
- the increasing amount of leisure and employment opportunities available to teenagers meant competing for the school team seemed less attractive
- the anti-competitive lobby became more vocal espousing the idea that competition was harmful to children

The focus of the 1995 government document Sport: *Raising the Game* is mainly on reinstating the status of school sport within school life.

extra-mural: inter-school competitions in the United States of America which can be informal or highly organised and serious. The students go through a more selective process than the *intra-mural* activities. The activities are widely reported by the press and the local community takes considerable interest.

extrinsic motivation: motivation for success based on the external rewards given to the performer which can influence behaviour. They are used for *reinforcement*, to shape behaviour in an attempt to encourage repetition of the action. Reinforcers can be tangible, such as cups, medals, certificates or money, but can also be intangible, for example, praise, a round of applause, social status, recognition or the glory of winning. Care must be taken not to over-use extrinsic rewards, as the performer may become over-reliant on them and if withdrawn the performer may lose the *motivation* to continue participating. Their use should be combined with a performer's *intrinsic motivation*.

extrovert: a person who is sociable, active, outgoing, optimistic and impulsive. These *traits* are said to be due to the relative insensitivity of their *reticular activating system* to incoming sensory information, leading to low levels of *arousal*. As a result they need to increase stimulation levels to avoid boredom and prefer situations that involve other people or challenges. It has been suggested extroverts cope better with competitive, pressurised, stressful situations and occupy positions of responsibility. In comparison, *introverts* possess the opposite traits and are placed at the other end of the *continuum*. These characteristics can be measured using *Eysenck's personality inventory (EPI)* or *Cattell's 16 personality factors questionnaire*.

Eysenck's personality inventory (EPI) measures the personality *traits* of an individual along two dimensions: introversion–extroversion and stable–neuroticism, using a questionnaire requiring a series of 'yes' or 'no' responses. A personal profile is then constructed with a score for each dimension. Usually most people do not fall into the extremes of each category. Within the test is a lie scale, which invalidates the results if exceeded. See also *trait theory*.

fag: a young public schoolboy who performs menial chores for an older boy or prefect. *Thomas Arnold* discouraged this system believing it to be open to abuse, leading to bullying. In relation to sporting activities, the younger boys would 'fag at *fives*', meaning they would collect the balls whilst the older boys played the game.

fair: travelling entertainment with side-shows. It was at the fair that the *working classes* had some fun, saw new faces and experienced fresh amusements. The fair, especially in medieval times, was granted by the king and could last up to three days. Both fairs and markets would bring in merchants and traders. They were usually granted to the Church and often landed on *holy days* or feast days in honour of a saint. Entertainment was a key feature with the jugglers, minstrels, freak shows, the unfortunate bear on his chain destined to be baited, cock fighting, dicing, wagering, dancing and so on.

fair play is defined by the *European Charter on Sport for All* as much more than playing within the *rules*. It incorporates the concepts of friendship, respect for others and always playing in the right spirit. It is defined as a way of thinking not just of behaving. It concerns issues such as the elimination of cheating, *gamesmanship, doping*, violence, exploitation, unequal opportunities, excessive *commercialisation* and corruption. Fair play is a positive concept. If practised fairly, sport is a culturally enriching experience and an individual is given the opportunity for self-expression and personal achievement. Sport promotes responsibility to others and for the environment. According to the European Charter on Sport for All, providers of sporting activities should make fair play a central concept.

far transfer: see *transfer of learning*

Fartlek training: form of endurance conditioning where the aerobic *energy system* is stressed due to the continuous nature of the exercise. The key to this type of training is that the speed or intensity of the exercise is varied so that both aerobic and anaerobic *energy systems* can be stressed. Fartlek sessions are usually performed for a minimum of 45 minutes, with the intensity of the session varying from low-intensity walking to high-intensity sprinting. Traditionally, this form of training has taken place in the countryside over varied terrain, but this alternating pace method could be practised anywhere in your local environment for, example:

- a 15-minute jog at 60 per cent *maximum heart rate* (MHR)
- a sprint for one lamp post/easy jog for three lamp posts
- repeat ten times
- walk for 90 seconds
- a 5-minute jog at 75 per cent MHR, and so on.

The benefits of this training are that it can be adapted to the individual, is easy to administer and can also be fun, offering variety to what some regard as the monotony of continuous jogging. Since both aerobic and anaerobic systems are stressed through this method of training, a wealth of sportspeople can benefit and it is particularly suited to those activities that involve a mixture of *aerobic* and *anaerobic* work, for example, games such as rugby, netball, soccer or hockey.

fast twitch muscle fibre: type of muscle fibre suited to high intensity, power activities involving anaerobic work. These fibres have a low oxidative capacity and a high glycolytic capacity. The physiological characteristics of fast twitch fibres differ greatly from *slow twitch fibres*, which include:

- possession of greater amounts of ATPase – the enzyme responsible for splitting *ATP*
- a more highly developed sarcoplasmic reticulum, which means greater amounts of calcium can arrive at the muscle cell initiating quicker contractile speeds. Indeed slow twitch fibres take approximately 110 milliseconds to reach maximal tension whilst fast twitch can reach it in a mere 50 milliseconds
- the ability to generate greater force than slow twitch motor units since there are more fast twitch fibres per motor unit than in slow twitch motor units.

Fast twitch fibres are also known as 'type 2 fibres' and are commonly sub-divided into:

- type 2a or fast oxidative glycolytic (FOG) fibres pick up certain slow twitch characteristics as a result of endurance training. They therefore tend to have a greater resistance to fatigue
- type 2b or fast twitch glycolytic (FTG) fibres can generate much greater forces
- type 2c have recently been recognised, and are recruited for extremely explosive activities such as the power lift.

fat: an organic lipid compound formed from glycerol and fatty acids. It exists in the body in many forms, including adipose tissue, triglycerides and *free fatty acids*. Fat is our major energy source with up to 70 per cent of our energy derived from it at rest. When sufficient oxygen is available to the muscle cell, fatty acids constitute the favoured fuel for energy production and during low-intensity exercise fat is a major source as the body tries to spare the limited stores of *glycogen* for higher intensity bouts of exercise. Due to the hydrophobic (low water solubility) quality of fat, energy production is slow so the body cannot use fat as its sole fuel source and energy production is therefore usually fuelled by a combination of fat and glycogen. One explanation of athlete 'hitting the wall' is that all their glycogen stores have been depleted and the athlete is trying to metabolise fat as a sole fuel source. Endurance training can encourage the body to utilise fat as a fuel, thus depleting glycogen less. However, the risks of excessive fat consumption are well documented, so it is recommended that an athlete's diet should not consist of more than 30 per cent fat of total calories consumed.

fatigue: occurs when the body is unable to resynthesise *adenosine triphosphate (ATP)* for energy. This is caused by three main factors:

- lack of oxygen – leading to a build up of lactic acid and lowering of the levels of blood acidity
- lack of phosphocreatine (PC)
- lack of glycogen and glucose.

The onset of fatigue can be delayed by utilising appropriate training methods to delay *onset of blood lactate accumulation (OBLA)* and improve the aerobic system.

faulty processes: the causes of a group not reaching its potential or fulfilling its goal. The *actual productivity* of the group does not match its *potential productivity*. The causes usually fall into the two categories of co-ordination problems and motivational losses. The former may include lack of teamwork, poor execution of tactics and poor concentration, while the latter is due to a lack of universal commitment to the same goals. Some group members perhaps feel less valued, illustrating the *Ringlemann effect* and elements of *social loafing*. See also *group productivity*.

federalism: where the powers of government are divided between the national and the state or provincial governments. For example, when the United States sought to free themselves from Britain, they created a system where the powers of the new national government were restricted but it could act on matters of national interest such as defence.

feedback: information received by the individual or group either during or after completion of the performance. It can be used for a variety of purposes including the detection and correction of errors, for providing *motivation* during the learning process and *reinforcement* of actions. The nature of the feedback given will alter depending on the performer's *stage of learning*, but it is vital that all information is accurate, limited to key points and relevant to the individual or group. Numerous forms of feedback are outlined below:

- Intrinsic or internal feedback – received from within the performer via *proprioceptors* developing a kinaesthetic awareness. As the performer becomes more skilled, they are able to detect and correct their own faults. For example, a more experienced gymnast completing a vault will be able to feel if they opened from the tuck position at the correct time.

- Extrinsic or external feedback – received from outside the performer usually via sound or vision, through their *exteroceptors*, from the coach, teacher, team mates or even spectators. This form of information is used extensively during the *cognitive* and *associative phases of learning*. For example, a less experienced gymnast completing a vault will rely on *guidance* from the coach concerning their performance, as they have not yet developed their kinaesthetic awareness fully. Also known as *augmented feedback*. See also *knowledge of results* and *knowledge of performance*.

- Continuous feedback – form of feedback received during the activity via *proprioceptors* or *kinaesthesis*. For example, a badminton player knows if he or she is hitting the shuttlecock properly because of the 'feel' and sound experienced during the rally. Information may also be received from an external source, e.g., a coach.

- Terminal feedback – received after the activity. For example, it may be given immediately by the coach or some time later, such as when analysing a video of the performance.

- Positive feedback – used as a form of *reinforcement* if the performance was successful, encouraging a repetition of the action. For example, the coach of a netball team would praise a good shot or attempt at the ring.

- Negative feedback – received if the performance was incorrect, to discourage a repetition of the action. For example, the coach of the same netball team would highlight faults in a poor attempt.

female education lagged behind that of boys for many years. This was based on the assumption that women required social accomplishments rather than intellectual development. The idea was challenged in the Victorian era when pioneers such as Frances Buss and Dorothea Beale founded the North London Collegiate School and Cheltenham Ladies College. These were to become serious educational establishments for the upper and middle classes.

The Schools Inquiry Commission 1868 encouraged the girls' foundation schools. In 1881 the universities recognised that girls fulfilled the degree requirements of boys. By 1898, following the Endowed Schools Act there were 80 *endowed* girls schools. The 1918 Act gave girls the same educational advantages as boys. Madame *Bergman Osterberg* was to have a long lasting effect in her role following her appointment in 1881 as Lady Superintendent of Physical Education for the London School Board.

femininity: characteristics associated with being a woman. The *stereotype* of femininity has tended to restrict the feminine role, constraining women to act out defenceless and helpless roles and effectively keeping them out of many forms of sport. This stereotype was a powerful force during the *Victorian era* with its emphasis on the 'medical vulnerability', emotional nature and social limitations of women. Women's sport struck a balance between the beginnings of physical liberation and what was considered socially respectable. Women are constantly trying to re-define their roles and therefore femininity is a changing concept.

fencing: the dextrous use of a sword for attack or defence. It has its roots in the traditions of knightly chivalry and today it is a sport practised throughout the world with three weapons: the **foil** (origin – sporting purposes), the **epee** (origin – infantry fighting) and the **sabre** (origin – cavalry weapon). By the sixteenth century the broadsword was made obsolete as its military function was no longer required but professional swordsmen still used it for staging exciting sporting contests. New fencing weapons and styles were imported from Europe and the rapier in the sixteenth century became popular, as were fencing lessons which formed part of a gentleman's education. Duels were commonly used as a means of settling disputes. Fencing developed popularity in the *public schools* and universities during the nineteenth century. In 1861 it was included in the curriculum of the army school of physical training.

Festinger's attitude theory: see *cognitive dissonance theory*

Fiedler's contingency model of leadership: see *contingency theory of leadership*

field sports: an umbrella term to cover activities such as *fox hunting*, hare *coursing*, angling, shooting and deer stalking.

fifty plus: a campaign in 1983 by the Sports Council to raise participation in physical and sporting activities for this age group. This age group is increasingly affluent as personal pensions have improved during the twentieth century and people have more disposable income. They are also generally more active and healthier than ever before and an increase in activity can help prevent the onset of ageing. The social benefits are also stressed as this can be a time of dramatic change for many people: some may be widowed, some may retire or be made redundant, and family obligations may change. Active lifestyles can help people overcome great social change. This group of people comprises a potentially rich market for sport.

fight or flight response: reaction of a person when faced with a situation of perceived danger or threat that occurs during the 'alarm' stage of the *general adaptation syndrome*. The secretion of hormones by the nervous system increases the *arousal* level causing physiological changes such as increased heart rate and breathing. The performer either deals with the situation or avoids it. For example, a footballer facing a penalty shoot-out, will either take their turn or decline, leaving the task to others.

fighting games: contests of the most direct kind between two individuals. Examples are *boxing*, judo, *fencing*, wrestling and *martial arts*. The modern versions have rule structures to contain potential physical harm to opponents. They use systems of points for hitting targets or the 'hold' as a form of domination, and take place within a confined area and a set period of time.

fine skill involves the performer executing accurate and precise actions using small muscle groups. These types of skill are placed on the same *continuum* as *gross skills*. Examples include a snooker shot or throwing a dart. Some skills combine both fine and gross skills, such as the use of the fingers during spin bowling combined with the overall run-up and delivery.

Fishbein's attitude theory: suggests a person's behaviour can best be predicted based on their 'behavioural intention'. If they have a positive *attitude* and intend to participate they are more likely to do so. The influence of *significant others* is also relevant and can affect a performer's intent, as they wish to conform to social *norms*, i.e., it is socially desirable. For example, an individual has a positive attitude toward watersports, but this does not mean they take part regularly in all watersports, due to lack of time, facilities, injuries, etc.

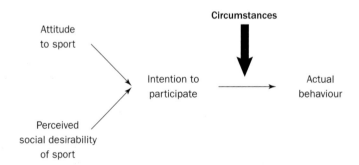

fitness: the ability to meet the demands of your environment or lifestyle. Each individual has different requirements depending on the nature of their job, circumstances and leisure activities. Fitness is generally sub-divided into:

* *health-related fitness* – includes strength, speed, stamina, muscular endurance, flexibility and body composition
* *skill-related fitness* – includes agility, balance, co-ordination, reaction time and power.

Components of fitness for different activities can be identified and developed according to the requirements and ability of the individual. See also *measurement of fitness*.

fitness testing: see *measurement of fitness*

FITT regime: the principles of training of **f**requency, **i**ntensity, **t**ime and **t**ype.

Fitts and Posner's stages of learning theory proposes that a performer will experience three progressive phases of development when learning a new skill. They are:

- the *cognitive phase of learning*
- the *associative phase of learning*
- the *autonomous phase of learning*.

fives: a ball game similar to squash but played with bats or hands. It was played at *inns* and other public places, becoming popular in the nineteenth century *public schools*, but as it was an individual game it did not gain favour with the masters. Therefore it was mainly played in recreational time by the boys and consequently did not establish well-known formal *rules* and individual schools had their own variations of the game.

fixator: muscles that allow the *agonist* to work effectively by stabilising the bones. They stabilise the *origin* of the agonist, so that it can pull against the bone to achieve an effective contraction. For example, during the bicep curl, the trapezius acts as the fixator, stabilising the scapula (the origin of the bicep) so that the bicep can pull against it to raise the lower arm.

fixed joint: bones connected by fibrous tissue which have no joint cavity. There is no observable movement and they include the sutures of the cranium. They are also known as fibrous joints.

flat bone: provides suitable sites for muscle attachment, with the *origins* of the muscles often attaching to them. Examples include the sternum, the bones of the cranium, the bones of the pelvis, and upon close inspection it can be seen that the bones of the ribs are also flat offering protection to the internal organs of the body. The pelvis, sternum and cranium also produce blood cells.

Fleishman's taxonomy of motor abilities: method of classifying a performer's *abilities*, which are sub-divided into 11 perceptual and nine physical motor abilities. The former include *co-ordination*, precision, aiming, *reaction time*, manual dexterity and *speed*; the latter are more linked to gross movement and components of fitness such as *strength*, *flexibility*, *balance* and stamina.

flexibility: the range of movement possible at a joint. Flexibility is determined by the elasticity of ligaments, tendons, the strength of the surrounding muscles and the shape of articulating bones. Often the degree of movement is determined by the type of joint, since joints are either designed for stability or mobility. Flexibility is lost very quickly through inactivity and must therefore be constantly developed by the athlete. Mobility training should be carried out at the end of a training session when muscles are usually warm, as part of a *cooldown*. Flexibility can be measured by the 'sit and reach test', providing an indication of the flexibility of the lower back and hamstrings.

flexion: movement pattern or joint action characterised by the decrease in angle between the two articulating bones. For example, in the performance of a bicep curl, where the lower arm moves towards the shoulder, the angle between the humerus and radius decreases, causing flexion at the elbow. A muscle which causes flexion is known as a *flexor*. In the case of a bicep curl, the bicep brachii is the flexor. (See appendix, page 268.)

flexor: a muscle which causes *flexion*. For example, the biceps femoris cause flexion of the lower leg at the knee joint.

folk sports: activities originating from or traditional to the common people of a country. They often originated from rustic festivals or rituals, for example, *mob games*, running events and *wrestling*.

football: any of various games played with a round or oval ball and usually based on two teams competing to kick, butt, carry or otherwise propel the ball into each other's goal or territory. Variations include Australian football, *American football* and *Association football*. The game originated as a *mob game* and as such there were many local variations.

Football League: an organisation that exists for the benefit of its membership, the professional clubs. Its strength is the week-by-week programme of League matches, but its role has always been different to the Football Association who formed the Cup competition. They are two separate bodies with similar but some competing interests. (See *Association football*).

Football Trust: an organisation founded in 1979 by the pools companies Littlewoods, Vernons and Zetters. The Trust's priority task is to help the Premier League, *Football League* and Scottish Football League clubs to meet the cost of implementing the recommendations of the Taylor Report (which outlined the need for improved safety at sports stadia), notably new grounds, new stands, seating and roofing. The Trust received the proceeds of a reduction in pool betting duty (RPBD) in 1990 to help fund this work. Some of the successes have been:

- new grounds have been created, for example, at Chester and Millwall
- contributions have been made to each of the home nations' national stadiums
- CCTV cameras have been installed to help combat *hooliganism*
- the Football in the Community Programme owes its existence to the Trust with investments exceeding £5.5 million
- investment has been made into training facilities and youth development
- football in schools and women's football (£800,000 since 1989) have all benefited
- funds from 'Spot the Ball' competitions were lucrative until the advent of the *National Lottery* resulted in them being curtailed in 1997.

forced expiratory volume (FEV1): the percentage of *vital capacity* that can be expired in one second. This is usually about 85 per cent and gives an indication of the overall efficiency of the airways.

Forster Education Act: see *Education Acts*

Foundation for Sport and the Arts: an organisation set up by the pools promoters in 1991 to channel funds into sport and the arts. The pools provide approximately £60 million annually that can be used for the benefit of sport. The Foundation works closely with the sports councils and administers grants while its main aims are to:

- support the improvement of existing facilities
- assist the construction of new sport venues
- help with appropriate sports projects (schools, disabled, *Olympic* and *Paralympic* teams).

fox hunting: the pursuit of a wild fox with a pack of hounds. Each hunt has its own designated area called the hunt country. The hunt meets at a predetermined place and moves off to a draw – particular woodland or other habitat where foxes are likely to be found. The hounds work as a pack and are bred for intelligence, stamina and speed. By the turn of the eighteenth century fox hunting had become one of England's premier sports with a fashionable following. It represented the power structure of the countryside. By the late *Victorian* and *Edwardian* times subscription packs developed where members of the hunt would contribute significantly to the master's expenses. Women and children were also included and the hunt was very much a social occasion. The *railways* enabled wealthy urbanites to join the event. This activity is still a highly controversial issue today with some wishing to curtail it and others defending the traditional pastime.

France: the area of France is 210,000 square miles. It has a similar population to Britain but France has twice the area and therefore has a lower population density and is more rural. Paris dominates France in wealth and political influence. Political power is shared between the president and parliament. The president appoints the prime minister who deals with the day-to-day running of the country. The figure on page 102 gives a summary of some of the physical and social features of France.

free fatty acids (FFA): the primary source of energy, which is derived from *fat*, that is used by the muscles. Once freed from the triglyceride molecule (the stored form of fat), free fatty acids enter the blood stream and can be transported around the body. Once inside the muscle cell the FFAs undergo 'beta oxidation', a catabolic process which takes place in the *mitochondria*. Beta oxidation produces *acetyl co-A* which can then enter the *Krebs cycle* and follow the same path of metabolism as glycogen. Fat metabolism can generate much more energy since the fat molecule contains more carbon, which produces more acetyl co-A and therefore more electrons can enter the *electron transport chain*. One fatty acid molecule can yield up to 131 ATP molecules when completely oxidated, compared to 38 molecules of ATP yielded from glucose.

French sports system: the sports movement is based on two networks: federation and Olympic. The former was developed from the club level up to the federation while the latter developed the opposite way, from the government level down, and is administered by the National Olympic Committee.

Summary of the French sports system:

* there is a *centralised* political approach
* the federation, similar to the British *governing bodies*, is the fulcrum of French sport and is answerable to the Minister of Sport
* there is a tradition of multi-sport federations unlike the British tradition of single sport clubs
* *elite* sport was encouraged by the policies of General de Gaulle and has received state aid and support with the development of elite centres like *INSEP*
* there are strong links between school and civil clubs
* the facilities in schools are generally poor and have led to the use of more municipal facilities
* *physical education* is an examination subject on a compulsory basis and a rigid programme is followed
* a programme of *sport pours tous* similar to our Sport for All is aimed at improving the health of the nation.

A B C D E F G H I J K L M N O P Q R S T U V W X Y Z

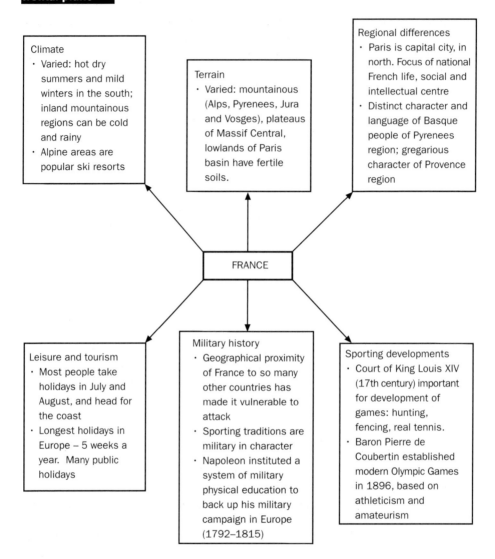

France

frontal plane: divides the body anterio-posteriorally, i.e. into front and back halves. Joint actions which work parallel to this plane are said to operate in the frontal plane. Such movement patterns include *abduction*, *adduction*, lateral flexion of the neck and trunk, scapulae elevation and depression and scapulae protraction and retraction. A knowledge of the planes of movement is essential when analysing movement. It is also known as the coronal plane. (See appendix, page 256.)

frontier: the limit of knowledge of a particular field. Sport is often called 'the last frontier' as we still do not know the limitations of human achievement in sport. It is an emotive term for Americans for it also links to the history of the settlement of their country as each frontier was moved from east to west. Qualities required to push back any frontier, be it geographical or of a sporting nature, are bravery, courage, strength and determination.

frustration–aggression hypothesis: this suggests that when the goal of a performer is blocked they become frustrated and this always leads to *aggression*. If released through an aggressive act, catharsis occurs and the performer is able to return to a stable emotional state. However if they are unable to release their frustration via an aggressive act, this merely causes more frustration and the cycle starts again (see the diagram below). For example, a basketball player who drives for a lay-up shot is constantly blocked by an opponent, causing frustration and the subsequent aggressive act may involve breaking the rules and fouling the defender. This results in a reduction in frustration allowing the player to refocus on the game.

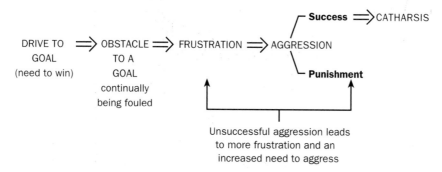

However the theory does not account for acts of aggression that are pre-meditated, learnt from others (see *social learning theory*) or purely instinctive. Also not all frustration experienced during performance will lead to an aggressive act as often performers employ various *stress management* techniques to control increasing levels of arousal. More recent studies have been developed based on the theory incorporating environmental factors and the effects of social learning (see *aggressive cue theory*).

functional classification: see *classification*

functionalist theory: that approach in *sociology* which seeks to explain the existence of social structures by the role they perform for society as a whole. It is a structural theory beginning its analysis at the level of society rather than the individual. It focuses on the interdependence of parts and how the functioning of parts is essential for the wellbeing of the whole. For example, how do the family unit, the economy of a country, the education system and the system of sport work together to contribute to the smooth running of the society as a whole? It proposes that social systems naturally seek to find a balance through an emphasis on consensus, common values and co-ordinated organisation. In relation to sport supporters of functionalism would ask questions such as:

- do sports provide *socialisation* experiences through which people learn the values of their society and can sport help relieve tensions that could cause conflict?
- do sports create unity and help integrate peoples?
- do sports tend to help people achieve and help social progress?
- do sports help people understand survival skills should their society face external change?

Criticisms of the theory suggest that it:

- is a conservative approach, stressing order at the expense of conflict

- ignores individuals in focusing only on the structural elements
- focusing on the present without any sense of the past.

See also *dysfunction*.

functions of sport: see *culture and sport*

funding for sport: sum of money set aside for the purpose of sport, which can be obtained from a variety of sources, including individuals, commercial interests and national governments. Funding is available to individuals as well as groups and organisations. See also *National Lottery, Department for Culture, Media and Sport, Sports Aid* and *sponsorship*.

fusiform muscle shape: *muscles* characterised by bundles of muscle fibres (fasciculi) which lie parallel to each other and have a tendon at either end of the muscle belly. Fusiform muscle shapes, such as the bicep brachii and tricep brachii, are designed for speed rather than strength since their fibres may shorten by up to 50 per cent of their resting length enabling a wider range of movement. See also *pennate* muscle shape.

What other subjects are you studying?

A–Zs cover 18 different subjects. See the inside back cover for a list of all the titles in the series and how to order.

galvanic skin response: see *biofeedback*

gamble: to risk or bet, usually money, on the outcome of an event/sport. The upper and lower classes enjoyed this pastime in almost all sports but it was something to which the *middle classes* with their reforming morality objected. First they attacked the *animal sports* of baiting and cock fighting and then gambling. In *horse racing* off course betting and pub betting were made illegal, effectively discriminating against those who could not afford to attend weekday race meets. As a consequence illegal street betting became the norm and the result was the publication of the Street Betting Act in 1906. The improved communications of the *railway*, the telegraph and the press combined to cause an enormous interest in betting, permitting a whole industry to arise which would encourage and profit from regular gambling. This was epitomised by horse racing and later greyhound racing.

game: a contest with *rules*, the result being determined by skill, strength or chance. This category includes *fighting games, invasion games, net games, innings* and *target games.* Games require territorial domination either through runs, goals or hits on target. The success of individuals or teams can be measured either quantitatively through number of goals scored or more subjectively by judges and their interpretations, such as in boxing. They are different to *athletic* and *gymnastic activities* because they are inherently interactive, apart from certain games like golf. This interactive nature requires decision-making by the players in response to their opponents' actions, for example, a scrum half deciding what to do following the scrummage.

gamesmanship: the art of winning games or defeating opponents by clever or cunning means without actually cheating. It involves bending the *rules* without actually breaking them going against the ideal of *sportsmanship.* An example is a tennis player faking an injury prior to the opposing player serving, in order to make them lose the flow of their movement pattern.

GAS: see *general adaptation syndrome*

gaseous exchange: the movement of gases into and out of the blood stream, taking place at two sites in the body: the lungs and the muscle or tissue cell. This occurs through the process of diffusion, which explains the movement of gases and other dissolved substances from areas of high concentrations to areas of lower concentration. The blood in the pulmonary capillaries surrounding the *alveoli* is low in oxygen content but high in carbon dioxide, while the air inside the alveoli is of high oxygen concentration and of low carbon dioxide concentration. Therefore oxygen diffuses into the blood stream at the lungs, attaching itself to *haemoglobin*, and travels around to the muscles. Carbon dioxide, on the other hand, diffuses into the alveoli, where it is breathed out. The opposite happens at the *capillaries* surrounding the muscle fibres. The muscle fibres have a relatively low concentration of oxygen, since they have used it up to produce energy, yet they have a high concentration of carbon dioxide, a by-product of that process to produce energy. Consequently oxygen diffuses into the muscle whilst carbon dioxide diffuses from the muscle into the blood stream, where it is transported around to the lungs to be expelled. During exercise, gaseous exchange occurs much more rapidly since there are greater differences between oxygen concentrations inside and outside the muscle. Training can also promote capillarisation, which improves the efficiency of the whole gaseous exchange process.

gender: used by sociologists to describe the cultural and social attributes of men and women, which are manifested in masculinity and *femininity.*

general adaptation syndrome (GAS): Seyle proposed that the performer experiences three stages of physiological reaction when faced with a situation that induces *stress.* The three stages are:

- alarm reaction stage – initiated when the perceived stressful situation occurs, causing increases in heart rate, blood sugar level, adrenaline and blood pressure. This may prompt the *fight or flight response*

- resistance stage – the body systems attempt to cope with the *stressors* if they are not removed, by reverting to normal functioning levels if possible, or a state of *homeostasis*

- exhaustion stage – the continued presence of the stressors will prove too much for the body to cope with, causing heart disease, stomach ulcers and high blood pressure. The body fails to deal with the continued demands placed upon it and is unable to fight infection.

gentleman amateur: a social class distinction of the *amateur* code. The gentleman amateur was drawn only from the *upper classes* and was regarded as having qualities of refinement associated with a good family i.e. being courteous, cultured and well- educated. Although they may have participated in some activities with their lower class *professional* counterparts, there was no shame should they lose, as they were not being paid, nor were they involved in serious training.

gentry: persons of high birth or social standing, usually denoting persons just below nobility in social rank.

Gestalt theory: developed by a group of German scientists who proposed learning occurred through the performer understanding the relationship of the whole action rather than individual parts. See *cognitive theories of learning.*

gladiator: a man trained to fight in arenas to provide entertainment. The gladiator began life in ancient Greece/Rome as someone who fought with weapons against another gladiator or with wild animals, but the term is now used in high profile *professional sport.* The similarities between a modern and ancient gladiator would be that both athletes:

- are involved in a physical contact sport relying on physical strength and speed

- have a strong likelihood of injury resulting in an early end to a career

- are treated as expendable

- might be bought and sold through transfer deals and treated as commodities

- are paid by results

- have little control as they are 'owned' by a coach/manager
- have high *media* status and are treated as heroes.

gliding joint: see *synovial joint*

globalisation: the process of the increasing interdependency of societies on a world-wide scale. This can be particularly evident in economic and cultural terms. In the latter the *mass media* images drawn from a world-wide arena are transmitted into people's homes through satellite or cable TV and as a result the most influential are those media companies that are spread throughout the world. There is a danger of different cultures losing their identities and pastimes as the values of Western sport become increasingly dominant across the world. Examples of globalisation in sport are:

- the influx of foreign players into home teams
- sport organisations like other businesses are expanding their markets into as many countries as possible
- the *International Olympic Committee* has gradually incorporated National Olympic Committees (NOC) from nearly 200 nations turning the event into the most successful and lucrative media sports event in history
- the use of well-known athletes to endorse company products.

glycogen: the stored form of carbohydrate in the body. It is composed by linking large numbers of glucose molecules together which are stored in the liver and muscles. Typically the liver can store approximately 80 g of glycogen, whilst the muscles store approximately 15 g of glycogen per kilogram of muscle tissue and it forms the preferred fuel in activities of fairly high intensity, such as an 800 metre run. However the body's stores of glycogen could provide sufficient energy to fuel a ten-mile run, if used as a sole source of energy – or even further when used in combination with fatty acids and a marathon runner will use a mixture of both glycogen and fatty acids through the duration of the event. Pace is a vital factor in the success of a marathon, since the faster the athlete runs the more heavily they rely on stores of glycogen. However, it is essential that stores of glycogen are not completely used up, since the body cannot rely on the use of fat as a sole source of energy, and the athlete may well 'hit the wall'.

glycogen loading: a manipulation of the dietary intake of *carbohydrate* prior to a competition in which athletes try to maximise stores of glycogen. This process involves depleting the glycogen levels seven days prior to the event through endurance-based training, followed by starving the body of carbohydrate for the next three days. On the remaining days leading up to the competition the athlete consumes high carbohydrate meals, whilst reducing training intensity. Some research suggests that the performer who follows this method can boost stores to almost double of that which can normally be stored by the muscle. Other research, however, does not fully support the benefits of glycogen loading. It is also known as carbo-loading.

A recommended carbohydrate loading regimen (Source: Williams, 1989)

Day 1   moderately long exercise bout (should not be exhaustive)

Day 2   mixed diet; moderate carbohydrate intake; tapering exercise

Day 3   mixed diet; moderate carbohydrate intake; tapering exercise

Day 4   mixed diet; moderate carbohydrate intake; tapering exercise

Day 5   high-carbohydrate diet; tapering exercise

Day 6   high-carbohydrate diet; tapering exercise or rest

Day 7   high-carbohydrate diet; tapering exercise or rest

Day 8   completion

Note: the moderate carbohydrate intake should approximate 200 to 300 g of carbohydrate per day; the high carbohydrate intake should approximate 500 to 600 g of carbohydrate per day.

glycolysis: literally meaning 'the break-down of sugar', and refers to the series of chemical reactions that degrades glucose to form *pyruvic acid*. This process takes place in the sarcoplasm of the cell in the absence of oxygen, which is more commonly known as anaerobic respiration, causing the release of energy to resynthesise a net gain of two *adenosine triphosphate (ATP)* molecules. Since glycolysis does not require oxygen, some energy can be released from glucose fairly rapidly and is therefore used as a form of energy production in those activities that are of fairly high intensity and last for up to three minutes in duration. The 400-metres hurdles event is an excellent example of where glycolysis will form the predominant energy pathway. If there remains insufficient oxygen in the body pyruvic acid is converted to *lactic acid* by the enzyme lactate dehydrogenase (LDH). Lactic acid causes muscle fatigue if it accumulates. Interval training can improve the body's glycolytic capacity.

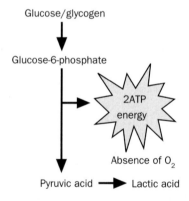

goal setting: method of enhancing the performance of an individual by increasing motivation, focusing attention and reducing anxiety levels. An achievable but challenging goal or target is set that is specific to the individual, usually by agreement between the performer and coach, which must be evaluated within a certain deadline. This can be simplified using the synonym, SMARTER, where:

S – specific

M – measurable

A – achievable

R – realistic

T – time related

E – exciting

R – recorded

For example, a young javelin thrower needs to develop his or her technique and certain aspects of fitness, including strength and speed. The weaknesses are measured, recorded for comparison in the future and used as a basis for the goals to be set. Each must ensure 'SMARTER' can be utilised. The targets set should be a mixture of short-and long-term goals to facilitate *motivation* and progression, which may be reviewed over a period of weeks or months. In comparison, an Olympic thrower may set goals over a period of months and years, planning their development towards major championships. If used correctly, the disheartening effect of *plateaus* in performance can be avoided or minimised. Different types of goal can be set, including *outcome goals*, *performance goals* and *process-orientated goals*.

golf: a *target game*, the origins of which are thought to derive from ancient activities played by Patagonian Indians, and from games called 'jeu de mal' in France and 'het kolven' in Holland. However, the Scots claim they were responsible for developing the game into its present form. The game was originally accessible to ordinary people but they were soon driven out of the game with the development of expensive equipment and private courses. The clubs were governed by the higher social classes and women were admitted on the understanding that a level of segregation was accepted. By 1898 there were 220 ladies clubs but the *Victorian* belief in the physical inferiority of women led to them playing on miniature versions of courses. Even today, women are discriminated against at club level, particularly in playing times, voting and shareholding.

Golgi tendon organ: proprioceptors found at the attachment of muscle and tendon fibres that are sensitive to changes in muscle tension and force of contraction. When tension is too great these receptors inhibit the contracting muscle (*agonist*) and excite the *antagonist*. In this way, damage to muscle and tendon can be prevented. It is thought that regular strength training reduces the sensitivity of Golgi tendon organs which enables the agonist to produce more forceful contractions.

goniometer: piece of equipment used to measure the range of motion at a joint. The 'head' of the goniometer is placed at the axis of rotation of a joint whilst the arms are aligned longitudinally with the bone. A measurement in degrees can be taken which gives a very objective reading (see *objectivity*) that can be used to assess improvement. One small disadvantage of this piece of equipment is that it is not always easy to identify the axis of rotation of a joint.

governing bodies: organisations responsible for their individual sport. Governing bodies were set up when *rules* for the sports needed to be agreed so that all clubs and individuals could compete on equal terms. Examples of governing bodies are the Football Association (FA) and the Amateur Swimming Association (ASA). Their main functions are to:

- establish rules and regulations, in accordance with the *international sport federations*
- organise competitions
- develop coaching awards and leadership schemes
- select national teams at international events
- liaise with relevant organisations.

In the United Kingdom governing bodies are 'autonomous' meaning they are free from political control with the *Central Council of Physical Recreation* representing their views to

Sport England. Governing bodies have had to cope with many changes in the latter half of the twentieth century, including:

- the growth of new sports, setting a challenge to the older traditional sports
- the decline in extra-curricular school sport and a dependence on governing bodies to fill this gap
- the blurring in definition between *amateur* and *professional* sport
- the need to compete internationally with countries who have developed systematic forms of training. This has meant that British governing bodies have had to devote more money to the training of their *elite* athletes just to be able to compete.

Funding is drawn from member clubs, associations and individual members or via grant aid from Sport England. Governing bodies also need to seek *sponsorship* in order to finance their responsibilities.

The figure below outlines the possible structure of a governing body.

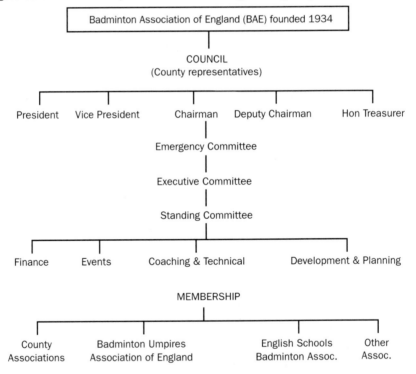

grammar schools: these are selective schools, with entrance via an 11+ examination. They were intended to cater for the most able children, effectively a small percentage of the population. It was hoped that they would provide quality educational opportunities for *working class* children but in reality a large percentage of entrants are still from *middle class* backgrounds.

grant maintained schools: schools which under the *Education Reform Act 1988* have been allowed to opt out of *local authority* control, receiving funding directly from central government. Initially funding was generous but this has fallen off considerably. It was a scheme introduced by the Conservative government who wanted schools to have more independence in how they managed their budgets.

grass roots: the lowest level of the *participation pyramid*. This is where the masses are encouraged to take part in active pursuits and occurs within the school physical education programme, recreational spheres and lower club levels.

Great Man theory: a theory proposed during the last century, stating that leaders are usually men born with innate traits or characteristics, such as intelligence, self-confidence, assertion, looks and a dominating personality. The theory has little credence today as many other factors influence the emergence and dominance of leaders, such as the situation and the nature of the group being led. (See also *emergent leader* and *prescribed leader*.)

gross motor ability: innate characteristics that allow movement to occur, such as speed, strength, stamina, flexibility and co-ordination. An individual during movement combines them, along with their *psychomotor abilities* to produce an effective performance. Different *skills* require different abilities, for example a gymnast and a tennis player both need speed, strength and flexibility but to differing degrees. See also *Fleishman's taxonomy of motor abilities*.

gross skill: skill that involves the performer executing actions involving large muscle groups and movement. These types of skill are placed on the same *continuum* as *fine skills*. Examples include running, throwing, jumping and swimming.

group: two or more people who interact with each other and influence behaviour, usually to achieve a common goal. Carron suggested they have a collective identity, shared objectives with structured interaction and modes of communication, which distinguishes them from a crowd, as shown below:

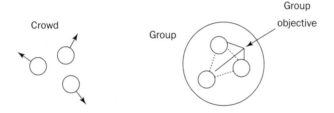

See also *group dynamics*.

group dynamics: a group is constantly developing and changing when interaction takes place. Tuckman suggests four key stages of development:

- forming – development of relationships
- storming – conflict between group members establishing roles
- norming – group gains stability and *cohesion*
- performing – individuals work together towards collective goal.

For example, a cricket team at the start of a season has a new coach, captain and several new players. During practice and warm-up matches discussions may take place as new members of the team establish themselves, but soon their roles are formed and each player knows what they are expected to contribute in order to achieve the team's *potential productivity*. See also *group productivity*.

group environment questionnaire (GEQ): this measures the cohesiveness of a *group* in sport-specific situations, based on the factors of task and social cohesion. Carron,

Widmeyer and Brawley (1985) based their questionnaire on the interaction, unification and motivation of individuals to remain in the group.

group productivity: the effectiveness of a group can be assessed using the formula:

actual productivity $=$ potential productivity $-$ faulty process

where potential productivity $=$ quantity and quality of the group's resources relevant to the task.

Steiner proposed that an effective *group* needs to be more than simply a collection of talented individuals, they must be able to work collectively together. For example, it is common for a manager to omit a player who appears to be the most skilful in favour of a less talented player, as they will contribute more to the overall team performance.

guidance: information that is provided for the performer by the coach or teacher to aid the learning of skills more effectively. The form of guidance used depends on the situation, the nature of the task as well as the ability and *personality* of the performer. The four main types of guidance are:

- visual – involves the performer attempting to create a mental picture of the action, by looking at a *demonstration*, video, OHT, slides, posters or pictures. Often the display can be modified by using cones, chalk marks, hoops or target areas. Useful in the *cognitive* and *associative stages of learning*

- verbal – usually provided by the coach to complement the visual guidance, highlighting relevant *cues* or providing *feedback*. This method can be utilised during all stages of learning, but can be more effective with experienced performers, who can translate the information into mental images more easily

- manual – involves the performer being physically placed, forced or supported into the correct positions. This is useful in situations that may be dangerous or require the performer to develop confidence, such as learning a gymnastic vault. It is used to develop the *kinaesthetic* awareness of a movement, for example the hands and arms of a novice batsman are held by the coach and guided through the shot to develop timing and co-ordination

- mechanical – provides support, similar to manual support, but involves some sort of device, for example, a swimming float or belt harness.

guided discovery teaching style: teaching in which the learners are led to explore various possibilities, but provided with information and questions to help them find a solution to the task. This method allows individuals to develop a greater understanding of the completed movements, which may be beneficial later if independent decisions have to be made. They may also have greater motivation and improved *self-efficacy*, as they are responsible for their own learning. It is useful for creative activities, such as gymnastic and dance routines. However, it is time consuming, performers do not all progress at the same rate and the teacher must constantly evaluate each person. See also *Mosston and Ashworth's spectrum of teaching styles.*

gymnastic activities rely on repetitive movement patterns. Examples are *gymnastics*, trampolining, ice skating and diving. Technical expertise and artistic interpretation are the two main factors that are assessed. The body is used as an art form, with appearance and individuality forming an important element. Judges usually assess the outcome and thus assessments are *subjective* and *qualitative* in nature.

gymnastics: practice or training in exercises that develop physical strength, posture and agility. The origin of the sport can be traced back to the ancient civilisations of China, Persia and Greece. The term derives from the word 'gymnos' meaning naked, which is the state in which Greek youths practised for military training. This took place in a gymnasium (meaning public place). Modern gymnastics developed along two fronts:

- the club system – following Jahn's system based on strength, via his inventions of the parallel bars and rings

- the education system – via Ling's *Swedish gymnastics*, that was to form the bedrock of early state school physical exercise in British schools. However, gymnastics could not rival team games in popularity in the nineteenth century public schools due to its foreign origin and lack of team-building qualities.

The English system was based on Archibald Maclaren's gymnasium which combined a mixture of activities such as fencing, climbing ropes, wrestling, vaulting and so on. This was considered suitable for the training of officers in that it developed physical skills and character-building qualities. The army formed the Army Gymnastic staff, which was to become the Army Physical Training Corps, following the realisation of the lack of fitness of soldiers in the Crimean War. Leading clubs formed a national *governing body*, the British Amateur Gymnastics Association in 1890.

Do you know we also have A–Zs for:

- **Biology**
- **Geography**
- **Travel and Leisure**
- **Health and Social Care?**

Ask for them in your local bookshop or see the inside back cover for ordering details.

A B C D E F G H I J K L M N O P Q R S T U V W X Y Z

haematocrit: the volume of red cells expressed as a fraction of the total volume of blood. It is therefore also a measure of the state of hydration of the blood, as it concerns the proportion of blood cells to plasma. Normal haematocrit for males occurs in the region of 42–45 per cent. If it is too high, there may be too many red blood cells in the blood relative to plasma, resulting in a blood viscosity increase, which slows down the flow and hinders oxygen transport to the muscles. This high value can also reflect that dehydration has occurred, which can cause serious problems in endurance events. Drinking plenty of fluids is essential to prevent performance from deteriorating and to keep the body in an adequate state of hydration.

haematology: the study of blood and its component parts.

haemoglobin: substance in red blood cells (erythrocytes) consisting of the protein 'globin' and the iron-based red pigment 'heme'. The main function of haemoglobin is to transport oxygen and carbon dioxide to and from the muscle cell. The recommended normal value for males is between 14–18 g per decilitre of blood and low haemoglobin levels can lead to premature fatigue as there is a limit to the oxygen-carrying capabilities of the body. However, low levels can be easily rectified by increasing the amount of iron consumed in the diet. Endurance athletes often attempt to increase their levels of haemoglobin prior to competition through *altitude training*, though its benefits are still under debate.

health-related fitness: considers the role that exercise has in the pursuit of healthier lifestyles. It has long been known that exercise can help in the prevention of so-called twentieth century medical problems such as *cardiovascular diseases* and *obesity*. It focuses on prescribing exercise regimes for the general population as opposed to the *elite* athlete.

Henley Regatta: see *regatta* and *rowing*

heuristic: comes from the Greek word 'eurisko' meaning 'serves to discover or reaches understanding of'. Through heuristic play children are satisfying their natural need to explore, and are discovering for themselves the properties and behaviour of different objects and materials. The play eliminates any sense of failure as is has open-ended possibilities rather than pre-determined goals set by adults. This type of learning began to be incorporated in '*Moving and Growing*' and '*Planning the Programme*' using a guidance style of teaching.

Hick's law states that reaction time will increase in a linear fashion as the amount of information to be processed increases. Therefore the greater the number of options a performer is faced with, the slower the reaction time: in other words their *choice reaction time* will be slower. For example, a badminton player who is able to execute a variety of shots will have an advantage over their opponent, as they do not know which to expect. In contrast, a player who has a limited range will be easier to play against, as they can only play the shuttle to certain areas of the court, thus making reaction time quicker. See also *simple reaction time* and *stimulus–response compatibility*. (See the figure below.)

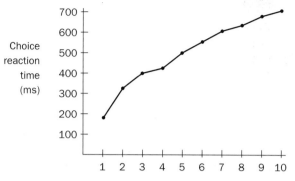

Number of stimulus–response alternatives

hierarchy of needs: see *Maslow's hierarchy of needs*

high culture: a term describing the arts, such as the opera and ballet, usually patronised by the *elite* in society. The arts usually reflect the privileges of wealth, education and free time. Activities pursued by this group of people are not made easily accessible to the lower social classes and there is a sense of cultural separatism. These activities are often considered to operate on a more intellectual and refined manner to those of *low culture*.

Highland Games: traditional festivals emerged from the struggles and developments peculiar to Scottish society. The activities were originally functional to the survival of society. Types of activities were hill racing, throwing of the strength stones/tossing the caber and recreational pastimes of labourers and woodmen.

Well known venues are Braemar, Lonach, Aboyne and Glenisland.

Images often linked to such games include:

* kilted athletes
* émigrés from all over the world
* subcultures of the 'heavies'
* bagpipes
* sponsorship by Scottish whisky industry
* clan chiefs.

The highland Games have been a symbol of *nationalism* following the destruction of Scottish culture by the British administration.

As an athletic festival they also provide employment for a band of semi-professional athletes who tour the basic circuit that developed in the north and the borders.

Higher Sports Leader Awards (HSLA): a progression from the *Community Sports Leader Awards* providing candidates of 18 years or over with the skills and experience to lead sport activities for a variety of community groups. The award is recognised as a stepping stone into employment in the sports and *leisure industry* and into higher education. It includes national *governing body* coaching, officiating and leadership awards. It is recognised by the *Duke of Edinburgh Award Scheme* at gold level.

hinge joint: see *synovial joint*

hockey: a field game played by 11 players each trying to score in the other team's goal with the aid of curved sticks. This is an example of an *invasion game*, with its origins in many ancient variations of stick and ball games. The word 'hockey' appears to have come into use in the nineteenth century when it became more organised. Blackheath is accepted as being the first hockey club, while the Teddington club used the game as winter exercise for their cricket players. The Hockey Association was formed in 1886, the Fédération Internationale de Hockey in 1924 and the Women's Hockey Association in 1895. Women adopted this game in the second half of the nineteenth century following the 'no-contact' rule in the men's game.

holism: the idea that the whole is greater than the sum of its parts. In sociological terms the entire social structure should be studied rather than focusing on small parts. In terms of the human being this translates to the idea that the mind, spirit and body need to be developed to produce the 'whole' man.

Holme Pierrpoint: see *national sport centres*

holy day: a day on which a religious festival is observed. Examples of such days were Shrovetide and the weekly holy day – Sunday. As well as national holy days of Easter, Christmas and Whitsuntide, many parishes had their own local festivals often numbering about 30. They mostly came between spring and autumn, giving opportunities for football, wrestling, *boxing, animal sports*, morris dancing and primitive forms of bowls. These occasions, particularly those with pagan associations, were criticised by the *Puritans* in the sixteenth century. Even Sunday was also considered too sacred for play. In the nineteenth century the holy days were significant for the working classes, as they were some of the few occasions they had free for recreational activities.

home advantage: in sport, the presence of others can be beneficial or detrimental to performance depending on the task, nature of the crowd and their proximity to play. The effects of *social facilitation* can be experienced by performers on home ground, which can help by increasing motivation and often lead to more victories, especially during the early rounds of a competition. However, performers might experience more pressure at home grounds if they are defending champions, due to higher expectations, which can negatively affect the result.

homeostasis: the process by which the body maintains its constant internal physiological state. For example, the body responds when experiencing stress by attempting to return to its stable state, e.g. slowing heart and breathing rates, or the body shivers if cold to raise the body temperature. See also *general adaptation syndrome*.

hooligan: a disorderly, noisy and violent person, often part of a gang. The term is mostly used in relation to the game of football, which has had a long and fluctuating history of crowd disorders dating back to the seventeenth and eighteenth centuries. Hooligans tend to go to matches with the intention of engaging in aggressive and violent behaviour.

The figure on page 117 outlines some of the factors and issues that underlie football hooliganism; it shows how these might impact on a football match, and the measures that the authorities might take to prevent and control hooliganism.

horizontal flexion: movement pattern that occurs at the shoulder joint, involving the arm being raised up and forward, for example when a swimmer at the start of the race throws their arms forward to gain additional momentum.

WORKING CLASS SUBCULTURE	RESOLVING CONFLICT	PSYCHOLOGICAL DEPRIVATION	FELT AROUSAL	LABELLING THEORY

Masculinity/excitement
Toughness/territory
Risk/novelty/adventure

Ritual ceremonial (Marsh)

Media stereotype

FOOTBALL HOOLIGANISM

Diminished responsibility

Violence of players

Displaced aggression

Pre-event hype

THE EVENT

Religion
Celtic vs Rangers
De-individualisation
Home and away
Historical traditions

Mass spectator sport

Importance of event

Chanting
Abuse
Missiles

Motivations of spectators

Size, structure of group

Penning

Segregation

Officials' decisions

Competition
Rivalry
Frustration
'the score'

Seater stadiums

PREVENTION & CONTROL MEASURES

Promote family

Security checks
Video monitoring
Liason between authorities
ID Cards

Media assumes responsibility

Control of alcohol

Tougher deterrents

Police and stewards
Effective policies

Hooligan

horse racing: equestrian activity derived from warfare, chariot racing and hunting. Two main types of racing emerged:

- across the flats – point to point

- over the sticks – steeplechasing under National Hunt rules.

By the 1750s the *Jockey Club* was in existence making it one of the first sports to develop a national administration, giving it a commercial and bureaucratic control over the activity. Racing became confined to thoroughbreds descended from Arabian, Turkish or Barbary steeds imported into England and it was initially an upper-class activity but became adopted by the lower classes as they could gamble without actually attending the meetings. The Derby held at Epsom downs is a fine example of the mix of the social classes at a sporting event.

Hull's drive reduction theory: see drive reduction theory

human growth hormone (HGH) is an artificial substance used (illegally) to stimulate *protein* synthesis and ultimately increase muscle mass. An increase in muscle mass is directly linked to increases in muscle *strength* and is therefore of benefit to a wide range of sporting activities from weight lifting to rugby. Other benefits include increased bone density and decreases in body fat that results from the increased metabolic activity that accompanies increases in muscle mass. However the risks of taking human growth hormone by far outweigh the advantages. These risks include abnormal development of bone and muscle tissue (particularly the broadening of facial features, hands and feet). Abnormal enlargement of internal organs, particularly the heart, can lead to heart disease and ultimately failure. Human growth hormone has also been linked to an increased risk of high *blood pressure* and diabetes.

hunting: the pursuit and killing or capture of game and wild animals. Hunting is a controversial issue: some people strongly oppose it, while others defend the activity. Also see *fox hunting*.

hurling: see *Cornish hurling*

hypertrophy: the increase in size or mass of a body organ or muscle, often associated with exercise. It is an adaptive response to training. For example, endurance training may well enlarge the heart which is known as 'cardiac hypertrophy', while *strength training* on the other hand can cause an increase in mass and cross-sectional area of skeletal muscle.

hypoglycaemia: low blood-glucose level. Blood-glucose levels can become depleted during low-intensity, long duration exercise, such as cycling or marathon running. An athlete may maintain their level of performance by keeping blood glucose levels to near normal levels by *carbohydrate* feeding during the exercise. It is not advisable, however, for athletes to ingest any carbohydrates between 15 and 45 minutes before the exercise period, since this can have an adverse effect, causing hypoglycaemia. It can cause a significant rise in insulin production, causing a very high and inefficient usage of glucose by the muscles, which leads to premature fatigue.

hypokinetic disorders: occur when the neural pathways from the *central nervous system* do not function properly, causing limited control and unco-ordinated movements. Such conditions include Parkinson's disease and Huntington's disease. The term hypokinetic disorders is also used for those medical conditions which arise directly as a result of an inactive lifestyle. They largely affect the musculo-skeletal and cardio-respiratory systems. Examples of such conditions include obesity, diabetes, arthritis and coronary heart disease.

hypnosis: method of relaxation used to reduce *anxiety* levels by placing the performer in a sleep-like state by altering their level of consciousness. At the present time it is not used extensively by sportspeople as the full effects are not fully understood.

Do you need revision help and advice?

Go to pages 274–287 for a range of revision appendices that include plenty of exam advice and tips.

ice hockey: hockey played on ice. It is an *invasion game* and one of the dominant *American sports*. It is one of the most violent team games – fighting is part of the action and is expected. The physical speed of the game and the implement used has made this game fast and brutal with the players dressed for protection. In contrast to *basketball*, ice hockey is predominantly played by whites and this is probably due to its origins in sub-Arctic Canada.

iceberg profile: see *profile of mood states*

Illinois agility run test: test designed to measure *speed* and *agility*. A ten-metre square is marked out with four cones at each of the corners in a sports hall. Four cones are placed 3.3 metres apart, bisecting the square. The subject lies prone (face down) at one corner and on the command 'go' runs the course as fast as possible weaving in and out of the cones. The time taken is recorded and compared to standard tables.

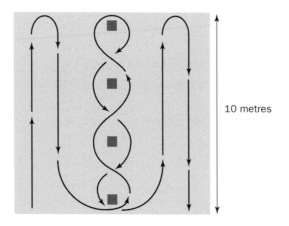

10 metres

Illinois competition questionnaire: see *sport competition anxiety test*

imagery: relaxation technique involving the formation of mental pictures to help reduce *stress* levels, increase confidence and concentration. It can be used in a variety of ways to either create the expected experience of a new situation or recall the feelings of a past situation. The performer can use the technique to develop a variety of sensations, as outlined below:

- pictures of escape to a calming place away from the pressure of competition
- recreation of the *kinaesthetic* feeling of a successful movement; for example what was the execution of a converted penalty like?

- creation of images of what may happen and how to deal with them. This can reduce *anxiety* levels and reaction times, since the performer feels they have been in the situation before

- creation of emotional feelings that may be experienced when placed in a stressful situation, such as success, victory and control

- creation of sounds in the situation, e.g. either the ball on the bat or external sources that may be distracting, such as the crowd during the execution of a penalty kick.

Imagery can be either internal or external. The former involves a sportsperson seeing themselves from within completing the action or in the situation, experiencing the kinaesthetic feelings. The latter, however, involves the sportsperson seeing themselves as if they were spectators or on film.

To be effective, the technique must be practised regularly, both during training and competitive situations; have realistic goals or targets; be used frequently in short periods of time with vivid pictures created; and be successful in outcome. It is also known as *visualisation*. See also *mental practice.*

inclusiveness: All people should be able to have their needs, abilities and aspirations recognised, understood and met within a supportive environment. These needs can range from learning and physical disabilities as well as needs arising for those who are disadvantaged or disaffected because of social or economic circumstances. All these people are at risk of social *exclusion*. The Government has a policy to promote social inclusion in the context of the National Strategy of Neighbourhood Renewal.

An inclusive approach is being developed by a number of organisations. An inclusive organisation would:

- put the individual at the centre of its policies

- recognise and support diversity by striving to meet the widest possible range of needs

- seek to achieve the best 'match' between provision and needs of the individual

- provide staff training and development

- liaise with other relevant organisations and foster 'joined up thinking'.

Inclusiveness recognises diversity of needs but in practical terms for disabled individuals it does not necessarily mean *segregation* or an integrated environment. For some an integrated approach that allows them to work alongside their peers, with additional support if required, may be the right option. But the fundamental principle remains always that the provision must be appropriate to meet the assessed needs of the individual.

Industrial Revolution: period in England in the middle of the 1700s which developed over a hundred years. It resulted in a dramatic movement of people from rural areas to the towns, transforming societies from their agricultural base to a factory system. During this time *rational recreation* developed on a large scale. See also *industrialisation*.

industrialisation: the process whereby a society moves from a predominantly agricultural base to one where the economy is dominated by manufacturing. Urbanisation is a consequence of industrialisation as a vast body of people moved to towns to seek employment and consequently live in smaller, cramped spaces. Transport and communications also develop with canals, roads and railways. Industrialisation caused many changes to many *popular recreations*. *Mob games* declined due to lack of space and the *civilising process* of society.

inequality: see *social inequality*

inferior: structure below or closer to the foot than another. For example, the inferior vena cava lies below the superior vena cava within the heart. (See appendix, page 253.)

information processing involves the performer gathering data, processing the relevant stimuli to form a decision, which is then executed by the muscular system. The process consists of three basic stages:

- Stimulus identification (*input*) – where information is collected from the *display*, via the *sensory system*. The process of *selective attention* eliminates any information that is deemed irrelevant. For example, during a middle distance race, the athlete may take note of his and other runners' positions, the speed, the distance to the finish and the crowd shouting at them. The noise from the crowd is irrelevant and will not form part of the second stage of the process.

- Response selection (*decision-making*) – the relevant information is assessed, a decision made based on previous experience is stored in the *memory* and an *executive motor programme* is formed. For example, a runner may decide to 'kick' for the finish 300 metres from the end of the race knowing his own and others' strengths and weaknesses.

- Response programming (*output*) – the motor programme is carried out via the *effector mechanism* and the muscular system. In this case the runner increases their pace in an attempt to win the race.

In order to assess the effectiveness of the decision and completed action, *feedback* is obtained from a variety of sources, either internally or externally. This allows the performer to develop a kinaesthetic awareness and make adjustments if required for the future if a similar situation arises. For example, the runner may have won the race and knows the tactics were correct and could be utilised again. However if the race had been lost the decision to increase the speed at that distance from the finish could be evaluated and taken into account in similar circumstances again.

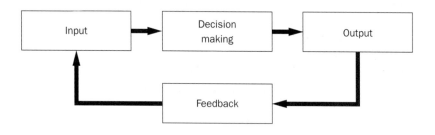

innings games: games where there is an 'in' team and an 'out' team, with each having an innings providing them with the opportunity to score. The playing area is defined as infield and outfield. The infield gives the opportunity for striking the ball in order to score runs, while the outfield is used to field or defend the ball and cut down the opportunities for the opposing side to score runs. The aim is to get the other team out. Examples of such games are *cricket*, rounders, *baseball* and softball.

inns: a pub or small hotel providing food or accommodation. The inn had always been the social meeting place in rural areas and was used by the *gentry* in the nineteenth century as a stopping place on long journeys. A tradition of games developed which was encouraged by the innkeepers to increase their business; examples are *fives*, rackets, *boxing, coursing* and *quoits*. Many of the new developing sports clubs met in such places and they formed mutually beneficial partnerships. For instance, the village cricket team perhaps used the field next to the inn; bowling greens and boxing rings were built on to the premises.

input: the first stage of *information processing*, where data from the surrounding area enters the body via the *sensory system*. For example, during a game of rugby, the player receives details of his or her own position on the pitch as well as those of their team mates and the opposition; the location, speed and direction of the ball; the decisions of the referee; instructions from the coach; reactions from spectators as well as a variety of *kinaesthetic* information. These cues are then transferred and filtered via the *selective attention* mechanism to the *decision-making* mechanism.

INSEP: the French National Institute of Sports and Physical Education. It is a *centre of excellence* and its aims are to:

- undertake scientific research
- produce highly qualified teachers, coaches and administrators
- enable selection by the federations and provide medical screening for coaches
- provide a venue for national team training
- provide a permanent sport study section for over a hundred children, catering specifically for swimming, gymnastics and tennis.

insertion: point of attachment for skeletal muscle. The insertion is the muscle attachment (tendon) on the bone that the muscle puts into action. For example, the insertion of the bicep is on the radius and when the bicep contracts the force is transmitted to the radius via the insertion, and *flexion* of the elbow occurs.

insight learning: see *cognitive theories of learning*

inspiration: the process of drawing air into the lungs, by the contraction of the diaphragm and external intercostal muscles. Contraction of the inspiratory muscles causes an enlargement of the thoracic cavity and therefore an expansion of the lungs. When the lungs have expanded, the air molecules within them have further to travel before striking a surface. Consequently the pressure within the lungs falls below that outside the body (atmospheric pressure) and creates a pressure differential. Since air always moves from areas of high pressure to areas of lower pressure, air rushes into the lungs. During exercise, to ensure maximal inspiration, other muscles help the respiratory muscles, including the sternocleidomastoid, scaleni and the pectorals. (See also *partial pressure*.)

inspiratory capacity: the total inspiratory ability of the lungs, the sum of *tidal volume* and *inspiratory reserve volume*. (See appendix, page 273.)

inspiratory reserve volume: the volume of air that can be breathed in following resting inspiration. This is an important aspect of our inspiratory capacity, since it enables greater expansion of our lungs during exercise, a time when more oxygen needs to be inspired. During exercise, the inspiratory reserve volume decreases to enable the increase in *tidal volume*. (See appendix, page 273.)

instinct theory: see *aggression*

Institute of Leisure and Amenity Management (ILAM): the professional body for leisure professionals. ILAM represents every aspect of leisure, culture and recreation management and is committed to the improvement of management standards. The institute plays a key role in the development of leisure management through education, research, information, debate and discussion with government and national agencies. Members are from the public, private, commercial and voluntary sectors.

Institute of Sport Sponsorship: this is one of the main organisations concerned with sport sponsorship in the United Kingdom. It was set up in association with the *Central Council of Physical Recreation* Sports Sponsorship Advisory Service and acts as a grouping of commercial companies and public bodies with an interest in sport. It works in conjunction with *Sport England* to co-ordinate the *Sportsmatch* scheme.

institution: an organisation or establishment founded for a specific purpose such as a hospital, church, school or sports club. Institutions are founded on certain principles and rules, which are embodied in codes of behaviour. They can perpetuate outdated sets of values and can retain and reinforce *discrimination*. Such organisations differ from random groups in various ways:

● individual members can come and go whilst the organisation will survive this movement

● goals guide the individuals as to how they are expected to behave

● decision-making and enforcement procedures operate in order to control members

● members have roles assigned to them.

instrumental aggression: see *assertive behaviour*

instrumental values: those linked directly with physical performance such as skilfulness and health development. These are some of the values with which we justify the benefits of participation in physical education and sport.

intangible reinforcers: see *reinforcement*

integration is the act of incorporating individuals into mainstream society. This can include religious and racial groups, disabled and socially disadvantaged groups.

In terms of disabled people it relates to the able bodied and disabled taking part together in the same activity at the same time; in contrast, segregation means disabled people participating among themselves. There are advantages and disadvantages with each approach. With integration the disabled participant may not be able to participate fully and the able bodied may find it unchallenging and obviously safety issues would have to be resolved. However, it can help the disabled participant feel more included in society and can help raise their self-esteem when they achieve success. Segregation on the other hand reinforces the notion of being different from the rest of society and there is a prerequisite of facilities being available for use by such groups and yet disabled participants may achieve more success in this environment.

interactionism: an analysis of society, which begins from the perspective of the individual to give meaning and intention to sociological theory. It focuses on the day-to-day activities of the millions of individuals who make up society, rather than seeing individuals as at the mercy of society (which is the perspective of *structural functionalism*) It recognises the constraints put upon individuals but allows for creative action. Research is based on the small-scale interactions of everyday life, such as those at a sports club. This would be seen as a product of the interaction of the various people involved and would not just focus on the power held by the administrators.

interactionist theory proposes that the personality of an individual is formed due to a combination of their innate traits and their interaction with the environment. This is often represented as:

$$B = f(PE)$$

where B is behaviour, f is function, P is personality trait and E is environment.

This helps to explain some of the weaknesses in the *trait* and *social learning theories*. For example, an experienced rugby player may appear extroverted and forceful on the field of play because of the nature of the game and their own skill level. However when playing other sports in which they are less skilled, such as golf, they may be more introverted and calm because the situational requirements are different. The coach can use this knowledge to identify particular behaviour patterns within specific situations and attempt to modify the actions of the performer if appropriate. For example, the coach may have to develop *stress management* techniques if the rugby player suffers from overwhelming *anxiety* every time they are faced with a kick to win the game.

intercollegiate sport: many colleges in the *United States of America* compete with each other in a wide range of sports. Intercollegiate sport has the following characteristics:

- there is competition for cash or non-cash prizes
- students compete against professionals
- spectators pay to watch matches and competitions
- athletes are subsidised
- athletes are recruited and paid and professional coaches employed.

Some complaints are aimed at the lack of importance placed on the academic programmes and this is especially the case in the *Big Time programmes*.

interference occurs when additional information is presented to the performer that may hinder the *information processing* time of the initial stimulus. This often takes place within the memory phase. As a result the coach should ensure instructions are short, precise and with sufficient time allowed for the performer to understand and take in the details. See also *single channel hypothesis*.

internalisation: the process whereby values and ideas are taken in by individuals as their own. The *socialisation* process is said to be the internalisation of values.

International Olympic Committee (IOC): the organisation that generates almost all international sporting activity. It was established in 1894 by *Baron Pierre de Coubertin* and is based in Lausanne in Switzerland. It is responsible for the control and development of the *Olympic Games* and the Olympic movement. There are two organisations:

- the Session – which takes decisions on issues such as *doping*, political boycotts, television contracts and the world sport development

- the Executive Board – which is responsible for the organisation of those policies. Attempts are made to make representation as balanced as possible, from poor to wealthy countries.

It is a powerful organisation with huge financial reserves. If the IOC gives a sport eligibility status, it can boost the profile of that sport considerably. It is under a lot of pressure from national Olympic committees, *international sport federations* and national governments. However, the nature of this organisation has allowed considerable corruption to take place, for example, the bribery of members for their vote by bidding host cities.

international sport federations: the organisations responsible for their individual sports. Their main responsibilities are to:

- formulate rules that will be adhered to by the national governing bodies

- organise events

- arrange *sponsorship* and television contracts.

See also *governing bodies*.

interval training: a method of training that involves alternating periods of exercise and rest (relief). This is probably the most popular type of training used in sport for training the *elite* athlete, as it is very versatile and can be used in almost any activity, although it is most widely used in *swimming, athletics* and *cycling*. Interval training can improve both *aerobic* and *anaerobic* capacities enabling the athlete to exercise at the specific intensity necessary to train the relevant energy system for that activity.

inter-war years: the period between the ending of *World War I* and the beginning of *World War II* (1919–1939). There were two dominant moods following World War I:

- to build a new country with values learned from the conflict

- to regain some sense of fun and frivolity.

The initial burst of lavish living by the upper classes was not to last. In the UK the General Strike of 1926 culminated in economic depression, high unemployment and similar trends in Germany led to the rise of Hitler in the thirties. Social deprivation and delinquency led to the need to occupy young men in physical recreation. This was to lead to the beginnings of formal Government policies for recreation provision. In 1937 the forerunner of the *Central Council of Physical Recreation* was established. The working classes participated mainly on Saturday afternoons. Football saw enormous crowds; dog racing was first held on a track in 1926; bowls and darts were still popular pub games. It was still the exception to go on holiday, apart from during the *wakes* week when the mills and factories closed down. Only the wealthy went abroad at this stage. International sport was continuing to develop with the *Olympic Games*, the cricket Test Series and media coverage began to make sport stars into national heroes (television started in 1938).

intra-mural sports: these are highly structured competitive sports and games in American schools. They are played to a high level as well as involving participation of a recreational nature, where the emphasis is on the social experience. They occur outside regular school classes or hours with teams organised on the basis of grade, class and house.

intrinsic motivation: internal satisfaction received by the performer, which can influence behaviour. It is used for *reinforcement*, to shape behaviour in an attempt to encourage repetition of the action. The desire of an individual to participate for the sake of the activity rather than the glory and prizes of winning is a powerful factor, and determines whether or not an individual may continue with and display commitment to an activity. For example, a rower may have the desire to train to develop personal fitness, to better their own performance, for the challenge the sport offers them and the enjoyment they receive from participating. Knowledge of an individual's intrinsic motivational factors could be combined with various forms of *extrinsic motivation* to maximise the performer's drive.

intrinsic feedback: see *feedback*

introceptors: see *sensory system*

introvert: a person who is quiet, unsociable, passive, careful and reserved. They display *traits* said to be the result of a highly sensitive *reticular activating system*, that causes a constantly higher natural level of arousal. This means that introverts do not need to seek additional stimulation to function at an optimal level. As a result they are said to avoid situations that cause over-arousal, choosing instead individual activities that require precision rather than force, e.g. shooting and archery. In comparison, *extroverts* possess the opposite traits and are placed at the other end of the *continuum*. These characteristics can be measured using *Eysenck's personality inventory (EPI)* or *Cattell's 16 personality factors questionnaire*.

Inuit: a member of a group of peoples inhabiting Nunavut (Canada), Greenland, Alaska and East Siberia having a culture adapted to an extremely cold climate. The Inuit were often referred to as Eskimos.

The Inuit on Nelson Island live in one of the last areas to be exposed to the outside world and earlier research was able to focus on an ancient way of life. They derive much of their subsistence from the ocean and economic pursuits for the most part are individual, where survival depended on personal skills, self-reliance and independence. Hunting skill and achievement are highly valued. Games of physical skill are preferred, especially those that require dexterity, strength and endurance. The games foster a competitive spirit but the social morality of the group places a high value on non-aggressive behaviour. There is little emphasis on equipment, which displaces possessiveness. They play marbles but do not win someone else's marbles. They know the competitive game but choose to ignore it. Theirs is essentially a co-operative society and has developed a culture which is less rigid and formal, with a lack of formal authority in leaders.

invasion games: games where teams are able to invade their opponents' territory. Examples are *hockey*, netball and *basketball*. Scoring is usually in the form of goals or points and the winner is the team who scores the most goals or points within the allocated time period. Invasion games are essentially about maintaining possession of the ball or object by passing effectively within the team, or creating possession by tackling or interception. Some allow contact whilst others forbid it. *Open skills* are mostly used as the environment is constantly changing and strategies are usually based on attacking and defending.

inverse stretch reflex: occurs when the *muscle spindle apparatus* detects the muscles stretching and triggers an opposing contraction for protection and prevention of injury. The faster the stretch, the stronger the reflex. Therefore there is a need to stretch gradually during a *warm-up* period before activities to increase the range of flexibility.

inversion: movement pattern or joint action taking place at the ankle, characterised by the turning of the sole of the foot medially inwards. For example, this occurs when a football player turns their foot inwards before executing a pass with the outside of the boot. (See appendix, page 272.)

inverted U theory proposes that as *arousal* levels increase, so does the level of performance, but only up to an optimum point, which is usually reached at moderate levels of arousal. After this point further increases will cause the performance to deteriorate, as shown in the figure below.

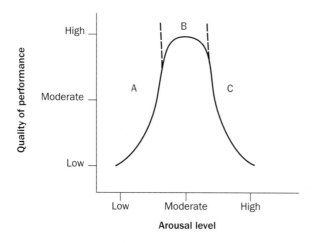

A – under-aroused (lack of concentration and attention)
B – optimal level
C – over-aroused (lose focus, miss cues and may become anxious)

However several factors need to be considered to determine the optimum level of arousal or *zone of optimal functioning*, including:

● the nature of the task – skills that are complex or require fine muscle movement, such as snooker, golf putting and archery, need a lower level than those of a gross or simple nature, for example, running, weight lifting or rugby tackle

● the skill level of the performer – those who are experienced may be able to cope with higher levels of arousal as their movements are autonomous, compared with novice performers who need to focus more carefully on relevant *cues*. For example a novice netball player will need to concentrate on the basic shooting action and become over-aroused when confronted with a defender, whereas an expert will be able to execute the skill under such pressure

● the personality of the performer – those who are more *extrovert* in nature can cope with higher levels of arousal and excitement compared with *introverts*.

The figure on page 128 shows three different zones of optimal functioning, depending on these factors.

See also *drive theory* and *catastrophe theory*.

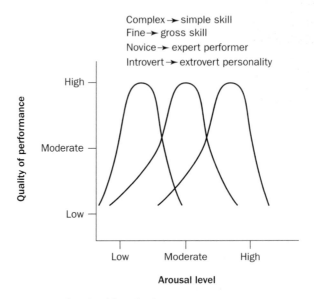

Complex → simple skill
Fine → gross skill
Novice → expert performer
Introvert → extrovert personality

Inverted U theory – zones of optimal functioning

IOC President: In July 2001 Jacques Rogge became the eighth IOC President after representing Belgium's National Olympic Committee.

irregular bone: type of bone so named due to its complex, individual shapes and the difficulty in classifying it. They have a variety of functions which include protection and muscle attachment. For example the vertebrae offer both protection of the spinal cord and attachment for muscles of the back and neck.

isokinetic muscle contraction: action that occurs when the speed of shortening of the muscle remains constant over the entire range of movement. Maximum force can also be exerted at all joint angles of the movement. This type of training relies on specialist equipment, either electronic or hydraulic where the speed of contraction can be preset. See also *isometric muscle contraction* and *isotonic muscle contraction*.

isometric muscle contraction: occurs when there is no active shortening or lengthening of the muscle, with the muscle length remaining static. Isometric contractions occur when the force of the muscle equals the weight or load of the object lifted. For example, the bicep contracts isometrically when holding a weight steady and the elbow joint remains at 90°, or holding a static balance. Alternatively isometric contractions can occur when the weight of the object is too great for the force generated within the muscle, for example when pushing against a wall. Isometric training can produce significant gains in strength and remain an important form of training for the rehabilitating athlete. See also *isokinetic muscle contraction* and *isotonic muscle contraction*.

isotonic muscle contraction: this occurs when the tension remains constant and where the muscle shortens by pulling on another structure such as the *origin*; for example, the legs during the running action. Isotonic contractions such as those experienced when using weight training equipment can greatly increase gains in muscular strength and endurance. (See also *concentric muscle contraction* and *eccentric muscle contraction*.)

Jacobsen's relaxation technique: see *progressive relaxation technique*

Jockey Club: the governing body that controls and regulates *horse racing* both on the flats and over the jumps. It was one of the earliest governing bodies to be established in the mid-eighteenth century.

joined up thinking: a term used to describe changes in Government thinking and policy when attempting to counteract huge social problems. It is an attempt to integrate policies by various organisations liasing with each other. In the past, schemes were often set up in isolation, for example to combat crime or to increase sport participation. Nowadays it is understood that such schemes can impact on other social needs. The *Best Value* policy is an example where Government sees that sport can make a valuable contribution to delivering the four key outcomes of employment, crime reduction, health and better qualifications.

In terms of funding there has also been a shift towards local authorities sharing costs for leisure provision as in *joint provision*.

joint provision: money made available from the education authorities for enhancing, enlarging and making additions to the facilities provided by the education authority. There is usually a centre manager and sound management has made these facilities available to the public in the evenings and weekends. It is different to *dual use* policies.

jousting: combat between two mounted knights tilting against each other with lances. It was popular in medieval times and took place in tournaments providing popular social occasions for the wealthy sections of society and military training for young knights. Jousting declined in popularity in the *Tudor* era as the ethos of society and warfare changed, becoming a relic of chivalry and courtly love.

Junior Sports Leader Awards (JSLA): the JSLA is intended for young people over the age of 14 working within a youth organisation or the school environment. The training and practical work is intended to give participants an appreciation of the skills required to lead sporting activities. Participants can graduate to the *Community Sports Leader Awards*.

Karvonen principle: method used to determine the correct intensity of training, through calculation of the training zone. Karvonen developed a formula to identify correct training intensities as a percentage of the sum of the maximum heart rate reserve and resting heart rate. The maximum heart rate reserve of a performer can be calculated by subtracting their resting heart rate [HR(rest)] from their *maximum heart rate* [HR(max)]:

maximum heart rate reserve = HR(max) − HR(rest)

where an individual's maximum heart rate can be calculated by subtracting their age from 220, i.e.

HR(max) = 220 − age

Karvonen suggests that a training intensity of between 60 and 75 per cent of maximal heart rate reserve should be used for the average athlete, although this can obviously be adapted to account for individual differences. An example of the calculation is shown below:

training heart rate 60% = 0.6 (max HR reserve) + HR(rest)

The benefit of this principle is that it gives the athlete and coach some precise figures to measure to ensure that they are training at the correct intensity.

Kenya: a republic in East Africa that became a British protectorate in 1895 and a colony in 1920. It gained independence in 1963 and is a member of the Commonwealth. The Kenya Amateur Athletic Association (KAAA) arranged to finance the Kenyan athletes as early as the 1950s, by providing them with international competition and training, recognising they could be of world class standard if they were given support. The community development officers organised meetings at local, divisional and district level. Standards rose and Kenyan athletes began to collect medals in the *Commonwealth Games*. The National Secondary School Championships were initiated and became a productive nursery of international talent. The first Olympic medal was won in the 1964 Tokyo Games, followed by eight more in the 1968 Mexico City Games. In Seoul, Kenya won the gold medal in each running event from 800 metres to 5000 metres. The country now has two world class stadiums – the Moi International Sports Centre and the Nyayo National Stadium.

The government has posted sports officers to all provinces and districts to develop sports programmes with the result that new talent emerges from rural areas. At the national level, the Kenya National Sports Council is supervising more than 30 individual sporting associations with world class potential in hockey, boxing, volleyball, karate and soccer. *Basketball* is the fastest growing sport in Kenya, boasting a national league, while the women's team featured in the World Championships in Australia and the men's is currently ranked fourth out of all African countries. Kenyan players have become a hot commodity within the highly competitive United States market, with players on *scholarships* at the American institutions. See also *emergent cultures*.

key stages: four sub-sections within the *National Curriculum* for different age groups.

- key stage 1 – ages 5–7. Activities include games, gymnastics and dance. The emphasis is developing simple skills
- key stage 2 – ages 7–11. Activities include those mentioned above and also athletic activities, outdoor and adventurous activities and swimming. Emphasis is on developing more complex skills and beginning to plan and evaluate performance
- key stage 3 – ages 11–14. Options are given as to which activities can be followed and students refine their motor skills and develop strategic understanding
- key stage 4 – ages 14–16. Students follow selected areas of activity as well as undertaking different roles such as coach and official.

kinaesthetic: describes sensations that are felt by the performer concerning movement of the body, weight distribution and muscle tension. This information is received via the *proprioceptors* and allows learning and evaluation of movement patterns to take place. For example, during a race a hurdler can alter particular aspects of the technique if they do not feel correct kinaesthetically.

kinesiology: the study of the movement of body parts. It considers the action of the musculo-skeletal system as well as the mechanics of movement. When studying kinesiology, it is helpful to consider the following:

- the names of the muscles contracting
- the function of the muscles contracting
- the role of the muscle, for example, is it an *agonist*, *antagonist* or *fixator*?
- the type of muscle contraction: *isotonic, concentric, eccentric, isokinetic*, or *isometric*
- the movement patterns occurring at the joints as result of the contraction
- the plane in which the movement takes place: *saggital, frontal* or *horizontal*?

See appendix, page 262 for table of kinesiology.

Kingsley, Charles: one of the most influential exponents of the *muscular Christianity* movement. He helped to combine the Christian and chivalric ideal of manliness, returning to the Platonic concept of, the 'whole man'. Kingsley believed healthy bodies were needed alongside healthy minds. He also led the hygienic movement that was to have a powerful effect on the working conditions of the poor in the nineteenth century.

knowledge of performance: information received by a performer about their execution of their technique or motor programme. This form of *feedback* is usually received from an external source, such as a coach, but can also be internal or *kinaesthetic*, if the performer is experienced or in the *autonomous stage of learning*. The technological development of visual guidance (see *guidance*) has improved the quality of the knowledge of performance that can be provided. For example, the coach of a sprinter may analyse his or her technique from the starting blocks with the use of video, identify weaknesses and adjust the training programme accordingly. If used effectively, not only does performance improve but so too does the athlete's motivation. See also *knowledge of results*.

knowledge of results: information received by a performer about the outcome of an action. The results may be obtained in a variety of forms, including the number of goals scored, recorded times or distances, number of rally wins or accuracy of the pass. This form of *feedback* is gained externally, either visually or through a coach, and is essential to the development of skills during the *cognitive* and *associative phases of learning*. When this information is combined with effective *knowledge of performance*, a player or athlete can modify their actions in the future.

Krebs cycle: the second stage of the *aerobic energy system*, where carbohydrate is broken down, allowing resynthesis of *adenosine triphosphate (ATP)*. The process reduces *acetyl co-A* to carbon dioxide and hydrogen atoms, which are in turn passed onto the *electron transport chain*. Three reactions occur:

1   citric acid is oxidised – the hydrogen is removed

2   carbon dioxide is formed and expelled via the lungs

3   energy for resynthesis of two molecules of ATP is released.

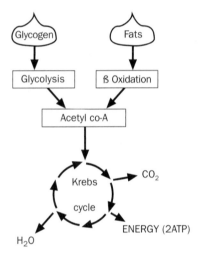

Do you need help with the synoptic element of your Physical Education course?

Go to page 274 for tips and advice.

lacrosse: ball game invented by the *native Americans*, now played by two teams who try to propel a ball into each other's goals by means of long handled rackets or crosses (French Canadian for hooked stick). It is thought to have survived the arrival of white settlers, as it was a fast, exciting game, which matched those of the developing *American sports*. English girls' schools adopted the game in the nineteenth century and it has retained its private school ethos. See also *baggataway*.

lactacid debt: the slow component of excess post-exercise oxygen consumption. It is the volume of oxygen consumed following exercise which is used to break down any *lactic acid* that may have accrued. The oxygen consumed during this phase may also be used to supply the respiratory muscles and the heart with energy to remain slightly elevated in the recovery period. Depending upon the intensity of the prior exercise, the lactacid debt may take up to 24 hours to complete. For example, a large lactacid debt will occur when running 400 metres or swimming 200 metres in a personal best time.

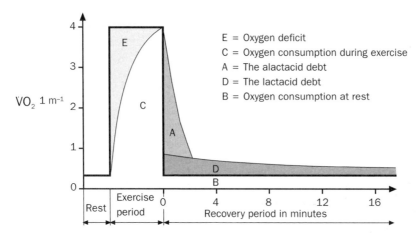

E = Oxygen deficit
C = Oxygen consumption during exercise
A = The alactacid debt
D = The lactacid debt
B = Oxygen consumption at rest

lactate: a salt of *lactic acid* often found in the blood. Lactic acid and lactate are not the same compound. When lactic acid is oxidised, hydrogen (H^+) is removed and the remaining compound when combined with sodium (N^+) or potassium (K^+) forms a salt – a lactate. Often the terms lactate and lactic acid are used interchangeably, since large quantities of blood lactate assume that large amounts of lactic acid has formed.

$$CH_3CHOHCOOH \longrightarrow CH_3CHOHCOO^- + H^+$$
lactic acid   lactate ion   hydrogen ion

lactate tests: the measurement of blood *lactate* which is used to determine the intensity at which an athlete is working. Many types of lactate tests can be used. For example, the performer could be required to run at speeds of 8, 9, 10 and finally 11 miles per hour, and at the end of each stage blood samples are taken by a small prick on the finger and analysed for blood lactate. The point at which blood lactate rises significantly indicates the point of *onset of blood lactate accumulation*, and the running speed which corresponds to this is recorded. Improvements in endurance ability can be observed, when lower lactate levels are recorded for the same intensity of exercise; this shows that the body has adapted to cope better with this intensity of exercise through *buffering* lactic acid.

lactic acid: formed when the body is exercising under *anaerobic* conditions and at quite high intensity and is a by-product of *anaerobic glycolysis*, formed when *pyruvic acid* is acted upon by the enzyme lactate dehydrogenase (LDH). As lactic acid is derived from glycogen (it is simply glycogen that has not been completely degraded) it is not, as many people mistakenly believe, a waste product but can be a source of energy. It is only once lactic acid has started to accumulate in the muscle that the fatigue associated with it takes its toll. Lactic acid accumulation is associated with activities of high intensity such as a 400-metre run or 200-metre swim.

lactic acid energy system: the means of energy provision, which breaks down glycogen in the absence of oxygen (see *anaerobic glycolysis*). Glycolytic enzymes work on breaking down the glucose molecule into *pyruvic acid* which is converted to lactic acid when there is not sufficient oxygen available. In breaking down glucose to pyruvic acid, sufficient energy to resynthesise two ATP molecules is released. However, this represents only five per cent of the energy stored within the glucose molecule, since in the absence of oxygen the lactic acid produced inhibits the further break- down of the glucose molecule. This system does, however, release energy relatively quickly and is therefore responsible for supplying ATP in high intensity, short-term exercise such as a 400-metre run or 200-metre swim. Although the lactic acid system is used in those activities that last between ten seconds and three minutes, it will also operate in more endurance-based activities when the *anaerobic threshold* is exceeded due to the lack of oxygen available to the working muscles (see the figure under *glycolysis* entry, page 108).

laissez-faire leader: a type of leader that allows the *group* to make their own decisions, offering them little help with the decision-making process. A laissez-faire leader generally adopts a passive role and as a result the task is less likely to be completed. Often if the group is left alone members become aggressive towards each other, do little work and give up easily. See also *democratic leader* and *autocratic leader*.

Lakeland sports: a traditional sporting festival based in the Lake District of northwest England.

'Upon Stone Carr there have been held, time out of mind, races and other sports, such as wrestling, leaping [high jump] tracing with dogs [hound trailing].'   (1787)

In the English Lake District one can draw a parallel between a sheep-based economy and many of the sporting occasions tending to have social significance during the early nineteenth century. Shepherds travel to buy and sell sheep. In this way a show would be born; families treat the occasion as a 'day out'. Following the showing and selling of sheep there would be sports and dances. Such events were based on a seasonal economy.

laminar flow: the smooth flow of air around a moving object. Most implements used in sport travel relatively quickly and are not uniformly shaped. This prevents the smooth flow of air around the object causing drag. Through *streamlining*, athletes have attempted to minimise drag and promote laminar flow. For example, cycle helmets have been shaped like a tear drop, the best shape to encourage laminar flow, and cyclists adopt more streamlined positions with their bodies. (See the figure below.)

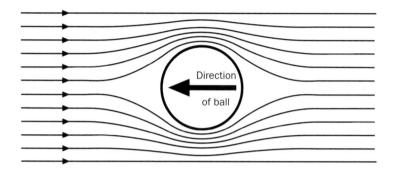

Direction of ball

lateral: a term of direction which means towards the outside of the body. Lateral rotation, for example, takes place at the shoulder during the recovery phase of the breaststroke arm pull, since the humerus rotates at the shoulder joint towards the outside of the body. (See appendix, page 253.)

lawn tennis: tennis played on a grass court. It was developed in the nineteenth century from the aristocratic pastime of *real tennis*, played on a sophisticated indoor court. Major Wingfield took most of the credit for the game's popularity. His invention which he called 'Spharistike' had an hour-glass court. He provided a commercial product which could be bought in kit form, consisting of a net, posts, rackets and balls, making it attractive to the *middle classes* eager to develop their own forms of recreation and who also had large suburban gardens. They were to go on to form the clubs and develop the administration.

The Marylebone Cricket Club took the game one stage further, calling it lawn tennis and adopting an oblong-shaped court. It ousted croquet from the lawns of the middle classes. It was also considered suitable for ladies to play, since they could play privately and it was not too energetic. In this way, lawn tennis reflected and encouraged the growing liberation of women in these social classes. It was adopted in the girls' schools as it was deemed respectable and accepted by the family. The game was popular in this increasingly leisured society but *working class* participation was delayed until the provision of public facilities and its introduction into state schools, which only happened well into the twentieth century. Lawn tennis was to change from an elitist *amateur* game to a highly *professional* one with all the trappings of *commercialisation*.

le plein air: love of the fresh air. This is a popular concept in *France* and underpins the policy of developing an appreciation of the natural environment through physical activity. France's varied climate and terrain provide plenty of opportunities.

leadership: the behavioural process of influencing another individual or group towards achieving their goal. Early psychologists proposed the *Great Man theory* suggesting people were born with leadership characteristics, whereas more recent studies refute this claim arguing that *social learning theory* is more relevant. Individuals who naturally evolve into leaders from within the group are known as *emergent leaders*, while those nominated by others outside the group are *prescribed leaders*. To be successful, both types should be flexible in their approaches varying their *leadership style* depending on:

- personal characteristics – experience, ability, age and personality
- group characteristics – size, age, experience
- situational demands – task complexity, goals and available resources.

See also *contingency theory of leadership* and *Chelladuri's multi-dimensional model of leadership*, which suggest the style most appropriate to employ after taking into account various factors.

leadership styles: the method adopted by an individual to lead a group. There are a variety of styles available depending on the nature of the group and the situation, including:

- *autocratic leader*
- *democratic leader*
- *laissez-faire leader*.

See also *leadership*.

learned helplessness: feelings experienced by an individual when they believe that failure is inevitable because of negative past experiences. For example, a young gymnast who has been unable to master a headstand balance will not attempt the skill in the future because they feel their failure is due to a lack of ability, rather than due to lack of effort or task difficulty (see *attribution theory*). The phenomenon can be either 'specific', as in the case of the gymnast's attitude towards balances, or 'general', in which they may feel negative towards all sport. It is important to develop the *self-confidence* of the performer and set them realistic, achievable goals, so they develop *need to achieve* characteristics (see also *achievement motivation*).

learning: any relatively permanent change in behaviour that occurs as a direct result of experience. An individual who trains and practises will know if learning has taken place, as their uncontrolled actions alter to become recognised *skills*. This occurs in phases, as suggested by *Fitts and Posner's stages of learning*.

LEDCs: less economically developed countries: see *emergent cultures.*

legislation: the act or process of making laws. There has traditionally been little sport legislation in the United Kingdom as a result of trying to keep sport and politics separate. However, there has been an increase recently as players are becoming more accountable for their actions on the field of play, and supporters are now bound by legislation following the growth of hooliganism in the 1970s (see *hooligan*). There has also been educational legislation, e.g. the 1988 *Education Act* that affects physical education through the *National Curriculum*. Increases in levels of legislation often reflect governments seeking more control in a given area. The money made through sport makes it of economic interest also.

leisure: time when there is an element of freedom for the individual to choose what to do. The time which provides this element of freedom is called 'surplus time'; that is, time left over from domestic responsibilities, work and satisfying essential bodily needs like eating and sleeping. This time is not evenly distributed across the population, for example, retired people have a lot of leisure time whilst a working mother probably has the least. This does not necessarily mean the retired group uses leisure facilities the most, as these people probably also have the least income and limited mobility. Leisure therefore is culturally determined and concepts such as *high culture* and *low culture* emerge. How people decide to use their leisure time will depend on many factors, e.g. their income and what activities are commonly practised amongst their peer group.

There are numerous uses of leisure time and these would be classed as recreational pursuits. Leisure should benefit the individual and have meaning in terms of personal development for relaxation, entertainment, self-fulfilment and self-realisation, whilst allowing people to develop skills. As such it has instrumental value.

Leisure can have either a high or a low status in *society* depending on the values of that society. For example, in Western societies leisure has traditionally been seen to have a lower status than work. This stemmed from the *protestant work ethic* whilst in the communist systems the term *purposeful leisure* is used. In recent time, the nature of leisure has changed and grown dramatically. The reasons for this include:

- working hours have been reduced by the application of technology
- labour-saving gadgets enable people to spend much less time on domestic chores
- increase in life expectancy
- increase in disposable incomes
- decline in the role of traditional structures like the church and family
- education for everyone
- mobility of a large section of the population
- public provision of leisure facilities
- early retirement
- unemployment.

Benefits to the individual	Benefit to society
Gives relief from stress/catharsis/relaxation	Keeps mass of population occupied/social control
Promotes physical and mental well being	
Provides a challenge	Recreates energies for work
Active leisure = health/fitness	Maintains cultural traditions
Entertains	Provides economic profit

leisure industry: collectively, those organisations where individuals pay for access to leisure facilities. The development of the leisure industry followed industrialisation, and leisure is now seen as part of a capitalist system with global interests.

leisure provision: various organisations are responsible for providing local communities with leisure and recreational facilities. They can be classed as private, voluntary and public.

Private sector	Public sector	Voluntary sector
Privately owned, registered companies	Business operations run by local authority departments	Business operations owned by members
Trading on normal profit/loss/ self-financed	Trading on set prices/charges etc. according to pre-set budget	Possibly on trust/charity basis; trading on normal profit/loss/breakeven
Managed by owners and their employees	Managed by local authority employees	Managed by members committee; may employ staff
Must operate and survive in open market/make a profit/ compete	May involve subsidies as a matter of policy/Council tax or equivalent	Financed by members fees/ fund raising/sponsorship

levers produce turning movements about a fixed point, called a fulcrum. In the human body bones act as levers, a joint as the fulcrum and muscles provide the effort or force to move the lever about the fulcrum. Levers are central to all movement that occurs in the body. There are three classes of lever that occur in the body and each is determined by the relative positions of the fulcrum (F), resistance (R) and effort (E):

- 1st class lever – one where the fulcrum lies between the effort and the resistance, for example, the elbow joint when throwing the javelin. This class of lever is particularly good if speed is required

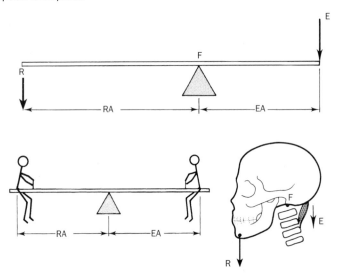

- 2nd class lever – one where the resistance lies between the fulcrum and the effort, for example when raising up onto tiptoe. It is best illustrated by a high jumper rocking onto the ball of their foot during take-off. This lever system can generate great force

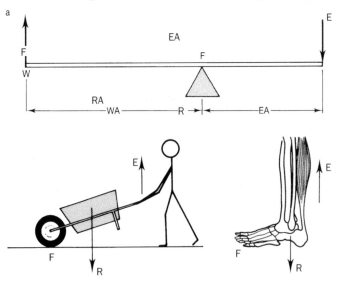

138

- 3rd class lever – occurs when the effort lies between the resistance and the fulcrum. This is the most common type of lever in the body and can easily be seen at the elbow when performing a bicep curl.

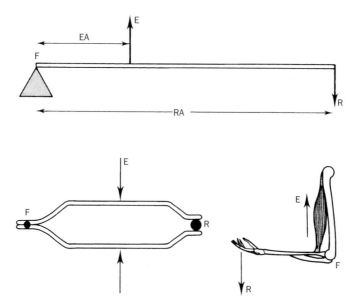

To determine the class of lever operating think of the component in the **middle** of the system, i.e. 'For F R E think 12 3'.

license system: a membership card which all French school-children have allowing them entry into a variety of multi-sport clubs. The license is a useful way of providing statistical evidence of sport participation and suggests trends from which projections and therefore policies can be made. It can also monitor standards for selection purposes and provides medical information.

lifetime sports: a range of activities which can be carried on throughout life, for example, badminton and rambling. All generations are encouraged to become involved and some believe the *physical education* curriculum in schools should reflect this trend with a move away from purely traditional activities. The emphasis is on lower energy output and participating for fun, attempting to dispel the myth that sport is the prerogative of the young. Veteran sections in clubs are also beginning to take this aspect into account.

ligaments: tough, fibrous connective tissue that attaches one bone to another. Typically ligaments occur at joints and are responsible for stabilising them to enable effective movement to take place. For example, the knee joint is composed of an intricate network of ligaments, including the lateral and medial collateral ligaments that prevent any sideways movement, whilst the *cruciate ligaments* prevent anterio-posterior (forwards and backwards) movement of the tibia.

This therefore limits the movement at the knee joint to *flexion* and *extension* and enables us to run and kick. The shoulder joint, on the other hand, allows a much wider range of movement since there is a less intricate network of ligaments.

Likert scale: questionnaire evaluating the attitude of an individual. It is composed of a series of statements, with which the individual has to indicate how much they agree or disagree. The scale usually has five gradings, ranging from 'strongly agree' to 'strongly disagree'. This allows the individual to express a wider opinion towards the *attitude object* than a *Thurstone scale*. See also *attitude tests*.

Lilleshall National Sports Centre: see *national sport centres*

linear motion: movement of an object or body occurring in a straight line when a force acts upon it. For example, a sprinter who runs down the track in an upright position, with no turning or rotation, experiences linear motion. In comparison, however, a gymnast performing a somersault would experience *angular motion*, during the rotation phase. See also *Newton's laws of motion*.

linear performance curve: see *performance curves*

lipoprotein: protein containing a lipid produced by the liver. It can combine with cholesterol and triglycerides to make them water-soluble allowing them to be easily transported by the cardiovascular system and used by the body. *Aerobic* exercise can increase high-density lipoproteins (HDLs) and has been proven to lower the risk of *cardiovascular diseases*.

Little League: well-established children's sport programme in the United States. A good example is Little League *baseball* that is now a big business employing full-time professional employees and volunteers. Parents initially set up such programmes, catering for different age groups with different divisions. Children are selected by competitive trials and winning is highly valued. Following local and regional playoffs, an annual world series is held. It is valued for its *competitiveness*.

local authorities: the political bodies that control towns, cities and rural areas which are distinct from national governments. They are administrative areas of government that look after local issues such as education and recreation. There are two tiers – county councils and district councils. Local authorities have a heavy burden in providing for *leisure* and now this is mainly the responsibility of one specialist department. However, as legislation is permissive, that is local authorities are not required by law to provide facilities, it is not surprising that wide variations in provision and expenditure can occur. Reasons why local authorities will provide for leisure are:

- leisure is in popular demand from local residents
- leisure is increasingly valued for its own benefits and not just to reduce other social problems like vandalism
- leisure is seen to be of economic benefit to a local area, particularly in its ability to attract tourism.

local management of schools (LMS): a system which has allowed individual schools freedom to run their own budgets and make their own choices away from the local education authority.

Lombardian ethic: dominant concept in American sport which is said to be based on the saying of the coach, Vince Lombardi, 'winning isn't the most important thing, it's the only thing'. This emphasises the competitive, achievement-orientated, reward-based type of sport behaviour.

long bone: cylindrical shaped bones found in the limbs of the body. Their primary function is to act as *levers* to facilitate movement. For example, in the action of running, the upper leg muscles (quadriceps) contract to raise the thigh (femur) and pull the foot off the floor; in a second contraction they pull on the shin bone (tibia) to cause extension at the knee and the foot is place back onto the floor. This forms one single stride; when this occurs repeatedly a running action takes place. A second vital function of long bones is the production of blood cells which occurs deep inside the bone (see figure below). Examples of long bones include: femur, tibia, humerus and phalanges (although the latter are not great in length they are cylindrical and so also fall into this category).

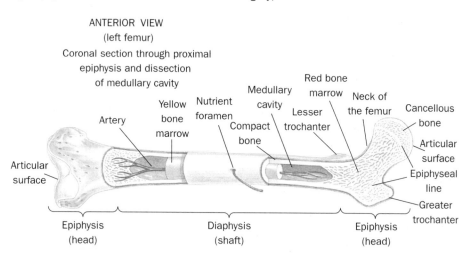

ANTERIOR VIEW
(left femur)
Coronal section through proximal epiphysis and dissection of medullary cavity

Epiphysis (head) — Diaphysis (shaft) — Epiphysis (head)

long-term memory: component of the *memory* process, which has the capacity to store vast amounts of information for an unlimited period of time. When a performer is faced with a new situation, the relevant stimuli are processed via the *short-term memory store* and a comparison is made with any similar past experiences. If any recognition occurs, the similarities are recalled and returned to the short-term memory store or *working memory,* so a decision can be made and a motor programme (see *executive motor programme*) constructed. Any relevant stored data can make the decision-making process quicker and therefore enhance the execution of the skill. For example, a rugby player who is faced with a situation involving a complicated set pattern of play will have the capability to complete the sequence if it has been practised sufficiently to be retained in the long-term memory. Similarly, if confronted with an overlap situation, the player will know which option is the most suitable, and *reaction time* can be reduced if a comparable scenario has been experienced in the past. The long-term memory can be improved through practice and 'overlearning' motor programmes, so that the performer progresses towards the *autonomous stage of learning*.

lottery fund: launched in 1994, the Sport England Lottery fund had a broad policy strategy:

- to introduce the Priority Areas Initiative for some of England's most deprived communities
- to set and achieve a target of funding 1000 community projects in the first year
- to fund a new national stadium and a *UK Sports Institute*
- to fund some of our talented young sport stars.

The Lottery Act (1998) and the revised directions from the Secretary of State for Culture, Media and Sport allowed for a more pro-active approach.

The two-fund approach:

- Community Projects Fund – will contain three parts: the small projects award up to £5000; capital awards (over £5000) concentrating on community provision, and revenue awards (over £5000) which will concentrate on combatting the social exclusion of young people who could progress given adequate support.

- World Class Fund – includes the UK Sports Institute *(UKSI)*; capital support for special- ist national facilities other than the UK site; revenue support through the world class programmes and world class events to support bringing international competitions to this country.

See also *National Lottery*.

low culture: this traditionally refers to the cultural pursuits of the mass of the population. Individuals choose their own leisure pursuits within the context of their own culture, values and identity. Low or popular culture does not usually require sophisticated levels of appre- ciation or understanding. It is accessible and therefore to some extent is defined by what is made available by the leisure market forces. It is usually exciting and dramatic, for example, *football* and *boxing*.

lower class: see *working class*

lumbar vertebrae: the third section of the vertebral column, consisting of five lumbar vertebrae which are the largest of all the individual vertebrae. Their large centrum or body offer a great deal of weight-bearing capacity, while their large *processes* secure the attach- ment of the muscles. This muscle attachment, together with the intervertebral discs of cartilage, form *cartilaginous joints*, which enable flexion and extension (forward and backward movement) and lateral flexion (side to side movement) of the trunk. For example, when performing a 'pike' jump in trampolining, it is the cartilaginous joints between the lumbar vertebrae that enable us to touch our toes. (See appendix, page 258.)

lymphatic system: network of vessels that carry excess fluid away from tissues, prevent- ing saturation and swelling of the tissues and muscles. Following exercise, excess fluid can cause swelling and pain in the associated muscles and tissues and a *cool-down* can help remove this excess fluid by draining it away via the lymphatic system. Training can improve the efficiency at which the lymphatic system drains away the excess fluid and thereby prevents muscle pain.

What other subjects are you studying?

A–Zs cover 18 different subjects. See the inside back cover for a list of all the titles in the series and how to order.

macro cycle: part of the *periodisation* process, the development of a macro cycle is central to effective training planning. Essentially, a macro cycle is based around the longterm *performance goal*. It could last one to four years. For example, training towards the *Olympic Games*.

Magnus effect: the *Bernouilli effect* applied to spinning objects is known as the Magnus effect. It is concerned with the flow of air or water past a moving object and the creation of differences in pressure between different parts of the object. When a spinning object travels through the air, the air molecules in contact with the object spin with it creating what is known as a 'boundary layer'. This boundary layer will eventually collide head on with the main air flow on one side of the object (see figure below). This slows the flow of air down on this one side of the object which causes pressure to increase and a pressure differential to occur. The pressure differential causes a Magnus force, directed from high pressure to low pressure. For example, playing a top spin shot in tennis causes a pressure differential between high pressure at the top of the ball and low pressure at the bottom of the tennis ball. As objects will always move from high pressure to low pressure the ball is pulled downwards. Furthermore, the Magnus force is heightened with new balls in tennis since the nap or fuzz of the ball traps a much larger boundary layer and causes a greater pressure differential.

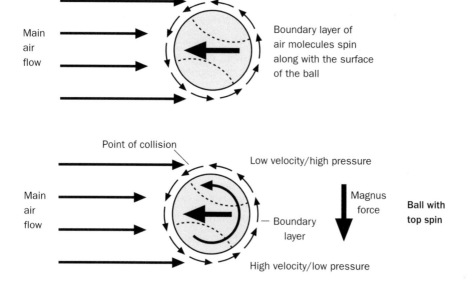

Main air flow

Boundary layer of air molecules spin along with the surface of the ball

Point of collision

Low velocity/high pressure

Main air flow

Boundary layer

Magnus force

Ball with top spin

High velocity/low pressure

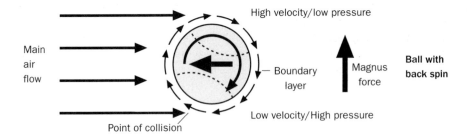

manual guidance: see *guidance*

manual labour clause: the formal exclusion of manual workers by the Amateur Rowing Association in 1882. It excluded anyone who was by trade 'a mechanic, artisan or labourer' but was abolished in 1890. It was a device to retain a social distinction in sport as the *gentry* amateurs did not wish to be beaten by lower-class *professionals* nor could they socialise with them after the sporting event.

Maori culture: the indigenous inhabitants of New Zealand, who before colonisation by Britain had an integrated, co-operative political system. A fixed rank in society from birth negated the need for competition. This is an example of a 'closed' social system similar to the Indian caste system. The individual identified with the tribe and the means of production were collectively owned. *Recreation* was an important element in Maori life with many of the games derived from tribal myths and it served to conserve the ancient folklore. In Maori culture, games to serve various functions include:

● training for war

● acquiring grace and skill

● contributing to economic efficiency

● *recreation*

● promoting tribal loyalty

● an outlet for healthy competition in an otherwise co-operative social system.

martial arts: activities which relate to, or are a characteristic of, war. Examples are judo, karate, tai kwando. They are *combat* activities and mainly derive from Eastern cultures, often being founded on certain philosophies or religions.

Marxism: a political and economic perspective that developed from the work of Karl Marx (1818–1883). He stressed the role of conflict between the social classes in society rather than *social order*. This conflict is based upon economic dimensions. The ruling classes (bourgeoisie) own the means of production and control the resources; thus they have economic and political control over the proletariat or lower classes.

This theory however:

● does not recognise the freedom of individuals to exercise their free will

● does not recognise social order as it exists in most societies.

Maslow's hierarchy of needs proposes that individuals have various levels of motivational needs, both physiological and psychological, that must be fulfilled in a specific order. People continue to strive to satisfy those needs lower down the hierarchy before progressing to the next level. For example, the basic needs of thirst, hunger and warmth must be satisfied before progressing to the higher needs of *esteem* and self-fulfilment. In terms of sporting activity, a performer may reach the highest level by achieving success, receiving acclaim or mastering a skill. However, this cannot be achieved until he or she feels safe and comfortable, allowing them to experience the *motivation* to explore new challenges.

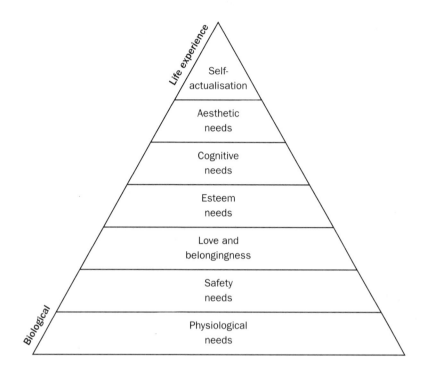

Maslow's hierarchy of needs

mass culture: see *low culture*

mass media: forms of mass communication to the general public, comprising newspaper, radio and television broadcasting. The initial developments occurred in the eighteenth century and towards the end of the twentieth century new technologies increased the influence of the media even more through satellites, computers, and the Internet.

Advantages to sport	Disadvantages to sport
Boost participation figures	Rule changes to be more media-friendly
Boost funds for the sport	Retain discrimination, e.g. less female sport shown
Higher profile can be given to minority groups	Commercial interest can come first, not the interest of the sport
Help detailed analysis of an event	Reduce funding for sports with less television coverage
Reach global audiences immediately	Lack of coverage can reduce participation
Help referees	Dictation of players' commitments and timing of events

mass participation: see *Sport for All*

massed practice involves the repeated practice of skills over a period of time, with little or no recovery periods. This form of *practice* is useful with well-motivated, experienced performers, who possess good levels of fitness and with tasks that are simple and discrete in nature, e.g. shooting at goal or racket strokes, such as the tennis serve or badminton smashes. Care should be taken when using this method to avoid boredom, fatigue and overtraining.

matrix: an area of the *mitochondria* where the *Krebs' cycle* takes place.

maximum heart rate (MHR): an individual can calculate an estimate of their maximum heart rate by subtracting their age from 220. For example, an 18-year-old student will have a maximum heart rate of 220 – 18 = 202 beats per minute (bpm). By exercising at a percentage of our maximum heart rate we have an objective method of calculating and monitoring training intensities. It is advised that the trained athlete work between 70 and 85 per cent of their MHR whilst the person exercising for health-related reasons work between 60 and 75 per cent of their MHR. Therefore if we took a trained 18-year-old student:

$$70\% = 0.7 \times 202 = 141 \text{ bpm}$$
$$85\% = 0.85 \times 202 = 172 \text{ bpm}$$

We now have two figures which represent the athlete's training heart rate or *training zone*. As long as their heart rate lies between 141 bpm and 172 bpm, benefits of training will occur. This has particular use for monitoring intensities in endurance-based activities such as long-distance running, *swimming* or *cycling*.

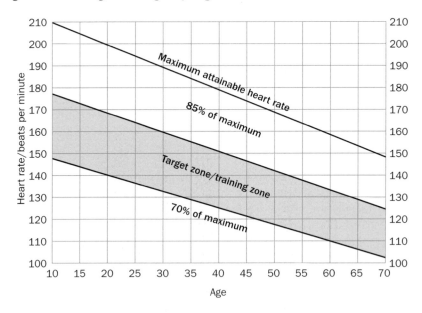

maximum oxygen uptake (VO$_2$max): the maximum volume of oxygen that can be taken in, transported to and consumed by the working muscles per minute. Maximum oxygen uptake is the best way of determining endurance performance. For example, a marathon runner who undertakes long periods of exercise using the *aerobic energy system* and whose muscles are extremely efficient at utilising oxygen, would be expected to have a high maximum oxygen uptake. It can only truly be measured under laboratory conditions whereby athletes undertake a task, such as running on a treadmill, that becomes progressively more difficult, and a computer analyses the relative concentrations of oxygen and carbon dioxide that are inspired and expired. The test continues until a point is reached when the body's oxygen consumption does not increase with increasing workloads. At this point, the athlete is working at their aerobic limit, i.e. their maximum oxygen uptake, and it can be recorded in absolute terms, 'l/min' for non-weight bearing activities, or relative to body weight in 'ml/kg/min'. The higher the value, the more efficient the body is at exercising under aerobic conditions.

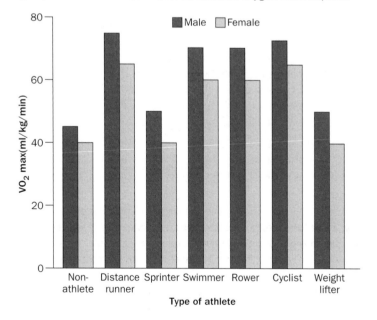

Maximum oxygen uptake is largely genetically determined and can only normally be improved by 10–20 per cent through training. The graph below shows the expected norms for different groups of athletes. Also known as maximal oxygen consumption.

May Day festivals: the first day of May, traditionally a celebration of the coming of spring. It stems from Roman times and hence was heathen in origin. The May games consisted of activities such as dancing round the maypole, archery, war-like shows, stage plays and bonfires. Some countries still recognise it as a day of holiday for workers.

measurement of fitness: a battery of tests used to assess an individual's components of fitness. These tests can identify strengths and weaknesses in performance, physiological potential, success of training programmes and can be used to compare against norms within their group. The table below outlines some common fitness tests.

Fitness component	Recognised test	Evaluation of test
aerobic fitness	multistage fitness test	compared to standard Sportcoach UK tables
anaerobic fitness	Wingate cycle test	objective data from computer printouts
strength	handgrip dynamometer	scores compared to standard tables
muscular endurance	NCF abdominal conditioning test	scores compared to Sportcoach UK standard tables
flexibility	sit and reach test	scores compared to standard tables
body composition	bioelectric impedance	objective values that can be compared to standard tables and norms
speed	30 m sprint	times compared to standard tables

mechanical guidance: see *guidance*

media: see *mass media*

medial: term of direction which means towards the midline of the body. Medial rotation for example, takes place at the shoulder during the 'pull' phase of the breaststroke arm action, since the humerus rotates at the shoulder joint towards the midline of the body. (See appendix, page 253.)

medical classification: see *classification*

medieval era: the years between 1066 and 1485 are generally known as the *Middle Ages*. The bulk of the population was rural but towns were emerging and with them came the development of the professions, e.g. medicine and law, from which the *middle classes* were to grow. Festivals and feasts played a large part in recreational pastimes though military activities still played a major role in times when defence was of paramount importance. Popular activities were mob football (see *mob games*), wrestling, *animal baiting*, skittles and bowls.

meditation: the use of controlled breathing to help clear the mind to focus on specific *cues* or thoughts. Specific words, sounds or chants, known as 'mantra', are learnt and practised allowing the performer to reduce levels of *anxiety* and relax. This should be carried out ideally in a quiet place, to induce feelings of calm.

melting pot: a term used to describe the influence of the universities, particularly Oxford and Cambridge, in pooling the experiences and developments that occurred in the gentry *public schools*. The different versions of games became codified at the universities, giving a national interpretation of rules that were to become adopted worldwide.

memory: system within the brain that allows information to be organised, retained and retrieved at a later date (see figure on page 149). It is a central component of *information* *processing* allowing *decision-making* to occur. The faster a performer can retrieve information from the memory about past experiences, the better the chances of a successful outcome. For example, a basketball player in the attacking half of the court detects certain *stimuli*, which are compared with similar situations previously experienced. If similarities are recognised the decision-making process is faster, allowing the player to execute the appropriate skill more quickly than a player who has not been in that position before.

Memory is sub-divided into several phases:

- *short-term sensory store* – information retained for up to 1 second
- *short-term memory store* – limited information retained for up to 30 seconds
- *long-term memory store* – permanent store with vast capacity

There are numerous methods that can be utilised to improve the efficiency of a performer's memory including practice, chaining (see *progressive part method practice*), *chunking*, *mental practice* and *imagery*.

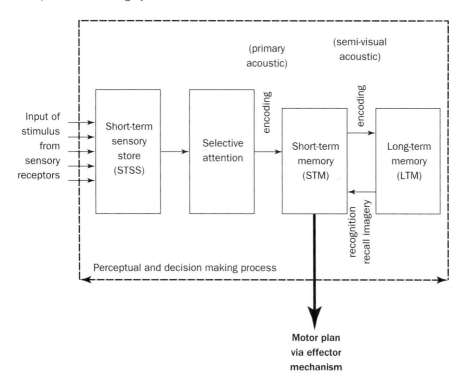

mental practice involves the mental or cognitive rehearsal of a skill without physical movement. An individual visualises the situation that has to be completed, which can reduce learning time for novices and prepare experienced performers for competition, reducing *reaction time* and improving *anticipation*. It is a useful technique to employ during the recovery periods of training to focus an athlete's mind and control their levels of *arousal*. The figure on page 150 shows the comparison of effects of mental practice and physical practice on performance over a period of days.

mental relaxation: see *meditation*

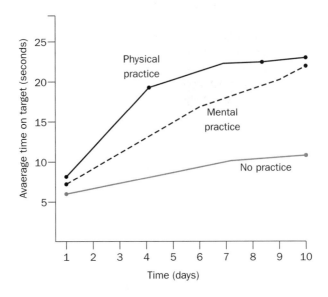

Mental practice

meniscus (pl. menisci): crescent-shaped pad of fibro-cartilage found between the articulating surfaces of the knee joint. Its function is to aid the *articular cartilage* in preventing wear between the tibia and femur as well as to increase the shock absorption properties of the knee joint which enable us to run and jump. The menisci may be torn by a violent blow such as a tackle in football or by a sudden twisting movement, sometimes causing loose bits of cartilage to float in the joint capsule and interfere with the joint action. The introduction of key-hole surgery has meant that such problems can be easily remedied with little long-term effect on joint mobility.

mental rehearsal: see *imagery*

meso cycle: part of the *periodisation process* the development of a meso cycle is central to effective training planning. A meso cycle comprises a number of *micro cycles* and lasts between one month and three months. An example of a meso cycle could be the development of *strength* in the pre-season phase of training.

Methodists: followers of a system of faith developed by John Wesley and which is a non-conformist denomination. In the nineteenth century Methodists believed popular recreations to be sinful, being associated with drinking and *gambling*. The Methodists were among the strongest opponents of *animal sport* in the eighteenth and nineteenth centuries and were to have a detrimental effect on *recreation* pastimes for the lower classes. They tried to provide alternative religious activities combining recreation with a spiritual cause.

micro cycle: part of the *periodisation* process the development of a micro cycle is central to effective training planning. Essentially a micro cycle is a group of training sessions or units, usually organised over the period of a week, but can last up to three weeks. They usually focus on one particular component of performance and can be either fitness or skill-related.

middle ages: see *medieval era*

middle classes: the traditional social class grouping which stands between the *upper* and *working classes* and is usually associated with non-manual work such as clerical or professional work such as teaching. The middle classes emerged through the *Industrial Revolution* and they had a civilising effect on nineteenth-century society and were a strong religious and moral force, restricting blood sports and rationalising many sports, i.e. they developed rules, structured competitions and *governing bodies*.

military drill: training in procedures or movements and use of weapons. Strict and often repetitious training or exercises used as a method of teaching in the nineteenth-century state schools. See *model course*.

Minister for Sport: a British government minister whose main responsibility is to oversee and co-ordinate sport at a national level. S/he works in the *Department for Culture, Media and Sport*.

minute ventilation: the total volume of air taken to the lungs per minute. It is the product of *tidal volume* (the volume of air taken to the lungs per breath) and frequency (the number of breaths taken per minute), and at rest this volume should lie between 6000 ml and 7000 ml per minute. Since both frequency of breathing and tidal volume increase during exercise there is a significant rise in minute ventilation. However, changes in minute ventilation following submaximal training are fairly insignificant.

mitochondrion (pl. mitochondria): the powerhouse of the muscle cell which plays a central role in the production of *adenosine triphosphate (ATP)* under *aerobic* conditions. Endurance athletes such as tour cyclists would be expected to possess larger and more efficient mitochondria in the muscles of their legs in order to optimise ATP and therefore energy production. Both the size and number of mitochondria can be increased through a programme of endurance training. (See figure below.)

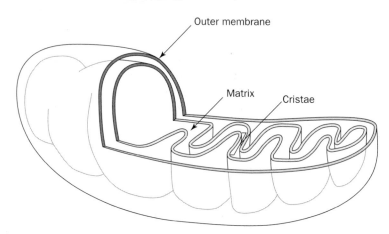

mixed economy: see *economic systems*

mob: an unorganised, unruly mass of people who are engaged in some form of disorder. The mob was symbolic in the nineteenth century of everything that the *upper classes* feared. Following the French Revolution, the mob came to represent a threat to their privileged lifestyle from the lower orders. See also *mob games*.

mob football: see *mob games*

mob games: games played by an unorganised, unruly mass of people such as mob football and mob hockey. These games were a form of *popular recreation*, characterised by:

- occasional play
- few, simple rules
- limited structure and organisation
- participation-based rather than spectator-based
- needing physical force rather than skill
- lower class development
- being local rather than regional or national
- limited equipment and facilities.

model course: policy of drill used in state schools, which was initiated in 1902 by Colonel Fox of the War Office. The lack of fitness, discipline and poor general health of the working classes had been noted in the *Boer War* and blamed for the heavy loss of life suffered. The aim was to improve:

- the fitness of the working classes for military preparation
- their familiarity with combat and weapons
- discipline and obedience amongst the working classes.

It was characterised by:

- the use of commands issued by the teacher or non-commissioned officers (NCO)
- children standing in uniform military-style rows and obeying commands
- large numbers being catered for in a small space
- movements that were free-standing requiring no apparatus, and therefore cheap.

However the problems of the course were that:

- that essentially adult exercises were performed by children
- that it did not take into account children's physical, mental or emotional needs
- there was no educational content
- individualism was submerged within a group response
- use of NCOs lowered the status of the subject.

moment of inertia: a measure of the resistance of an object to *angular motion*. This is dependent on the mass of the object and the distribution of that mass around the axis of rotation. For example, when performing a somersault, if the gymnast is in a tuck position the moment of inertia is smaller than if they are in an open position. It is calculated using the formula:

$$I = mk^2$$

where I = moment of inertia, m = mass and k = radius of gyration.

momentum: the amount of motion a moving object or individual possesses and is the product of its mass and velocity:

$$Mo = m \times v$$

For example, a prop forward in rugby with a mass of 90 kg and a velocity of 10 m/s has a momentum of 900 kg m/s. As the mass of an object or person tends to remain constant in sporting situations, any change in momentum must be as a result of change in velocity. A long jumper, for example, will change their run-up so that they are travelling at their highest velocity at take-off, in an attempt to optimise their momentum.

mood states: see *profile of mood states*

Mosston and Ashworth's spectrum of teaching styles: a continuum of teaching styles based on who makes the decision about the learning environment. The type of teaching style is chosen by the teacher based on a number of factors, including the nature of the task, the situation, the ability of the performer as well as the personality and experience of the teacher. The coach or teacher should take note of these variables and be flexible in their use of the styles in order to maximise the learning environment. There are numerous styles as indicated on the figure below, with the most common being:

- A – *command style* – all decisions made by the teacher, no pupil input
- C/D – *reciprocal style* – decisions made predominantly by the teacher with some input from the performer
- F – *discovery style* – decisions made by the performers with some guidance and input from the teacher
- I/J – *problem solving style* – all decisions made by the performer, no teacher input

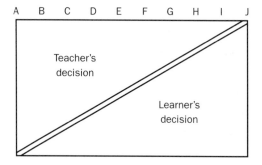

motivation: the internal mechanisms and external stimuli, which arouse and direct behaviour. It is generally suggested that we have two basic motives that require fulfilment, our physiological and psychological needs (see *Maslow's hierarchy of needs*). Each performer has differing needs that motivate them to participate, which fall into two broad categories:

- *intrinsic motivation* – involves gaining self-satisfaction or pride from achievements; the desire to challenge oneself; or simply the enjoyment of taking part. For example, an individual, may decide to learn how to play squash as a form of recreation, to develop their fitness levels and to see if they can master the game
- *extrinsic motivation* – involves receiving either tangible or intangible *rewards*. The former includes medals, cups, certificates or money, while the latter may involve praise from a coach, family, peer group or the media, as well as glory, social approval or achievement records

Many of the latter examples can be utilised to reinforce learning, but should be used with care, as the over-use of extrinsic rewards can undermine the intrinsic values needed for long-term participation. For example, a novice swimmer may be encouraged to learn to swim for numerous reasons including the safety, enjoyment, social and health benefits received. However to maintain their interest, awards and badges may be used, but care must be taken to ensure the swimmer does not simply continue because of the next reward – otherwise what happens after the final badge? Ideally, a performer should be motivated by a combination of intrinsic and extrinsic rewards, in order to optimise learning. See also *arousal, achievement motivation* and *attribution theory.*

motor abilities: see *gross motor abilities*

motor control: the regulation and adaption of bodily movements. It is suggested that individuals achieve this on three levels, depending on the extent to which the central nervous system is involved:

- level 1 – *open loop control,* automatic, requiring no conscious control; for example, catching a ball or running

- level 2 – *closed loop control*, some *feedback* received via kinaesthetic awareness and any adjustments are made subconsciously with little conscious attention from the performer; for example, holding a balance

- level 3 – closed loop control, feedback received and conscious decisions are made to adjust the movement, requiring attention from the performer, for example, a beginner learning to dribble has to continually evaluate and adapt their actions.

The majority of situations may require each performer to alternate between all three levels and will vary depending on the level of experience. For example, the novice will have to concentrate while dribbling more than an expert, who can perform the skill without apparently thinking about its execution.

motor end plate: the functional junction between the nerve and the muscle cell. It is the point at which the motor nerve stimulates the muscle fibre and causes contraction.

motor neurone: a nerve cell which conducts nerve impulses from the brain and spinal cord to muscles and to initiate contraction. See the diagram on page 155. Neurones have three distinct parts:

1 – a cell body which contains a well-defined nucleus

2 – dendrites which receive impulses and conduct them towards the cell body

3 – an axon, a single, long, thin extension that sends the impulse towards the muscle.

The ends of the axon terminals contain bulb-like structures known as synaptic end bulbs which form part of the *neuro-muscular junction*. Without the complex structure of motor neurones, it would not be possible to perform the co-ordinated movements required for sporting activities.

motor programme: see *executive motor programme*

motor skill: the physical execution of a movement by combining various *abilities*. Each skill requires different abilities to be effective and usually combines with *cognitive* and *perceptual skills*. Motor skills include a tennis serve, hurdling, running and rock climbing.

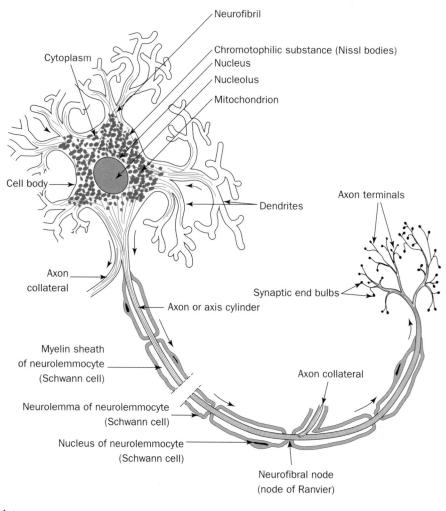

Neurofibril

Chromotophilic substance (Nissl bodies)
Nucleus
Nucleolus
Mitochondrion

Cytoplasm

Cell body

Axon terminals

Dendrites

Axon
collateral

Synaptic end bulbs

Axon or axis cylinder

Myelin sheath
of neurolemmocyte
(Schwann cell)

Axon collateral

Neurolemma of neurolemmocyte
(Schwann cell)

Nucleus of neurolemmocyte
(Schwann cell)

Neurofibral node
(node of Ranvier)

Motor neurone

motor unit: consists of the motor neurone plus all the fibres which that neurone inner-vates. Muscle fibres within a muscle are under the control of different motor neurones, just like pupils within a school are assigned to different forms or tutor groups. The number of motor units that are recruited for a specific contraction is determined by the strength needed for a given action. For example, when performing a bicep curl to a maximum, all the motor units within the biceps are recruited to enable the highest possible force to be generated. However, if a lighter weight is lifted, then only the number of motor units required to lift the weight will be recruited. A motor unit follows the *all or none law* so that if a motor unit is recruited then all the fibres within the unit will contract to their maximum possible extent. Furthermore, the number of fibres assigned to a particular motor unit varies depending upon the precision of movement required. For example, a motor unit of the eye may only have as few as ten fibres under its influence, since such movements require great control, whilst the gastrocnemius which is designed for strength may have up to 2000 fibres per motor unit. In this way, efficient yet effective muscle contraction can occur in all movements undertaken within the sporting arena.

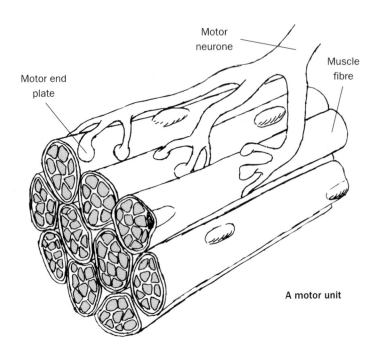

A motor unit

movement analysis: see *kinesiology*

movement approach: freedom, self-discovery and self-expression were encouraged in *physical education* lessons following World War II. Much of this was based on the philosophy of Dewey who proposed that activities could be educationally valid because of the intrinsic value of movement for its own sake. Emphasis was placed on individual discovery of solutions to physical problems and personal interpretation replaced the group response. The movement approach was readily adopted in primary schools, while in secondary schools educational gymnastics and dance were distinguished from the more traditional work of Olympic gymnastics and games.

movement pattern: a visual description of the movements possible at a joint. It is central to analysing movement. See appendix, page 268.

movement time: the time taken between the start of a movement and its completion. When the performer has made their decision based on the various *stimuli* from the environment, and the message has been sent to the muscular system (see *reaction time*), the time taken to complete that *executive motor programme* is recorded. For example, it would be the time a water polo player takes from the start of the shooting action to the finish of the action. See also *response time*.

Moving and Growing: a Ministry of Education publication in 1952 which combined with *Planning the Programme* replaced the old *Syllabuses of Physical Training* and were developed for use in primary schools. They combined the two influences of obstacle training from the army and movement training from the centres of dance. These publications developed as a result of changes in educational thinking which was to make learning more child-centred. The activities focussed upon included agility, playground and more major game skills, dance and movement to music, national dances and swimming. The key characteristics that distinguish them from earlier forms of physical activity in state schools are that it was 'exploratory', 'creative', 'individual' and 'fun'.

Much Wenlock Olympian Games: a festival of sporting activities established in 1850 at Much Wenlock by Dr Penny Brookes who formed a National Olympic Association. It had all the trappings of a rustic festival, with the events including football, *cricket*, *quoits*, a blindfold wheelbarrow race, and chasing a pig through the town. By the 1870s the events included track and field *athletics*, such as the pentathlon and tilting at the ring (a version of the jousting tournament). It was based on the spirit of *amateurism* placing the ideals of *fair play* and team spirit high above any material objectives. *Baron Pierre de Coubertin* visited these games in the years preceding the foundation of the modern *Olympic Games*.

multicultural: a society that incorporates the cultures of other groups, particularly other *ethnic groups*. The food, customs and religious beliefs of these groups can have an effect on the *dominant culture*. Different views exist about whether ethnic groups should be assimilated into the main culture or can co-exist alongside it. Education policies have had to adjust to cater for the requirements of these groups. Traditional sporting activities in the West are not always appropriate for different cultures. See *accommodation* and *assimilation*.

multi-stage fitness test: test used to predict *maximum oxygen uptake* (VO_2max). Devised by the *National Coaching Foundation*, it is a progressive shuttle run test that starts off easily and becomes progressively more difficult. Subjects are required to run as many shuttles of 20 metres as possible, keeping in time to the bleeps emitted from a pre-recorded tape. This becomes more difficult, however, since the difficulty increases with each level attained and the speed and intensity of running must be increased accordingly. Subjects continue to run as long as possible until such a time when they can no longer keep up with the bleeps. Once the subject withdraws from the test the level and shuttle number attained can be recorded and compared to standard tables which translate the score into a predicted VO_2max value.

Municipal Reform Act 1835: this Act provided local councils that were elected by local authorities, the legislation allowing them to raise money to provide the means for improving the moral, mental and physical state of the masses. Recreational facilities began to appear in the 1850s whereas prior to this, only the *upper classes* had access to such facilities. Provision included libraries, museums and parks. The parks were popular and constructed to:

- encourage rational sport that was rule-based with underlying moral qualities
- provide socially acceptable alternatives to the public house and gambling and thereby gain social control of the masses
- encourage a fitter, healthier workforce
- acknowledge an increase in social justice and reform
- appease the growing pressure from the lower classes for more facilities
- raise the profile of local areas for urban prestige.

muscle pump: aids the blood's return to the heart via the veins and is an essential part of the *venous return mechanism*. The contraction of skeletal muscle compresses upon localised veins which squeezes blood towards the heart. Pocket valves in the veins prevent any backflow and therefore ensures the smooth return of blood. During exercise the venous return increases dramatically, since there are more frequent and stronger muscular contractions ensuring that blood returns to the heart quickly, ready to be pumped around the body once again. If exercise is stopped suddenly without performing a *cool-down,* the venous return mechanism slows due to the cessation of the muscle pump and this may cause blood to pool in the veins and hinder the removal of *lactic acid* that may have accumulated.

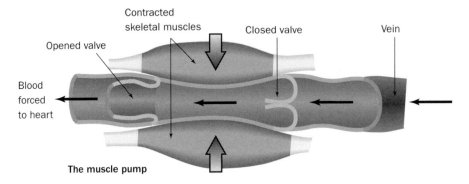

The muscle pump

muscle spindle apparatus: receptors that lie between the muscle fibres detecting the degree of stretch within the muscle. They transmit information to the spinal cord and brain concerning the muscle's length. In order to perform specific movements, the brain must know the current state of the muscle so that it can be adjusted appropriately, essentially preventing the muscle from overstretching and causing injury. When performing *plyometrics,* for example, on jumping down from a box the quadriceps are stretched, the muscle spindles detect the degree of stretch, and to prevent the muscle from stretching too far cause an instant *concentric contraction* which shortens the muscle and causes an explosive jump upwards. (See the figure below and on page 159.)

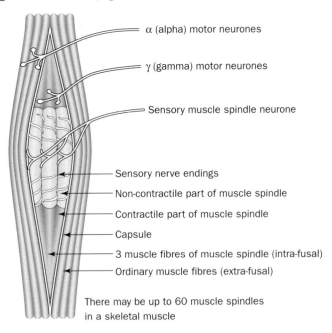

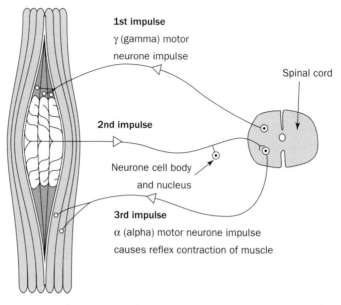

1st impulse
γ (gamma) motor
neurone impulse

Spinal cord

2nd impulse

Neurone cell body
and nucleus

3rd impulse
α (alpha) motor neurone impulse
causes reflex contraction of muscle

Muscle spindle apparatus (see page 158)

muscle tone: sustained partial contraction of portions of skeletal muscle. A muscle may be in a state of partial contraction at any given time, since some fibres may be contracted whilst others relax. This tightens the muscle but contraction is not sufficient to initiate movement. Muscle tone is essential for maintaining posture, for example, the neck muscles will contract to support the weight of the head but do not contract enough to pull the head all the way back. When performing a handstand in gymnastics, muscle tone in the arms and shoulders is essential to maintain balance.

muscle twitch: the response of a muscle fibre to a single stimulus.

muscular Christianity: an evangelical movement combining the Christian and chivalric ideal of manliness. It was the return of the Platonic concept of the 'whole man'. It aimed to improve one's ability to be courteous, gentle, brave and enterprising, reverent and truthful, selfless and devoted. It included the belief that healthy bodies were needed alongside healthy minds and moreover that moral understanding could be developed through athletic activity. However, it was not just any type of activity – muscular Christianity encouraged *rational recreation* and pursuits that took place in the *natural environment* such as cycling and rambling.

muscular endurance: the ability of a muscle to undergo repeated contractions and avoid fatigue. Muscular endurance is a major component of fitness required in activities where one or more muscle groups work at medium to high intensity for periods of time lasting up to five or six minutes. A good example is competitive rowing, where muscles of both the upper and lower body work continually throughout the race. This aspect of fitness is largely based upon the efficiency of the *lactic acid energy system* and the *buffering* capacity of the body, but can be improved through training. Any training for muscular endurance should work at improving these systems, for example, by undertaking *interval training* with a work:relief ratio of 1:1. Various tests can be performed to measure muscular endurance, including the National Coaching Foundation abdominal conditioning test.

myo-: a prefix meaning pertaining to 'muscle'.

myocardial infarction: the death of cardiac tissue which results from an insufficient blood supply reaching the *myocardium*. It is also known as a heart attack.

myocardium: the thickest portion of cardiac tissue (lying between the *pericardium* and the *endocardium*) which is responsible for pumping blood around the body. The heart of a trained athlete is larger than that of a non-athlete and is characterised by a thicker myocardium allowing the heart muscle to contract with a much greater force and pump more blood out of the heart per beat (*stroke volume*). At rest, this means that the heart does not need to pump as many times per minute to get the same volume of blood flowing to the muscles. However, during exercise, the increased thickness of the myocardium together with an increased heart rate means that the volume of blood flowing to the muscles (*cardiac output*) increases substantially.

myofibril: a thread-like structure, many of which combine to make up a muscle fibre, forming the contractile unit of skeletal muscle. They run longitudinally through the muscle fibre and are composed of two *myofilaments*, one thick protein named *myosin* and a thinner protein called *actin*. The interaction of actin and myosin occurs via the *sliding filament theory* which explains the process of muscle contraction at molecular level.

myofilament: extremely fine molecular proteins which make up a *myofibril*. The action of the myofilaments is responsible for the contraction of the myofibrils and therefore the muscle as a whole. There are two types of myofilaments: a thick *myosin* filament and a thin *actin* filament. It is the interaction between these two myofilaments via the *sliding filament theory* that can explain muscle contraction and which is therefore central to our understanding of movement.

myogenic: the capacity of the heart to generate spontaneous *action potentials* (impulses) which cause the heart to contract. Essentially the heart does not need to wait for an action potential to arrive from the brain, but can emit its own from the pacemaker (see *sino-atrial node*). This means that during exercise, the heart can respond quickly to ensure adequate supply of blood, hormones and nutrients to the muscle cell.

myoglobin: form of *haemoglobin* that occurs within the muscle cell that transports oxygen to the *mitochondria*, in order to produce energy via the aerobic energy pathway. The *slow twitch fibres* used for endurance-based activities contain more myoglobin than *fast twitch fibres*, due to their need for oxygen. It is also myoglobin, an iron-based protein, that gives slow twitch fibres their characteristic red colour. Endurance training has shown to increase muscle myoglobin content by up to 80 per cent.

myosin: the contractile protein that makes up the thick myofilaments of muscle fibres and enables the muscle to contract according to the *sliding filament theory*.

nAch: see *need to achieve*

nAf: see *need to avoid failure*

narcotic analgesics: any of a group of drugs such as opium and morphine that produce numbness and stupor. They are taken to reduce or mask pain but also for the pleasant feelings they induce. Side effects associated with them are respiratory problems, depression, dependence and addiction. Also see *doping*.

National Collegiate Athletic Association (NCAA): responsible for the inter-scholastic athletic programmes in the larger American colleges. It was established in 1906 to control and create order in American college athletics. There are four major membership divisions according to the size and quality of the sport programmes. The NCAA acts as a monopoly in its control and in the 1980s when women's sport began to attract revenue of its own, the NCAA took over from the AIAW – Association for Intercollegiate Athletics for Women. The NCAA is able to make considerable sums of money from selling broadcasting rights for revenue-producing sports. The courts restricted its monopoly in the 1980s but it remains a powerful organisation in amateur sports.

National Curriculum: introduced by the *Education Reform Act 1988*, which laid down what should be taught to children between the ages of 5–16 in state schools. It was an attempt to raise standards in education and make schools more accountable for what they teach. League tables are published so comparisons can be made between schools. *Attainment targets* and programmes of study have been laid down within *key stages*. This was a move towards the *centralisation* of education. For the subject of physical education the following points were made:

- an enhanced role for team games
- a minimum recommended time of two hours per week for PE and sport in formal lessons
- teaching standards to be monitored by OFSTED (Office for Standards in Education).

For the advantages and disadvantages of a National Curiculum see *centralised*.

national governments: various governments, individuals and administrators have sometimes used sport and physical activity to serve certain political ends. These are summarised in the figure on page 162.

National Governing Bodies: see *governing bodies*

national identity: a state or country possessing unique identifying characteristics; something by which a state is recognised. Sport represents and reinforces images of regional and national identity. Powerful symbols are used, for example, national anthems, team colours, flags and ceremonies. For example, the Scottish rugby ground at Murrayfield evokes vivid messages and images of Scottish identity and nationhood, and the Tours de France epitomises French national identity. Some newly developing countries use success in sport to help create a national identity, for example, Kenya and running. *Globalisation*, however, has served to confuse cultural identity as communities become fragmented and genetic mixing of ethnic groups occurs.

National Institute of Sport: a national organisation founded to promote *elite* sport. Each country has its own system to develop talented performers, who often progress to use specialist facilities, with top quality coaches and scientific support. Examples of such centres include the *United Kingdom Sports Institute*, the *Australian Institute of Sport* and the French centre in Paris, *INSEP*. (See also *academies of sport*.)

National Junior Sports Programmes: launched in 1996 by the English Sports Council (now *Sport England*) in conjunction with the *Youth Sports Trust*. Its aim is to encourage young children from the age of four to become involved in sport. It provides kit, coaching and places to play, as well as identifying the more talented performers from a wider base. Many teachers have received training with the aid of funding from the *National Lottery*, Sport England (formerly the Sports Council), the Youth Sports Trust and business *sponsorship*. There are four main elements:

- *Top Play* – aimed at 4–9-year-olds, general introduction to movement skills
- *Top Sport* – aimed at 7–11-year-olds, sport-specific skills developed
- *Champion Coaching* – for talented performers within the region
- *Top Club* – aimed at 11 years and over, specialising in an activity.

See also *World Class England*.

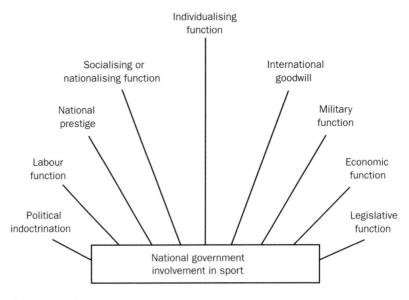

National governments

National Lottery: a game of chance set up on a national scale in which tickets are sold, one or more of which may later qualify the holder for a prize. In Britain this was established in 1994 and is run by the company 'Camelot'. Billions of pounds have been raised which has been divided between the five good causes: the arts, heritage, the Millennium Fund, charities and sports. It has provided grants for projects ranging from village halls, athletic clubs, new major sports venues and the individual sports themselves, making a difference at local, regional and national level.

National Parks: areas of land controlled by the state in order to preserve its natural beauty and wild life. There are ten National Parks in Britain, including, for example, those in the Brecon Beacons, Dartmoor, the Lake District and Snowdonia. These areas are governed by the national park authorities, which are local government bodies consisting of local council-lors plus members appointed by the Secretary of State for the Environment. National Parks can cater for a wide range of interests: they provide walkers with pleasant open countryside for enjoyment, accommodation for tourists and a livelihood for farmers and foresters, quarrymen and gamekeepers. They were established for two reasons: to ensure landscape *conservation* and to allow access to mountains and moorlands.

national sport centres: sport centres run by *Sport England* to provide appropriate training facilities for the elite performer but which are also open to the public. They are used exten-sively by the *governing bodies* of sport and there are currently five in Britain:

- Bisham Abbey, Buckinghamshire – major facilities include tennis courts (indoor and outdoor courts with various playing surfaces), two artificial turf pitches, grass pitches, weight-lifting platforms and associated conditioning rooms.

- Crystal Palace, London – major facilities include athletics track, indoor athletics area, two artificial turf pitches, ski-slope, four swimming pools, various indoor arenas and associated conditioning rooms. There is also a specialist sports injuries clinic.

- Holme Pierrepont, Nottingham – National Water Sports Centre. The major facilities include a regatta lake, white water slalom course, water ski lagoon, sports hall and associated conditioning rooms.

- Lilleshall, Shropshire – major facilities include indoor and outdoor tennis courts, spe-cialist gymnastic areas, several sports halls, squash courts and associated conditioning rooms.

- Plas y Brenin, Snowdonia – National Mountain Centre. The major facilities include climbing walls, indoor canoe training pool, ski slope, fitness room and easy access to the Snowdonia National Park.

nationalism: a sentiment based on common cultural characteristics that binds a popula-tion. It often produces a policy of national independence or separatism. Sport can develop the feelings of patriotism and loyalty to one's country that are characteristic of nationalism. For example, during a major championship the progress of the team is followed and nation-alism can intensify as the later stages are reached.

native Americans: the original inhabitants of North America – the American Indians. There are nearly 2 million native Americans in the *United States* made up from over 200 cultural groups, though Anglos (British settlers) have tended to *stereotype* them into one group and generally refer to them as 'Indians'. Sport amongst these groups has traditionally been associated with ritual and ceremony, though little research has been carried out, as Indian culture has undergone many changes following the colonisation of the United States. In modern sport, only when success and achievement have been notable in *American football* and *baseball* has any *media* attention been focused on them. Native American participation in sport has generally been limited due to:

- poverty and poor health
- lack of equipment and programmes
- prejudice
- cultural isolation.

In 1983 the Iroquois national *lacrosse* team was established reflecting the origins of the game. The term 'Hispanic' is a generic term used to describe people whose origins can be traced to Spanish-speaking countries (approximately 22 million) and whose cultures are related by language, colonial history or Catholicism. Examples are Chicanos and Puerto Ricans.

There are approximately 6.7 million 'Asian Americans' in the United States, but very little sociological research has been done on any of these groups in relation to sport participation. Generally they are discriminated against in terms of racial stereotypes which make belonging to sports groups difficult and also their traditions may not always coincide with the true American sports.

natural environment: usually associated with the natural world, including land, air and sea. The latter half of the twentieth century saw an increase in concern for its survival. Pollution, loss of the green belt and increasing inroads into more isolated areas of the countryside are some of the issues that environmental groups are raising at a political level. In terms of *recreation,* the natural environment was valued in the eighteenth and nineteenth centuries as an *escape* from the polluted towns. The trend for outdoor activities began with rambling, climbing and *cycling* , firstly with the *upper* and *middle classes,* and then with the *working classes* as they gained more free time and transport enabled them to access the countryside.

Country parks, nature reserves, green belt areas and areas of outstanding natural beauty as well as *National Parks* are all seeing an increase in use. Conflicts can emerge between landowners and recreation users and *conservation* is a key issue.

near transfer: see *transfer of learning*

need to achieve (nAch): personality characteristics possessed by individuals that are used to explain their levels of motivation towards a task. The *achievement motivation* theory suggests such performers gain pride and satisfaction from participation; display perseverance while completing the task quickly and efficiently; are prepared to take risks and challenges and they like *feedback* and personal responsibility. For example, a club-standard tennis player will be happy to play someone of a similar or better ability if offered the opportunity without worrying about the outcome. They would rise to the challenge and use the experience they may gain in the future. See also *need to avoid failure (nAf)*.

need to avoid failure (nAf): personality characteristics possessed by individuals that are used to explain their levels of motivation towards a task. The *achievement motivation* theory suggests such performers will attempt to avoid shame and humiliation when participating: they will avoid situations of risk i.e. those with a 50–50 chance of success and hence choose tasks that are either very easy or very difficult in nature. They also dislike personal *feedback* or positions of responsibility and tend to attribute reasons for their actions to external factors, such as the opposition, luck or other circumstances beyond their control.

For example, a club tennis player high in nAf will tend to choose opponents who are better or worse than themselves, because they are not expected to win or should do so easily. As a result, the outcome will not be a reflection of their ability and they are therefore motivated to avoid failure. See also *need to achieve (nAch)*.

negative performance curve: see *performance curves*

negative reinforcement: see *reinforcement*

negative transfer: see *transfer of learning*

net games: games in this category involve opponents being separated by a net, for examples, *tennis* and volleyball. They can be individual and team games, the winner being decided by who wins the most games, sets or rubbers. Mainly *open skills* are utilised except when the game is started by a serve. Domination is achieved by playing shots which the opponent is unable to return.

neuromuscular junction: the area of contact between the motor nerve (*neurone*) and the muscle fibre. It is the point at which muscle fibre innervation occurs providing that there is sufficient *acetylcholine* available to diffuse across the synaptic cleft and produce an *action potential*. (See the figure below and on page 166.)

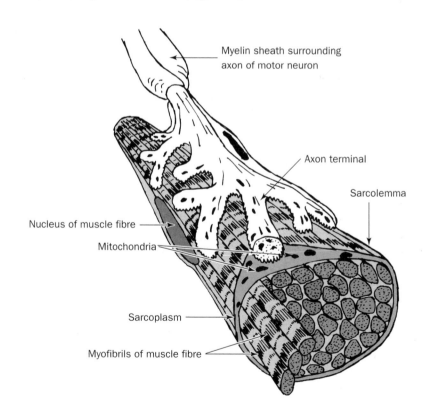

Myelin sheath surrounding axon of motor neuron

Axon terminal

Sarcolemma

Nucleus of muscle fibre

Mitochondria

Sarcoplasm

Myofibrils of muscle fibre

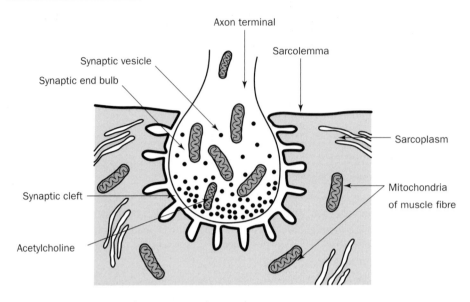

Neuromuscular junction (see page 165)

neurotic personality: a person who is touchy, restless, aggressive, moody and anxious. They display traits linked to their autonomic nervous system, which responds very quickly and powerfully to stressful situations, causing such emotional reactions. In comparison to those with a *stable personality*, they possess the opposite traits and are placed at the other end of the *continuum*. These characteristics can be measured using *Eysenck's personality inventory (EPI)* or *Cattell's 16 personality factors questionnaire.*

New Zealand: an independent dominion within the Commonwealth, comprised of two main islands (North Island and South Island) plus Stewart Island, the Chatham Islands and a number of minor islands in the south-east Pacific. The original *Maori* inhabitants surrendered sovereignty in 1840 and were finally subdued by 1870. The game of *rugby football* has been used to develop a *national identity*, with the All Blacks a clear symbol of the country they represent.

newton (N): the standard unit of force. One newton represents the force required to give a 1 kg mass an acceleration of I m/s^2. This stems from Newton's second law of motion which states that F = mass × acceleration. If we know the mass of a sprinter and their acceleration over three seconds it is possible to determine the amount of force that was necessary to produce that acceleration.

Newton's laws of motion: motion can be described via the three laws of motion.

The first law of motion (N1)

This is the law of inertia, and states:

> 'Every body at rest, or moving with constant velocity in a straight line, will continue in that state unless compelled to change by an external force exerted upon it …'.

So, in order to change the motion of an object or performer a force must be applied. For example, to move a golf ball off a tee, a force must be applied to it from the club head. Likewise, for a sprinter to move out of the blocks, the sprinter must exert a force from their muscles. Furthermore once the golf ball is in flight it will continue to move at constant velocity until acted upon by a force, in this instance air resistance acts as the force to slow the ball down, as does gravity which causes the ball to land on the fairway.

The second law of motion (N2)

This is the law of acceleration, and states:

> 'The acceleration of a body is proportional to the force causing it, and the acceleration takes place in the direction in which that force acts'.

This is often expressed as $F = ma$ (where F is the force acting, m is the mass of the body or object and a is the resultant acceleration). This suggests that the greater the mass, the greater the force required to give the same acceleration, and also that if mass remains constant, then the greater the force applied, the greater the acceleration. For example, more force is applied to the shuttlecock in an overhead clear to create a greater acceleration than compared with performing a drop shot!

The third law of motion (N3)

This is the law of reaction, and states:

> '... when one action exerts a force on a second object, there is a force equal in magnitude but opposite in direction exerted by the second object on the first ...'

or more simply:

> 'to every action there is an equal and opposite reaction'.

When a swimmer, for example, exerts a force upon the starting blocks the blocks exert an equal and opposite reaction force upon the swimmer, propelling them into the water. Once in the water, the swimmer must exert a backward force on the water in order to move forward!

noise: information that is gathered from the environment that is irrelevant to the performance. This can cause the performer to take longer to detect relevant *cues* and slow the *information processing* system. During a game, a player may have to ignore shouts from the crowd, effects of the weather or any tactics employed by their opponents to distract them.

noradrenaline: a hormone released from the adrenal medulla via the *sympathetic nervous system*. Noradrenaline has many functions in the body but specifically prepares the body for its *fight or flight response*. It is the action of noradrenaline that increases heart rate and causes the force of contraction of the cardiac muscle fibres to increase during exercise. This, together with its function of increasing blood glucose levels, enables the athlete's muscles to receive the necessary nutrients required for optimal performance. Also known as norepinephrine.

norms: established standards of behaviour shared by members of a social group and to which each member is expected to conform. They include expected patterns of behaviour such as etiquette and can also have moral dimensions. They are learned through the process of *socialisation*.

obesity: a condition which accompanies a sedentary or inactive lifestyle, caused by an imbalance between energy intake and expenditure which results in an excessive increase in the body's total quantity of fat. Typically, men with more than 25 per cent body fat and women with more than 35 per cent are clinically defined as obese. Obesity can lead to increased incidence of *cardiovascular diseases* such as *atherosclerosis*, hypertension, heart disease and strokes as well as other complications including gall bladder disease and diabetes.

Since obesity is the result of an imbalance between energy intake and expenditure, it follows that by increasing energy expenditure through exercise, obesity can be prevented. Exercise also suppresses appetite, and increases the basal metabolic rate. However, care should be taken when prescribing an exercise programme for the obese, and account taken of their limited exercise capacity. Activities should be of low intensity, low impact and *aerobic* in nature, such as walking, swimming or cycling, and the intensity should only be increased very gradually. Obesity can be determined by the *body mass index*.

OBLA: see *onset of blood lactate accumulation*

objectivity: the ability to perform an investigation and to collect data without allowing personal interpretation or bias to influence the result. Where possible testing should be objective, allowing for comparison of results that are meaningful. For example, various physiological and psychological tests, including the *multi-stage fitness test* and the *SCAT* questionnaire, produce results that cannot be open to individual interpretation or *subjective* analysis.

observational learning: see *social learning theory*

Ogive performance curve: see *performance curve*

old boy: a male ex-pupil of a school. The old boys in the nineteenth centuries would financially support their schools, would often go back into teaching, and sport fixtures would be held against current students. See also *old boy network*.

old boy network: the appointment to power of former pupils of the same small group of well-established public schools or universities. It has served to perpetuate traditional *elite* values in society and can repress *social mobility* of the lower classes.

Olympic bids: the way in which national governments, sport organisations and cities bid, in competition with others, to win the approval of the IOC to host the *Olympic Games*. They do this for a variety of reasons:

- civic and national pride
- political gain
- economic benefits.

The selection of the host city is vitally important, as the success of the Games can often be dependent on the chosen site. Each candidate city must demonstrate to the IOC that its bid to stage the greatest multi-disciplinary event in the world has the support of its people and its political authorities. A manual containing evaluation criteria is available and the Evaluation Commission evaluates each city bid. Following allegations of misconduct during the Salt Lake City bid for the 2002 winter Olympics changes were made. A selection college was put in place for Turin 2006. This selection college selects two cities from among six finalists. The selection of the host city takes place immediately after on the same day. Th IOC President was unable to vote on this occasion.

Olympic Games: the greatest *Panhellenic* festival, held every four years in honour of Zeus at ancient Olympia, which lasted over a thousand years. The modern revival consists of international athletic and sporting contests held every four years in a selected country, since their inception by *Baron Pierre de Coubertin* in Athens in 1896. Contestants were inspired by his vision of countries drawn together in healthy competition, where the taking part was important, not necessarily the winning. Baron de Couberin established the *International Olympic Committee* to oversee the running of the Games and each member country now has a National Olympic Committee. The Olympic flag shows five interconnecting rings, in different colours displayed on a white background, representing the five continents – Europe, Asia, Africa, Oceania and the Americas.

The Olympic motto is 'Citius, Altius, Fortius' which means 'swifter, higher, stronger' and the six goals of the Olympic movement are to develop:

*   personal *excellence*
*   sport as education
*   cultural exchange
*   *mass participation*
*   *fair-play*
*   international understanding.

The games have been affected by political situations as they are given prominent *mass media* coverage and thus can be used to promote political messages. For example, the Soviet boycott of the Los Angeles Games in 1984 was one of the most dramatic occasions following the 1980 American boycott of the Moscow Games. The Games were founded on an amateur basis, as de Coubertin was disappointed with the growing *commercialisation* of nineteenth century sport. Today some countries could not host the Games as commercial considerations are high due to the enormous cost involved. Nevertheless, there is fierce competition to host the games and put in an *Olympic bid*. This has also led to incidents of corruption at the highest levels, both within the administration and performer levels.

Olympism: a philosophy of life, exalting and combining in a balanced whole the qualities of body, will and mind. Blending sport with culture and education, Olympism seeks to create a way of life based on the joy found in effort, the educational value of good example and respect for universal fundamental ethical principles.

onset of blood lactate accumulation (OBLA): the point at which *lactic acid* starts to accumulate in the blood, usually taken when blood lactate reaches 4 mmol per litre of blood. It typically occurs when the body converts to *anaerobic* means of energy production.

Below this point the body can work aerobically and therefore sustained low-intensity exercise can take place, since no lactic acid has accumulated. However, exercise above the point of OBLA can usually only last for approximately one minute. For example, imagine how your legs feel at the end of running a flat-out 400-metre run!

OBLA always occurs below the performer's *maximum oxygen uptake* (VO$_2$max). The higher the percentage of VO$_2$max at which OBLA occurs, the better that individual is at endurance-based activity. Typically, OBLA in the untrained performer occurs at approximately 50 per cent of VO$_2$max, whilst in trained endurance athletes, it may be delayed until 80 per cent of VO$_2$max has been attained. Following a training programme that includes bouts of both aerobic and anaerobic work, the point of OBLA can be delayed and improvements in performance take place. (See the figure below.)

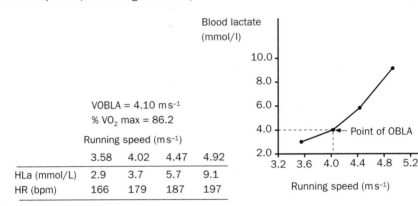

VOBLA = 4.10 m s^{-1}
% VO$_2$ max = 86.2

Running speed (m s^{-1})

	3.58	4.02	4.47	4.92
HLa (mmol/L)	2.9	3.7	5.7	9.1
HR (bpm)	166	179	187	197

The test shows that this squash player is using a large percentage of his VO$_2$ max, resulting in a more successful endurance performance

open loop control theory suggests that some movements are performed without conscious control because they are so well learned and appear automatic. The *executive motor programmes*, which are stored in the *long-term memory*, can be retrieved very quickly when required and are performed without the need for *feedback* and adjustment during the execution of the task.

Input ➤ Executive mechanism ➤ Effector mechanism ➤ Output

This process usually occurs during the completion in a *closed skill* (for example, skipping or running), but can also take place in an *open skill* such as catching a ball. However, most sportsmen and women experience both open loop and *closed loop* control throughout their performance, alternating between each depending on the task difficulty and level of skill performance.

open skill: a skill performed in an unstable, changing, unpredictable environment to which the performer must continually react, adjusting their position and actions as required. It is usually an *externally paced skill* requiring the performer to evaluate the situation quickly, and select and adapt an appropriate response. Such skills, for example, include all games involving passing and receiving a ball, or racket sports where the position of an opponent on court will determine the selection of the stroke to be played (see also *closed skill*).

open societies: those societies where there is a great deal of *social mobility* in the class structure. They are more common in the Western democracies where *capitalism* is prevalent. Based on meritocracy, social mobility is usually achieved through qualifications gained via the education system. Sport can also be used for this purpose; for example, performers who excel in their chosen sport can often reap financial rewards and improve their lifestyle.

operant conditioning: a theory which states that learning is more effective if the performer is concerned with the action and its consequences, as it increases or decreases the probability of it reoccurring. It is one of the *associationist theories*, but differs from *classical conditioning* because the action of the performer is shaped through manipulating the environment and reinforced, either strengthening or weakening the *stimulus–response bond* depending on the outcome. For example, to develop accuracy, a games player has to hit a target and receives reinforcement by observing his of her success or failure. The coach may provide three forms of reinforcement:

- *positive reinforcement* – increases the likelihood of the action being repeated
- *negative reinforcement* – decreases the chance of repetition
- *punishment* – could be used to strengthen or weaken the stimulus–response bond.

Some complex skills may need to be broken down into *subroutines* and learned in stages, reinforced and developed progressively. For example, a high jumper may practice the run-up, take-off, layout and landing in isolation, receiving reinforcement, such as praise, to ensure the correct technique is repeated when the complete action is performed. However, care should be taken not to provide too much positive reinforcement, so that the performer constantly seeks praise and becomes over-reliant upon it, and causing a reduction in performance levels if withdrawn. *Thorndike's laws of learning* were based on trial and error learning, which when utilised help to strengthen the stimulus–response bonds and support these theories.

organisations: see *institutions*

origin: the point of attachment of a muscle (*tendon*) onto a stationary bone against which the muscle can pull. It occurs at the opposite end of the muscle *insertion* and usually occurs on the nearest flat bone. Major muscle origins and insertions are highlighted in the table on page 172.

Osgood's semantic differential scale: see *semantic differential scale*s

ossification: the process of bone formation. Some bones are formed directly in membranes, known as direct or intramembranous ossification. Examples include the *flat bones* of the skull, and the patella. Other bones gradually replace hyaline cartilage from the foetal stage through to full maturation in our late teenage years. This is known as 'indirect or endochondral ossification' and examples include the short and long bones of our limbs.

osteocyte: a mature bone cell. Throughout life, bone is constantly remodelled so that it is stronger along the lines of stress. Unwanted cells are reabsorbed by 'bone- breaking cells' (osteoclasts) and then replaced by 'bone-making cells' (osteoblasts) along lines of stress. For example, when running, greater stress is imposed on the bones of the leg; osteocytes are therefore laid down along these lines of stress to increase the strength of the bone.

Origin of major muscles and insertions

Muscle	Function	Insertion	Origin
pectoralis major	flexes upper arm adducts upper arm	humerus	sternum clavicle rib cartilage
latissimus dorsi	extends and adducts upper arm	humerus	vertebrae (T5–L5) iliac crest
deltoid	abducts, flexes and extends upper arm	humerus	clavicle scapula acromion
biceps brachii	flexes lower arm	radius	scapula
triceps	extends lower arm	olecranon process	humerus scapula
iliopsoas (iliacus/psoas major)	flexes trunk flexes thigh	ilium vertebrae femur	ilium vertebrae femur
gluteus maximus	extends thigh	femur	ilium sacrum coccyx
gluteus medius gluteus minimus	abducts thigh	femur	ilium
hamstring group biceps femoris semimembranosus semitendinosus	flexes lower leg extends thigh	tibia fibula	ischium femur
quadricep group rectus femoris vastus medialis vastus lateralis vastus intermedius	extends lower leg flexes thigh	tibia (via patella tendon)	ilium femur
sartorius	flexes hip and knee	anterior superior iliac spine	tibia
adductors longus magnus brevis	adducts thigh	femur (linea aspera)	pubic bone
gastrocnemius	plantar flexion flexes knee	calcaneus	femur
soleus	plantar flexion	calcaneus	fibula tibia

As a rule of thumb, the origin of a muscle is the nearest flat bone, the insertion is the bone that the muscle puts into action

outcome goal: goal that is set to judge the performance of the individual against others and the end result. For example, a sprinter may be set the goal of either winning the race or finishing in the top three places to qualify for the next round. The efficiency and manner of their performance is not relevant, only the final result. If the *goal setting* is realistic and within the performer's capability, when they achieve the aim, their motivation is increased. However, it can be demotivating if the performer is unsuccessful, especially after repeated attempts. If this is the case, it may be more appropriate to use *performance goals* or *process-orientated goals.*

outdoor education: participation in outdoor pursuit activities in the *natural environment* in order to develop educational values. For example, a school may offer orienteering within the school grounds or arrange a visit to a *National Park* or other area where adventurous activities may be undertaken.

outdoor pursuits: see *adventurous activities*

outdoor recreation: participation in outdoor pursuit activities within the *natural environment* in an individual's free time.

output: the third stage of *information processing*, involving the completion of the selected action or movement. This occurs as a result of the effector mechanism, or system of nerves and muscles, implementing the *executive motor programmes* which have been formulated during the *decision-making* process. For example, a rugby player during open play may pass the ball to a player in close support having made a decision based on the available information from the *display*. Various mechanisms have been suggested as to how such movements are controlled and executed including those discussed in the *open loop theory*, the *closed loop theory* and *schema theory*.

Outward Bound Trust: a world-wide organisation that began to pioneer outdoor activities in the 1940s. It works in partnership with the *Duke of Edinburgh Award Scheme*, aiming to promote personal development training for young people by placing them in challenging situations such as expeditions and skills courses.

overtraining: caused by an imbalance between training and recovery, which usually occurs when insufficient time has been left for the body to regenerate and adapt before embarking upon the next training session. In the search for the best possible performance in competition, *elite* athletes are often tempted and prone to increase training loads and frequency of training above optimal levels, which can lead to symptoms of overtraining. These symptoms include enduring fatigue, loss of appetite, muscle tenderness, sleep disturbances and head colds. The coach can identify overtraining syndrome by physiological testing, which may show the athlete having an increased oxygen consumption, heart rate and blood lactate levels at fixed workloads. In order to combat overtraining, the coach should advise prolonged rest, and a reduction in training workloads for a period of weeks or months. This should hopefully restore both performance and competitive desire.

Oxbridge: a word used to refer to the most prestigious universities in Britain, Oxford and Cambridge. Despite some democratisation of student recruitment the large majority of students are still the products of the *public school* system who go on to occupy positions of power in many of our social structures such as politics and business. Several annual sporting occasions between the two capture the attention of the public and media, for example the Varsity rugby match and the Boat Race.

oxygen debt: the amount of oxygen consumed during recovery, above that which normally would have been consumed at rest in the same period of time. An oxygen debt will accrue when the body has undertaken some form of *anaerobic* exercise. This will occur at quite intense levels of exercise, lasting up to three minutes or when the *anaerobic threshold* has been exceeded. Typically an oxygen debt consists of two stages.

1 A fast stage or 'alactacid debt' – the oxygen is used during recovery to resynthesise fuels used in the alactic energy system, i.e. ATP and CP. This happens very quickly and lasts for about two or three minutes and explains why a 100-metre sprinter can perform repeated bouts of very high intensity with very little rest.

2 A slow stage or 'lactacid debt' – the oxygen is used to clear the body of lactic acid that will have accrued during the exercise period. This is a much longer process and the heart rate and respiratory rate can remain elevated for up to one hour.

By performing a *cool-down* following exercise, the oxygen debt can be replenished more rapidly, since oxygen delivery to the muscles is increased which is necessary for *lactic acid* removal. It is also known as *excess post-exercise oxygen consumption*.

oxyhaemoglobin (HbO$_2$): haemoglobin which is saturated with oxygen. In order to be transported in the blood, oxygen must combine with *haemoglobin* to form oxyhaemoglobin. The oxygen is then released at the tissue or muscle site to enable metabolism to take place. Males generally have higher levels of haemoglobin than females which explains their greater potential for aerobic activity.

Panhellenic Games: all-Greek festivals, the most famous of which is the *Olympic Games.*

Paralympic Games: originated as an annual sports meeting for semi-paralysed competitors. It is properly called the International Stoke Mandeville Games after the founding hospital in Buckinghamshire, England and was originally known as the Paraplegic Games. The idea of such athletic activity was conceived during World War II as recommended treatment for patients whose lower limbs and trunk were paralysed, and developed into regular competition. The international aspect to the Games was strengthened in 1960 when they were held in the Olympic city of Rome and they have expanded considerably with the Sydney 2000 Games attracting over 4000 athletes, 2000 coaches and many other supporting officials. 'Paralympic' means parallel to the Olympic Games – not paraplegic Olympics, and the Games are concerned with ability, athletic endeavour and *elite* performance. The symbol of the Games consists of three 'Tae-Geuks' symbolising the most significant components of the human being: mind, body and spirit; likewise the Paralympic motto is 'mind, body, spirit'.

parameter: information stored within a *schema*, which helps to initiate a response using the appropriate speed and force required. A performer who develops a wide range of parameters will have a better chance of successfully completing the skill, as they will be more familiar with the requirements when confronted with them in a game situation. For example, a netball player who executes their shots from a variety of positions on the court will need to use a slightly different action for each in terms of direction, force and speed. If during training they have practised from varied locations, they can modify their action more effectively than a player can who has only developed their shooting action from one or two places.

parasympathetic nervous system: primarily responsible for conserving the body's energy and its effects tend to oppose those of the *sympathetic nervous system*. It is one of the two sub-divisions of the *autonomic (or involuntary) nervous system*. Following exercise, the parasympathetic nervous system restores the heart rate and respiratory rate to normal resting levels.

part method practice: a performer attempts to develop specific subroutines of a skill in isolation before putting them into the correct sequence. This *practice* method lends itself to long sequences (gymnastic routines), *complex skills* (hurdling), low-level organisation skills (swimming) or dangerous tasks (gymnastic vaulting). It is useful for those performers who are beginners, have limited motivation or attention span, and for those who need to rectify particular faults in technique.

partial pressure: the pressure exerted by an individual gas when it exists within a mixture of gases. Partial pressure of a single gas is denoted by 'p' and to calculate the total pressure of a gas we simply add together all the partial pressures. For example, atmospheric pressure is composed of three main gases, nitrogen, oxygen and carbon dioxide:

$$\text{atmospheric pressure (760 mm Hg)} = p\text{N}_2 + p\text{O}_2 + p\text{CO}_2$$

If the fractional concentration of the gas is known, it is possible to calculate the partial pressure that each gas exerts. For example, approximately 21 per cent of atmospheric pressure is made up of oxygen. The pressure that oxygen therefore exerts in the whole gas can be computed as follows:

$$\text{atmospheric } p\text{O}_2 = 760 \text{ mm Hg} \times 0.21 = 160 \text{ mm Hg}$$

However, the reason why partial pressure is so important to us is that it determines how much oxygen we can get into the body and how much carbon dioxide can be expelled, since a gas will always move from areas where there is more of it to areas where the concentration is not so high. Quite simply, because the concentration of oxygen is greater outside the body than inside, a 'pressure gradient' is formed and oxygen moves into the body's blood stream. The greater the pressure gradient across the respiratory membrane, the more rapidly oxygen diffuses across it. When exercising, more oxygen is used up in the muscles and causes a greater pressure gradient enabling a quicker uptake of oxygen. Outlined below are partial pressures of respiratory gases at various sites in the body.

Partial pressures (mm Hg) of respiratory gases and nitrogen in atmospheric air, alveolar air, blood and tissue cells

	Atmospheric air (sea level)	Alveolar air	Deoxygenated blood	Oxygenated blood	Tissue cells
$p\text{O}_2$	160	105	40	105	40
$p\text{CO}_2$	0.3	40	45	40	45
$p\text{N}_2$	597	569	569	569	569

participation pyramid: a sport development continuum intended to enable people to learn the basic sports skills with the possibility of reaching a standard of sporting excellence. (See figure on page 177.)

- Foundation – learning basic movement skills, knowledge and understanding; developing a positive attitude to physical activity. The *physical education* programme in schools can represent this stage.

- Participation – exercising one's leisure option for a variety of reasons, including health, fitness and social. This stage is represented by *extra-curricular sport* at school, club level and during recreational time.

- Performance – improving standards through coaching, competition and training. The higher club and regional levels of performance would represent this level.

- Excellence – reaching national and publicly recognised standards of performance. National and international competition would represent this level.

patron: a person who sponsors any kind of athlete or artist from their own private funds. Patronage tends to occur amongst a privileged class within a hierarchical society. In the nineteenth century, wealthy aristocrats who wanted to be associated with new styles and trends would sometimes spend large amounts of money on sporting events and particular athletes, especially those involved with *boxing* and *pedestrianism*. A group of patrons would join together to form an association which would then organise the sport. When patrons withdrew their funds, the effect was similar to a modern day sponsor pulling out of an event, usually leading to a decline in the activity or athlete.

```
                    EXCELLENCE
              ▲ ▼ ▲ ▼ ▲
                      ◄
                      ►
                      ◄
                      ►
    PERFORMANCE   ◄  PARTICIPATION
     ▲   ▲   ▲   ►  ▲   ▲   ▲
        Introduction and reintroduction
              ▲           ▲
            FOUNDATION
         (primary school-aged only)
```

Participation pyramid

pedestrianism: an early form of race walking. In the eighteenth and nineteenth centuries, with only *horse racing* and *boxing* as rivals, pedestrianism was very popular with much *gambling* involving men against time, distance and other walkers. Captain Barclay was a famous walker who in 1809 walked 1000 miles in 1000 consecutive hours. A pedestrian was also a lower class individual who earned part of his money by competing in sporting activities for money, particularly *rowing*, footraces and *cricket*. It was the forerunner to the term *professional*.

pennate: a muscle shape designed for strength. The pennate (featherlike) muscles are characterised by an arrangement of muscle fibres around a central tendon and exist in the body where strength is required. For example, the tibialis posterior (unipennate) and soleus (bipennate) occur at the back of the lower leg and are responsible for lifting the whole body's weight off the floor when performing the high jump. Other examples of pennate muscles include the pectoralis major (multi pennate) and the orbicularis muscles of the eyes and mouth (circum pennate).

perception: the interpretation and analysis of information gathered from the environment by the sensory system. The various stimuli enter the *short-term sensory store*, where the relevant information is extracted by the process of *selective attention* before being transferred onto the *decision-making* phase. For example, when a tennis player receives details of their opponent's location on court, together with the speed and direction of the ball, they will use that information to analyse what options are available before deciding which shot to play next in the rally.

perceptual motor abilities: see *psychomotor ability*

perceptual narrowing: see *attentional narrowing*

perceptual skill: the accurate interpretation of information received via the *sensory system*, which allows the appropriate movement to be executed. For example, a good batsman will usually analyse the delivery of the bowler accurately before deciding which stroke to play. See also *perception*.

performance curves: curves plotted on a graph to provide a visual representation of the performance of an individual over a period of time, allowing analysis and evaluation. Often they are comprised of several types of curve, which need to be interpreted in order to assess the development or regression of the performer. The four types of curve are illustrated on the following page:

1   negatively accelerated curve – indicates a large improvement initially with little development in the later stages

2   positively accelerated curve – indicates minor improvements initially with large developments in later attempts

3   linear curve – indicates gradual improvements in relation to the number of attempts or time taken

4   ogive or S-shaped – any combination of curves 1, 2 and 3.

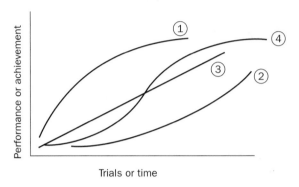

Trials or time

Often an individual will reach a *plateau* in their performance, showing a period of no improvement.

performance goal: a goal used to judge the performance of the individual against their own standards, rather than in comparison with their competitors. For example, a sprinter may set a number of goals for a race, including a good reaction to the starter's gun, effective arm action and how close they ran to their personal best time, rather than the finishing position. If the *goal setting* of the coach is realistic, the performer can evaluate their own actions and not worry about comparison with others. This helps to reduce *anxiety*, allowing the runner to remain motivated wherever they finish. The performance goals may influence the *outcome goals* that are set.

performance pyramid: see *participation pyramid*

pericardium: the outermost layer of the heart. It has many functions, but its primary role is to protect the *myocardium*. However, it also prevents over-distension of the heart, particularly when it beats maximally during exercise and serves to anchor the heart in position. Pericardial fluid prevents friction between the membranes and tissues of the heart as it beats. It is also called the *epicardium*.

periodisation: the organisation of training throughout a season so that an optimal physiological and psychological peak can be reached. Periodisation is an essential ingredient to any training programme which should contain several phases.

●   First, a solid training base is needed, which will include both general strength and endurance training. For a runner this might involve hill running, long interval training or circuit training with weights.

●   After this foundation has been laid, the runner can develop more specific skills and training sessions will become more intense, focusing on a pace more closely related to that required in competition.

- In order to prepare for competition the runner will need to taper their training. Here, the quantity of training may be reduced to enable the body to recoup maximum energy stores prior to competition, and more race-specific training, such as sprint starts for a sprinter, will be the norm. Also the athlete will prepare psychologically through techniques such as *mental practice*. This should enable the athlete to peak for their most important race of the season and this would normally last for between one and three weeks.

- The final phase is arguably the most important – the transition period. This is essentially a period of active rest, where the athlete can escape the stresses and strains of training and competition and prepare themselves for the following season.

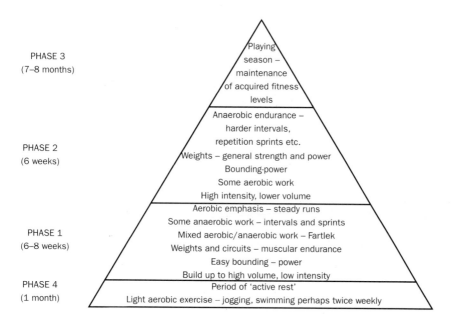

PHASE 3
(7–8 months)

Playing season – maintenance of acquired fitness levels

PHASE 2
(6 weeks)

Anaerobic endurance – harder intervals, repetition sprints etc.
Weights – general strength and power
Bounding-power
Some aerobic work
High intensity, lower volume

PHASE 1
(6–8 weeks)

Aerobic emphasis – steady runs
Some anaerobic work – intervals and sprints
Mixed aerobic/anaerobic work – Fartlek
Weights and circuits – muscular endurance
Easy bounding – power
Build up to high volume, low intensity

PHASE 4
(1 month)

Period of 'active rest'
Light aerobic exercise – jogging, swimming perhaps twice weekly

periosteum: thin membrane covering the surface of all bones. It is an important feature of the skeletal system as the periosteum enables *tendons* to attach to the bones (via *Sharpey's fibres*) which allows movement. It is also responsible for bone growth, since the periosteum contains the bone-building cells known as osteoblasts. Thus the periosteum is responsible for strengthening the bones as a result of an exercise programme.

person-orientated leader: see *contingency theory of leadership*

personality refers to the more or less stable, enduring, unique pattern of traits which determine our behaviour. Researchers have attempted to link personality with sporting performance, but with few conclusive results. Various theories suggest how our personality is formed:

- *trait theories* – personality is innate and stable over time

- *social learning theories* – personality is formed due to the effect of the environment and learnt experiences, which can alter over time

- *interactionist theories* – personality is formed due to a combination of traits and the environment.

For success in sport, the coach must view and treat each individual differently, according to their own personalities. Also each performer must evaluate their personality and understand how their traits can affect performance, and so learn to control their moods and arousal levels depending on the situation.

Hollander (1967) suggests personality is constructed of three layers (see diagram below), each separate but inter-related layer causing some aspects of behaviour to alter depending on the environment.

- *Psychological core* – basic attitudes, values, motives and self-worth which remain fairly constant.

- *Typical responses* – the middle layer represents the usual behaviour in a given situation based on the psychological core, for example, displaying acts of sportsmanship.

- *Role-related behaviour* – the outer layer depends on the specific situation and may cause personality and behaviour to alter considerably. The pressure or demands of the situation may require different behaviour, for example an experienced performer may appear quiet and thoughtful when being coached within their own team but when the roles are changed and they are coaching a junior team appear loud and assertive.

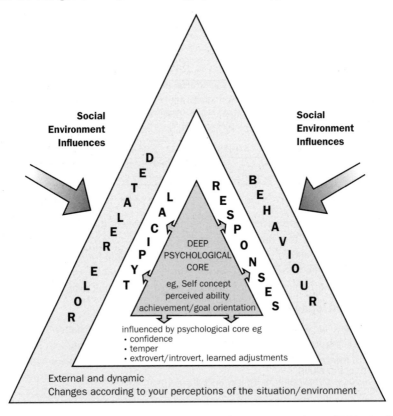

personality tests: methods used to assess the characteristics of an individual, which are used to formulate their unique *personality*. A variety of methods can be used, the most common of which are:

- *questionnaires* – the most commonly used methods, involving a series of questions. For example, *Eysenck's personality inventory (EPI)*, *Cattell's 16 personality factors questionnaire* and the *sport competition anxiety test (SCAT)*.

- observation – the behaviour of the individual is watched and recorded. This is very subjective and there are problems with validity.

- interviews – one-to-one discussion, sometimes involving projective tests, such as the *Rorschach inkblot test*.

Testing for personality is difficult, due to the problems of *reliability* and *validity* of procedures.

persuasive communication: technique to alter the *attitude* of an individual. The person is exposed to new information or experiences in an attempt to change their mind. The effectiveness of employing this method depends on the status of the person delivering the message, the quality of that message, the nature of the audience and the situation at the time. For example, within a young football team several players display a negative attitude towards training and only want to play matches. The coach may arrange for a well-known player to visit a coaching session to outline the type of training they follow, explain the reasons why they practise skills and the benefits they have received as a result. See also *cognitive dissonance*.

Philistine schools: the *middle class* copies of the established *public schools* for the *gentry*. Examples are Cheltenham College, Marlborough and Clifton.

phosphocreatine (PC): see *creatine phosphate*

physical activity readiness questionnaire (PAR-Q): questionnaire designed to assist individuals in determining whether they should see their doctor before undertaking a physical exercise programme. Typically this questionnaire asks up to 12 'yes/no' health-related questions. If participants answer 'yes' to any of the questions, they are advised to discuss the exercise programme with their doctor before becoming physically active. Such a questionnaire is essential for all participants commencing a programme for health-related reasons, and anyone over the age of 60 should always consult their doctor first.

physical education: the instilling of knowledge, skills and values through the medium of physical activity in an educational setting. It is an academic discipline that has, as its primary focus, the study of human movement with the aims of enhancing total human development and performance. It aims to do this through the experience of a range of physical activities, such as team, individual, competitive and non-competitive sports. Total development means acquiring activity-specific skills and knowledge, as well as fostering positive *attitudes* and *values* that will be useful in later life. Physical education can help us achieve a quality of life and vitality that can be lacking in sedentary lives. The key words which characterise physical education are:

- range of physical activities
- movement
- activity-specific skills
- knowledge
- values
- educational setting.

See also *National Curriculum*.

physical recreation: physical participation opportunities for all members of the community in their *leisure* time. The participant is still involved in skilful, competitive and strategic activities but at a less sophisticated level than the performance end of the *participation pyramid*. For example, individuals may play badminton for a club or simply book a court at a local leisure centre in their free time.

physical training: exercise which is wholly to do with training the body for fitness, commonly termed PT. This concept was strong in the nineteenth and early twentieth century state schools where the *Syllabuses of Physical Training* were taken from the army field books. There is no element here of the cognitive, social or moral development associated with the later term *physical education.*

ping-pong diplomacy: term developed following the visit of the American table tennis players and later swimmers to China as part of an attempt by the USA to restore diplomatic relations with China, which refuses to recognise Taiwan as an independent nation. Even now the pressures are evident.

pivot joint: see *synovial joint*

Planning the Programme: a primary school publication issued by the Ministry of Education in 1953 which was to replace the existing *Syllabuses of Physical Training* and ran parallel to the *Moving and Growing* initiative.

plantar flexion: movement pattern characterised by the increase in angle at the ankle, when pointing the toes. Plantar flexion occurs in the median (*saggital*) plane and occurs at the ankle when performing a handstand or swimming freestyle. (See appendix, page 269.)

Plas y Brenin: see *national sport centres*

plasma: a pale yellow fluid that forms the liquid component of the blood. Its components are water, (90 per cent) proteins (8 per cent) and salts (2 per cent) and plasma makes up to 55 per cent of blood volume. Plasma is a very important constituent of the blood since it helps transport hormones as well as assisting in the transport of fats and fat-soluble vitamins – important ingredients for successful exercise performance. However, for trained athletes, endurance training brings about a significant increase in plasma volume (haemod-ilution) which, in turn, causes an increase stroke volume due to its decreased viscosity. This improves the ability to transport oxygen to working muscles, thus facilitating energy production within the *mitochondria*.

plateau: a period of time in which no improvement occurs in an individual's performance or level of attainment. This may be indicated in a *performance curve*. It may occur for a number of reasons including:

- the complexity of the task
- the need to consolidate the skill level whilst progressing between the *stages of learning*
- lack of *motivation*
- boredom or lack of variety in practice
- fatigue, injuries or overtraining
- performer's natural ability level
- limited coaching knowledge
- unrealistic targets or goals.

A plateau should be avoided if possible in order to prevent demotivation. When required the coach should evaluate in conjunction with the athlete why this has occurred and discuss appropriate methods to overcome the situation, including developing an understanding of the concept of a 'plateau'.

play: 'a voluntary activity or occupation exercised within certain fixed rules of time and place, according to rules freely accepted but absolutely binding, having its aim in itself and accompanied by a feeling of tension, joy and the consciousness that this is different from ordinary life' (Huizinga).

The characteristics and values of play are:

Play

is spontaneous

↓

is voluntary

↓

is fun

↓

is serious

↓

has intrinsic value

↓

brings satisfaction

↓

heightens arousal

↓

is creative

↓

is uninhibitive

plural societies: the existence in society of different *ethnic groups* having distinctive ethnic origins, cultural forms, religions and so on. This is usually as a result of a policy of *accommodation*. Examples of such countries would be Western democratic cultures, such as France, the United Kingdom and USA.

pluralism: a state of society in which several groups have *autonomy* but are interdependent and have equal power. This theory does not accept that only an *elite* makes decisions but that the state considers the opinions of many different interest groups and then acts in the best interests of everyone.

plyometrics: a type of training designed to improve both power and strength. It commonly takes the form of 'bounding' and 'depth jumping' in which an athlete drops down from a box, lands and immediately rebounds onto a second box top. The theory behind it is that when the athlete drops down and lands on the floor, the quadricep muscle group undergoes an *eccentric muscle contraction*, i.e. it lengthens and pre-stretches the muscle. This pre-stretch enables the muscle to exert great forces when it eventually shortens, and the greater the pre-stretch, the more force is exerted by the quadriceps when they shorten. Furthermore, when the muscle is lengthening it actuates the stretch reflex which prevents the muscle from overstretching and causes a rapid, forceful *concentric muscle contraction*.

Plyometrics is often performed by sprint athletes, hurdlers and jumpers, as well as being part of a general conditioning programme for most activities.

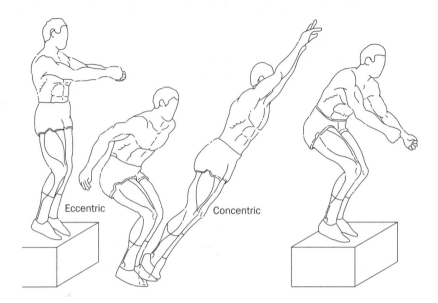

Eccentric   Concentric

PNF: see *proprioceptive neuromuscular facilitation*

politics: the science and art of government; dealing with the form, organisation and administration of a state or part of one, and of the regulation of its relations with other states. 'Political' means belonging to or pertaining to the state, its local and national government and policy. Politics is very much about power and the groups that wield it. See *national governments*.

POMS: see *profile of mood state*

popular recreation: recreation pursuits popular before the onset of the *Industrial Revolution*. These activities were characterised by:

- being occasional, due to little free time
- having few, simple and unwritten rules
- the activity being participation-based rather than spectator-based
- physical force rather than skill
- lower class involvement
- local rather than regional or national events
- limited structure, equipment and facilities.

See also *mob games*.

positive feedback: see *feedback*

positive performance curve: see *performance curves*

positive reinforcement: see *reinforcement*

positive transfer: see *transfer of learning*

posterior: a term of direction which refers to the rear of the body. For example, the 'tibialis posterior' is a muscle which exists at the back of the tibia, whilst the tibialis anterior muscle is situated at the front of the tibia along the shin. When describing the body or movements of the body it can be particularly useful to use these terms of direction. Also known as dorsal. (See appendix, page 253.)

post-school gap: the dropout rate in sport participation on leaving full-time education. Following the Wolfenden Report on Sport and the Community in 1960 the Sports Council (now *Sport England*) made this group (13–24 years) one of its target groups. Reasons for the decline are due to:

- the cost of participation

- the unfamiliarity with local facilities

- the facilities being less accessible

- a widening of other interests.

potential productivity refers to the best possible performance of the members of a group, taking into account their ability, skill level, opponents, task difficulty and expected outcome. However, rarely does each individual within the group perform to their maximum potential and it is usually the role of the coach to eliminate any *faulty processes*. For example, the USA Olympic basketball team composed of the top players from the NBA would be expected to have higher potential productivity than most other national teams. However, simply having the best players does not guarantee success, as they may not work effectively as a team. See also *group productivity*.

power: the work done per unit of time, which when considering human movement is the product of strength and speed. Power is obviously of benefit in activities in which the highest intensity of work is required, such as in weightlifting or indeed during a 100-metre sprint. If a performer can increase their power this can improve their performance as:

- the same amount of work (strength) can be performed in a shorter period of time (speed)

- an increased amount of work (strength) can be done in the same period of time (speed).

Plyometrics can be used to improve an individual's power.

POWERbreathe: A piece of apparatus designed to improve the *strength* of respiratory muscles. The POWERbreathe uses a form of *resistance training* to develop the inspiratory muscles. The POWERbreathe claims to improve endurance performance by up to 30% if used for 30 breaths, twice a day. It is therefore particularly useful to endurance athletes such as marathon runners and swimmers.

practice: allocated time, that allows the performer to reinforce, develop and refine learning. Constructive use of the time is vital to maximise the individual's potential and several factors should be considered before deciding on the nature of the practice session. These include the size and structure of the group, the personalities and abilities of the performers within that group, the complexity of the task as well as the time and facilities available. Practice is classified in two ways:

- methods of practice – depending on how the skill can broken down into phases. See also *whole method practice, part method practice, progressive part method practice* and *whole-part-whole method practice*

- types of practice – the structure of the session in terms of active work and recovery. See also *massed practice, distributed practice* and random/*variable practice.*

The coach or teacher should be flexible in their use of these methods and types of practice, to ensure the sessions are relevant, specific to the performer and maintain levels of *motivation.*

prejudice: an opinion or attitude, especially an unfavourable one, based on inadequate facts, often displaying intolerance or dislike of people of a certain race, religion or culture. Where possible, such negative attitudes should be broken down, although this may be difficult, even when the prejudiced person is presented with contradictory evidence. As a result *stereotypes* may be formed, which if acted upon, can lead to *discrimination.* Within a sporting context, this may limit the opportunities for individuals or groups. For example, women's sport may be viewed as less exciting when compared with men's and as a result may receive less media coverage and *sponsorship.*

prescribed leader: gains their position of authority through being appointed to the *group* by an external source. This type of leader is in contrast to an *emergent leader.* For example, the manager or national governing body nominates the captain of a national football team.

prime mover: see *agonist*

primitive culture: non-industrial, tribal societies where the emphasis is on subsistence living with ritual and religious meanings attached to many aspects of life, including physical activities and sports. These would also have had a functional purpose to them such as defence or food hunting, which required speed and accuracy. The cultures of *native Americans, aborigines* and early Samoans would be such examples.

principle of moments: an equation used to explain how a lever system can remain balanced about a fulcrum. The moments of force must be equal. In other words:

$$\text{total clockwise moment} = \text{total anticlockwise moment}$$

where

$$\text{clockwise moment} = \text{force} \times \text{distance to fulcrum}$$

$$\text{anticlockwise moment} = \frac{\text{force}}{\text{(of muscle)}} \times \frac{\text{distance of muscle insertion}}{\text{from the joint}}$$

therefore

$$y \text{ (force of resistance)} = z \text{ (force of muscle)}$$

principles of training: the rules or laws that underpin the effectiveness of a training regime. The main principles include *specificity, progressive overload, reversibility warm-up* and *cool-downs* and the FITT principle. Essentially, for improvement to occur and for the training programme to be successful, the principles of training must be followed.

prize ring: originally this was a contest where almost anything was allowed, from wrestling to weaponry. Jack Broughton excluded weaponry and wrestling and established *pugilism* (bare knuckle fighting) in its place. The supporters of the prize ring were called 'the fancy' and gambling was an inherent part of the activity. The prize ring was eventually driven underground due to government legislation banning the sport.

prizefighting: individuals were taught to defend themselves in gladiatorial schools in 'sword and buckle' contests. It was patronised by the wealthy and powerful, who wagered huge sums on the outcome of contests though would never have been combatants themselves. The activity employed a virtually professional core of men fighting in regular circuits, mostly concentrated around London. Rules were fairly loosely enforced and death was not uncommon. When the sport was outlawed contests were organised on private land away from magistrates. Notable figures were Jack Broughton, Daniel Mendoza and Tom Cribb.

proactive transfer: see *transfer of learning*

problem-solving teaching style: refers to a teacher setting a problem, with the learner attempting to find a solution. It is an open-ended and creative approach, similar to the *discovery teaching style*, and contrasts with the *command style*. It is useful in developing the cognitive and performance elements of the performer, allowing them to explore various possibilities and take responsibilities for their actions depending on their own strengths and abilities. For example, a team of basketball players may be placed in a specific situation and set the task of devising set moves and exploring attacking options available to them. However, this method can be time-consuming, and requires the performers to possess more experience, knowledge and skills. See also *Mosston and Ashworth's spectrum of teaching styles.*

process: bony projections which aid in the smooth articulation of the skeleton. When flexing the arm at the elbow, the bony point that can be felt at the tip of the elbow is known as the 'olecranon process' which disappears into a depression on the humerus when the arm is straightened. Sometimes processes are also used in the attachment of muscles.

process-orientated goals: goals that are specifically related to the development of the tactics or technique of the performer. For example, a sprinter may set the goals of developing their leg action or dip finish in order to improve their overall performance. These goals are closely linked to *performance goals* and their effective use should help to motivate the athlete.

professional sport: a sporting activity that is engaged in for financial gain or as a means of livelihood. Training is synonymous with improving standards and specialising in an activity. The term 'professional' came into use in the 1850s but the term did not always imply a monetary distinction. It also signified a *social class* distinction.

The Football Association and the Rugby Football Union were both to feel the effects of professionalism in their games as commercialisation took root with large numbers of spectators willing to pay. In rugby this led to the north–south split in 1894 with the formation of the professional sport of rugby league and the amateur code of rugby union.

Cricket had always had a form of professionalism and had managed to create a system which maintained the social class divide whilst allowing both social classes the opportunities to play the game. The term 'gentlemen and players' was used, indicating the former being the *gentry*, while the latter came from the *working classes*.

Rowing could not cope with competitions between the watermen, the lower class rowers and the gentry. Eventually the Amateur Rowing Association (ARA) brought in the *manual labour exclusion clause* which excluded manual workers whether or not they were professional sportsmen. This resulted in the formation of the National Amateur Rowing Association in 1890, which only excluded those who earned money through rowing.

profile of mood states (POMS): based on the proposition that an individual with positive mental health will be more successful in a sporting situation. A profile is constructed of a performer's mood states before competition with levels of tension, depression, anger, vigour, fatigue and confusion being recorded. Those with good mental health will produce an 'iceberg profile', displaying more vigour, but less tension, depression, fatigue and confusion when compared with unsuccessful athletes.

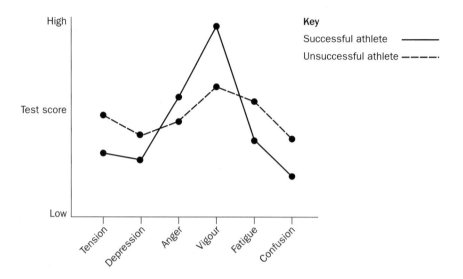

However, although this theory is widely accepted, many non-elite performers display an iceberg profile, but not all elite athletes do so. For those that do, it may alter if training regimes are excessive causing a loss of vigour, with a corresponding increase in the 'negative' moods.

profiling: a term used in *disability sport*, for the method of classifying sportsmen and women, using the degree and nature of their disability. It uses a side view outline or representation of a body, which exhibits certain tested characteristics.

progressive overload: a principle of training based around two important concepts. The first 'overload' suggests that in order to improve the body's strength or endurance, we must put it under some kind of stress. For example, to gain strength the muscles must be placed under great stress and loaded to a level greater than normal. The second concept, 'progression' suggests that as the body becomes stronger or better at coping with endurance-based activity, then further increases in muscle loading or distances run must follow to stimulate further improvement.

progressive part method practice: a method of practice in which the performer learns one part of the skill, before linking it to the next phase of the action. It is often referred to as 'chaining'; for example, a rugby team may have to learn a sequence of moves in order to complete a specific play. During training, the coach develops each move in isolation and gradually links them together, so they can be performed at speed with each player executing their own role. Similarly, this could apply to individual skills, such as a basketball lay-up shot. This method is useful for complex tasks and places less demand on the attention span of the performer, when compared with other forms of *practice*.

progressive relaxation technique involves the performer becoming aware of the alternating sensations of tension and relaxation of the muscles. Specific muscle groups are identified in succession, gradually reducing the tension throughout the body. Initially this may take time, but with practice athletes can focus and relax the whole body almost immediately. This is particularly useful prior to competition to facilitate sleep and during the event in periods of high *anxiety*. Also known as PRT. See also *autogenic training* and *self-directed relaxation*.

pronation: movement pattern characterised by the rotation of the forearm medially so that the palm of the hand faces downwards. Pronation occurs in the horizontal or transverse plane about a longitudinal axis, for example when performing a top spin forehand in tennis. (See appendix, page 271.)

proprietary colleges: *middle class* privately owned schools which were set up to emulate their *gentry* counterparts; for example, Malvern College was based on Winchester College. See also *philistine schools*.

proprioceptive neuromuscular facilitation (PNF): a stretching technique used to develop flexibility and mobility. Essentially PNF seeks to inhibit the stretch reflex that occurs when a muscle is stretched to its limit, so that a greater stretch can occur. By isometrically contracting the muscle that is being stretched to its limit, usually with the aid of a partner, the stretch reflex is diminished. (The stretch reflex is initiated by *muscle spindle apparatus* and *Golgi tendon organs*.) In the absence of the stretch reflex, the muscle can be stretched to a greater extent and with continued practice of PNF, a new limit of muscle stretch can occur enabling a greater range of movement and therefore greater mobility. This is obviously of benefit to all athletes but particularly in activities where flexibility and strength are a necessity, such as gymnastics or activities involving jumping.

proprioceptors: see *sensory system*

protein: energy-providing nutrient supplying up to ten per cent of the body's total energy requirements. It is made up of amino acid chains that provide the building blocks for tissue growth, *enzyme*, hormone and *haemoglobin* production, all of which are important for improvement in athletic performance. Typically, protein should comprise approximately 15 per cent of the total calorie intake and good sources include red meats, fish, poultry, dairy products, beans and pulses. The benefits of protein supplementation remain unclear, but it is generally thought that sufficient protein can be gained from the athlete's diet. However protein supplementation still occurs in activities such as weightlifting and bodybuilding.

Protestant work ethic: the belief of the Protestant religion associated with the Calvinists and Lutherans of the seventeenth century. The ethic emphasised that worldly work should be treated as a duty and as a means of earning salvation from God. Worldly success was seen as a sign that you were one of the 'chosen' to be saved, though reckless spending and enjoyment were not encouraged. Instead, a thrifty outlook towards life was valued. Leisure time and recreational activities therefore were given very low status. This was to be a particular constraint for the *working class* who had no private means for recreation and were subjected to the values of the moral *middle classes*.

Protestants: see *Protestant work ethic*

proximal: term of direction used to describe a structure or body part closer to the point of attachment of the trunk. For example, the proximal aspect of the femur would be the head of the femur which articulates about the hip. (See appendix, page 253.)

PRP: see *psychological refractory period*

PRT: see *progressive relaxation technique*

psychological refractory period (PRP): the delay caused by an increase in information-processing time when the initial stimulus is closely followed by a second stimulus. This slows the *reaction time* of the performer, as the first piece of information needs to be cleared before the second can be processed (see *single channel hypothesis*). This theory explains why 'dummy' or 'fake' moves can be successful. For example, a badminton player appears to be preparing to play a smash shot, but at the last moment executes a drop shot. The opponent prepares to receive the smash, but may not be able to alter their action to return the drop shot. The time delay is the psychological refractory period, as shown below.

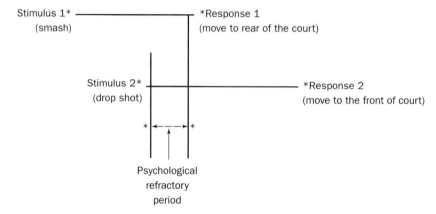

psychomotor ability: the capacity to process information, make decisions and execute a movement. *Reaction time*, limb co-ordination, dexterity, precision and aiming all depend on psychomotor abilities. They combine with *gross motor abilities* in varying degrees depending on the nature of the task. They are also known as perceptual motor abilities.

pub games: the pub was the focal point for the *working classes* in the industrial towns. Pubs were often found on the corners of most streets and they were associated with sporting activities. Ex-boxers and professional footballers often became landlords and continued the old tradition of the *inns* by providing recreational activities, but replaced the *animal sports* and cockfighting with games such as billiards, darts and skittles. The pub was often used as a base for a football team who played in the rapidly expanding league system.

public school: a private, independent fee-paying school. Public schools have a long tradition in Britain dating back to the original nine *barbarian* schools. The characteristics of these nineteenth century public schools include:

- being *elite* establishments for the *upper classes*
- fee-paying
- owned by trustees
- spartan
- fagging system (prefects or sixth formers having control of younger boys)
- single sex school
- non-local and rural
- boarding or residential.

The development of games occurred as the boys brought their local variations of activities, for example, *mob football*, to the school. These were played regularly in their free time, gradually developing unique school rules and an established competitive structure within a house system. Later, codified rules allowed inter-school fixtures to be played on a regular basis. The influence of public schools in spreading games in society was enormous because:

- *old boys* left schools and moved into positions of leadership
- universities codified rules
- employers spread games to workers
- officers spread games to troops throughout the Empire
- clergy spread games to parishes
- teachers spread games to schools
- diplomats spread games abroad.

In America, the term has a different meaning, as it refers to schools within the maintained sector.

pugilism: the art, practice or profession of fighting with the fists. The term comes from the Latin word 'pugus' meaning bare fist and mostly is used to refer to the time before *boxing* became an organised sport. Initially wrestling was allowed before the rules were drawn up and more rigidly enforced. It was one of the first activities to have formal rules drawn up as early as 1743.

pulmonary artery: vessel carrying deoxygenated blood from the heart to the lungs where the blood is subsequently oxygenated.

pulmonary circulation: the transport of blood between the heart and the lungs. The pulmonary artery carries blood from the right ventricle to the lungs where it becomes oxygen-rich and unloads carbon dioxide. The pulmonary vein then transports the freshly oxygenated blood back to the heart and into the left atrium, from where it can be pumped around the body to the working muscles.

pulmonary diffusion: the exchange of gases between the lungs and the blood. See *gaseous exchange*.

punishment: form of stimulus that is used to weaken behaviour, to reduce the likelihood of reoccurrence. For example, a player could be dropped from the team, penalised, booked, fined or substituted if they continually commit aggressive acts during a match. The continual use of punishment may cause emotional distress and resentment, so it may prove useful to use negative *reinforcement* as an alternative. It is important to understand the difference between punishment and negative reinforcement. The former is used to decrease the likelihood of the unwanted behaviour reoccurring, while the latter attempts to increase the chances of the desired action being repeated.

Puritans: the more extreme *Protestants* in the sixteenth and seventeenth centuries, who wished to purify the Church of England of most of its ceremony and other aspects which it associated with Catholicism. They were a growing body of influential townspeople with a strict, moral outlook to life shunning the more pleasurable activities. Play was considered to be idleness and a sinful waste of time. By the early seventeenth century the argument between the pleasure-seeking cavaliers and the Puritans had escalated. It prompted James I to write his *Book of Sports*.

purposeful leisure: a term used in *communist* governments who, as they operate an authoritarian system, require as much control over their population in leisure as in other areas of social life. This is *social control*, extolling the belief that rebellious tendencies can be curbed and political messages can be equally learned through the leisure situation. For example, activities that develop health and fitness were encouraged whilst those considered more anti-social, such as any that promoted gambling, were discouraged.

PWC$_{170}$ test: PWC stands for 'physical work capacity' and this sub-maximal test measures an individual's aerobic capacity. Subjects are required to perform three consecutive workloads on a cycle ergometer, whilst the heart rate is monitored. Initially a workload is set that increases the subject's heart rate to between 100 and 115 beats per minute. The heart rate is measured each minute until the subject reaches steady state. The test is repeated for a second and third workload which increases the heart rate to between 115 and 130, and 130 and 145 beats per minute respectively.

Each steady-state heart rate and respective workload are graphed and used to predict a workload that would elicit a heart rate response of 170 beats per minute. The score can then be compared to standard tables and a prediction made of *maximum oxygen uptake* (VO$_2$max).

pyruvic acid: the end product of *glycolysis*. The initial stages of energy production result in the breakdown of glucose to two molecules of pyruvic acid which provides sufficient energy to resynthesise two ATP molecules. In the absence of oxygen, for example, during very high intensity exercise such as a 400-metre run, pyruvic acid is converted into *lactic acid*. However, during aerobic activities such as jogging or cycling which are less intense, pyruvic acid is converted to citric acid from which a lot more energy can be produced via the *Krebs cycle* and *electron transfer chain*.

Do you need revision help and advice?

Go to pages 274–287 for a range of revision appendices that include plenty of exam advice and tips.

qualitative: relating to the quality (rather than the quantity) of something. The assessment of sports like *gymnastics* is qualitative. This can involve opinions and judgements rather than relying on *quantitative* data. In other words, it is more subjective than objective. Many would argue that this makes it prone to more bias and is not an entirely just method of declaring a winner.

quango: acronym for 'quasi-autonomous national government organisation'. An example is *Sport England*. A large number of quangos exist outside government departments, with varying degrees of independence. They are not under the direct control of parliament but linked to the government in some way, either financial, or through policy accountability or statutory obligations. They share common characteristics, which include the tendencies:

- to be funded directly by the Treasury
- for the board in control to be elected by the appropriate government minister
- to perform promotional or developmental activities
- to have specialist expertise not found elsewhere in the government
- to remain slightly detached politically from sensitive issues such as racial and sexual equality, creating a 'buffer zone' for the government.

They are often fragmented, lack co-ordination and contain increasing numbers of interested and sometimes competing parties.

quantitative: something that is capable of being measured using numerical data. Many believe this is a fairer method of deciding sporting outcomes, as it is less prone to bias when compared with *qualitative* methods. Developments in technology have meant that an even finer measure of success can be achieved. For example, the time of a race can now be recorded accurately to one-hundredth of a second.

questionnaire: a series of questions, whose purpose is to collect statistical information. Sports psychologists who wish to analyse *personality*, *attitude* and levels of *anxiety* often use them. Questionnaires are useful as athletes can complete them quickly in a variety of situations, questions can be specific to particular topics and responses can be confidential. However, numerous problems, such as misinterpretation or lack of understanding of the questions are inherent in this method of gathering information. Moreover, the respondents may not answer honestly, as they may wish to appear in a positive light, or they may give the answers they think are required. Also inappropriate questions may be used, which may lead to biased results, and even the actual time of completion may influence the responses. Commonly used questionnaires include, *Eysenck's personality inventory*, *Cattell's 16 personality factors*, *SCAT* and *CSAI-2*.

quintain: a military activity where Roman soldiers would 'run at the quintain', which was usually a tree or post. They would be either on foot, horseback or in boats, and needed skill, accuracy of aim and a steady eye. It was an activity enjoyed by all social classes and continued into the seventeenth century though by then it was used mainly ritualistically at festivals and wakes.

quoits: a game in which quoits, which are rings of iron, plastic or rope, are tossed at a stake in the ground in an attempt to encircle it. It has always been a popular rural and pub game.

Do you need help with the synoptic element of your Physical Education course?

Go to page 274 for tips and advice.

race: a group of people sharing the same inherited physical characteristic. Various assumptions developed as a consequence of trying to divide population groups on this basis. Throughout history, theories of the physical and mental inferiority of some races have been used by others to justify their suppression. See also *racism* and *ethnic groups*.

racism: a set of ideas or beliefs based on the assumption that races have distinctive characteristics determined by hereditary factors, endowing some races with an intrinsic superiority. *Discrimination* often results and in sport this is evident in a variety of ways, for example in *stacking*, and in the difficulty players often have in reaching the administrative and managerial positions. Campaigns such as Let's Stamp Racism Out of Football, which began in 1993, have attempted to cut racial harassment out of football. It is supported by the Commission for Racial Equality and Professional Footballers Association.

rackets: a game similar to squash played in a large four-walled court by two or four players using rackets and a small hard ball. The game began in fairly humble circumstances in England and is mentioned in 'The Pickwick Papers' as being played at Fleet Prison. Open courts existed in the backyards of taverns and *inns* and in many towns, while it was taken up by the *public schools* for its simple qualities and the possibilities of using architectural features within the school grounds. It was a game that suited the cult of *athleticism* containing *rules*, *etiquette* and *sportsmanship*.

radian: the unit of angular velocity. One radian is approximately equal to 57.3°. A knowledge of radians will enable a coach to calculate optimum rotational speed for a trampolinist or gymnast when performing complex somersaults.

radical ethic: one of the sport ethics in the *United States*, which expresses the view that the outcome of a sporting event or contest is important, but so too is the process. It is probably the closest to the British stance and is characterised by slogans such as Lifetime Sport, *Sport for All* and their *intra-mural programmes*. The quest for excellence can be strived for and achieved, but it should not be at the expense of other values.

railways: the effect on sport of the development of the railways in the nineteenth century was immense as trains allowed:

- spectators and teams to travel to fixtures
- fixtures to became more regular and held further afield
- the re-birth of the *Olympic Games*
- ramblers, cyclists and mountaineers easier access to the countryside
- the sport of angling to develop, as a publication titled 'The Rail and the Rod' revolutionised fishing, providing a guide to angling spots which could be reached within a 30-mile radius of London.

- factory owners to arrange special excursion trains for their employees to places like Blackpool.

Raising the Game: a government statement in 1995, outlining the then Prime Minister John Major's aims for sport in Britain. It supported the following initiatives to encourage participation and raise the standards of school sport:

- *Sportsmark* and Sportsmark Gold Awards/Sport College status
- schools were encouraged to make links with external clubs
- standards were recommended for the amount of opportunity for playing *sport* in physical education lessons and during extra-curricular activities
- Community Sports Initiative
- the training of teachers to run sports clubs and teams
- The *National Junior Sport Programmes.*

The aim was to provide opportunities, from sport at primary schools through to Olympic levels, and it highlighted the benefits of competition and the lessons which could be learned for life.

RAS: see *reticular activating system*

rational recreation: a term used to signify sporting activities which were characterised by:

- regular participation
- complex, written rules
- highly structured in nature
- being spectator-based as well as participation-based
- the need to use refined skills rather than force
- being a *middle* to *upper class* development
- being regionally and nationally based
- the use of sophisticated equipment and facilities.

Rational recreation became prevalent following the *Industrial Revolution* when the middle classes wished to change the recreational habits of the *working classes* from the more rowdy elements of *popular recreation*. They now required a more civilised population with orderly working habits and they wished to use sport to develop the moral qualities they admired. The movement was not only confined to sports – libraries, museums and parks also played their part.

reaction time: the time between the onset of a stimulus and the initiation of that response. The speed at which the *information processing* system interprets the stimuli is a critical factor determining the chance of success. For example, when a water polo player thinks he or she has a goal scoring opportunity and decides to attempt a shot, the time taken to analyse the situation and start the shooting action is the reaction time. There are two forms of reaction time: *simple reaction time* or *choice reaction time* and numerous factors affect the speed at which the process occurs, including age, gender, intensity of the stimulus, previous experience, arousal levels and the *stimulus–response compatibility*. The timing and number of stimuli can also affect the performance, causing a *psychological refractory period*. The time taken can be reduced through practice and *anticipation*. See also *movement time* and *response time*.

reactive strength: this is developed when an athlete performs a movement directly following an *eccentric muscle contraction*. For example, when a trampolinist drives from the trampoline bed directly after landing from a previous move.

real tennis: an ancient form of tennis, played in a four-walled indoor court with various openings, a sloping roofed corridor along three sides and a buttress on the fourth side. It is also called 'royal tennis', as the game was the sport of royalty and noblemen in France and England. The game originated in France and was made popular in England by the *Tudors*, but there were restrictive acts in the sixteenth century forbidding servants and labourers to play, enabling it to retain its privileged status. This game was one encouraged as *rational recreation*.

recall schema: see *schema theory*

receptors: see *sensory system*

reciprocal inhibition: the process of one muscle contracting whilst its opposite relaxes. For example, the muscles in the upper arm work in an antagonistic manner to cause flexion and extension of the elbow. As the biceps contract, the triceps relax and they are in the process of reciprocal inhibition.

reciprocal style teaching: a teaching style in which a teacher sets a task, which individuals have to complete in pairs, alternating roles as observer and performer. This allows them more responsibility, although the teacher retains overall control and monitors the progress, possibly offering assistance when appropriate. It helps to develop personal and social skills, evaluation and actual performance, as well as *self-confidence* and a greater understanding of the skill. For example, the teacher may give the group a demonstration, provide handouts to assist them and set the task of learning new dribbling techniques in pairs or small groups. However, it is difficult for the teacher to monitor all pairs or groups and fully assess their level of development and understanding. It can also be ineffective if the performers are unable to analyse and communicate, allowing poor and incorrect technique to develop. See also *Mosston and Ashworth's spectrum of teaching styles*.

recognition schema: see *schema theory*

recombinant erythropoietin (Rh EPO) is a synthetic form of *erythropoietin* (EPO), which is artificially manufactured. Some athletes abuse this substance by injecting it into the body where it can boost *haemoglobin* content and therefore improve the oxygen carrying capacity of the blood. It has also been shown to improve the *maximum oxygen uptake* (VO_{2max}) of a performer. The IOC and all governing bodies outlaw this form of blood doping. Although it has proven benefits with respect to performance enhancement, there are some serious side effects. These include an increase in *blood viscosity* (thickness) an increased risk of blood clotting and heart failure. The use of Rh EPO also reduces the production of the bodies' natural *erythropoietin* (EPO) that produces red blood cells.

recovery: period between training sessions during which time adaptation can take place. Training can inflict some severe damage to the body: muscle tissue can tear, be poisoned by acidic substances such as *lactic acid* and have all its energy stores thoroughly depleted. During the recovery period, however, the muscle can take time to rebuild, oxygen delivery and toxin removal mechanisms improve and the energy stores fully replete themselves. But in order not to suffer the same fate through training, the body actually supercompensates and adapts to be able to cope with greater amounts of stress. If the body is stressed repeatedly through training and adequate recovery is not allowed, symptoms of *overtraining* can result and performance can actually deteriorate. It is essential that the coach and athlete builds into the training programme sufficient recovery periods to enable adaptation to occur.

recreation: activities carried out during *leisure* time. Examples of activities would be reading, gardening, listening to music, *tourism* and participating in sporting activities. The word originates from the Latin word 'recreatio' which means to restore health. Recreation has long been associated with relaxation and recuperation of the individual, particularly useful in restoring people's energies for work. Recreation can be viewed in different capacities:

- as an extension of the *play* experience
- as a personal experience, of value to the individual
- in terms of the nature of an activity, such as *physical recreation* or more sedentary activities such as reading
- as an institution having a structured framework
- as a process – part of personal development

regatta: an organised series of races for *rowing* boats, yachts or other such craft. The earliest account of a regatta was on the River Thames in 1775 and later the famous Henley Regatta was established in 1839, purely as a means of boosting trade for the town. It soon became a traditional event, reflecting the *Victorian* love of combining sporting events with a grand social occasion and now has many prestigious school and club events, for example the Elizabeth Cup. The Henley Regatta reflected distinct social divisions between the classes, which are maintained even today.

reinforcement: the process used which increases the probability of behaviour reoccurring in the future. It is generally used in two forms:

- positive reinforcement – involves the use of a stimulus to create feelings of satisfaction to encourage a repetition of the action, for example, praise from a coach or the feeling of completing a skill successfully
- negative reinforcement – involves the withdrawal of an unpleasant stimulus when the desired response occurs, for example, the coach stops shouting at the team if their actions are correct.

In comparison, *punishment* is used to reduce the probability of the action being repeated.

relaxation: the reduction of muscle tension and levels of *stress* and *anxiety*. This can be achieved using either 'cognitive' methods, which utilise thoughts to induce a calmer state, or 'somatic' methods, involving the control of muscle tension. Either can be used in training or competition, but care should be taken with some techniques if employed too close to an event as this may lead to under-arousal. See also *stress management*.

reliability: if the findings of a test can be repeated, it is said to be reliable. For example, when a performer completes a personality questionnaire, the data collected after analysis should reach the same conclusion on each occasion concerning their traits. Tests also require *validity* to be of true value.

religion: belief in a supernatural power considered to be divine or to have control over human destiny. Over the centuries different religions have exerted considerable influence over the acceptance or non-acceptance of sporting activities. See also *evangelism, sabbatarianism, Methodists, Protestants, Puritans* and *Church*.

republic: a form of government in which the people or their elected representatives possess the supreme power. The head of state is an elected or nominated president, unlike a monarch who inherits the title. *France* and the *United States of America* are examples of republics and there are many people in *Australia* who would like their country to become a republic.

residual volume: the volume of air that remains in the lungs following maximal expiration. Its approximate value is 1200 ml, and changes are minimal during exercise. (See appendix.)

resistance training: a method of training which encompasses all types of exercising where resistance is applied to the body; for example, sand dune running or running up hills (resistance of gravity) together with harness running or running in weighted belts. Perhaps the most common type of resistance training is weight training which is explained fully under *strength training*.

respiratory exchange ratio (RER): a method of determining which energy-providing nutrient is predominantly in use during exercise. It is calculated by analysing oxygen consumption and carbon dioxide production, and is represented as follows:

$$RER = \frac{\text{volume of } CO_2 \text{ expired per minute}}{\text{volume of } O_2 \text{ uptake per minute}}$$

The closer the value is to 1.0, the more likely the body is to be using glycogen as a fuel, whereas the expected value for fats is 0.7. Intermediate figures suggest that a mixture of fuels is being utilised which is the expected norm. It is known as the respiratory quotient.

respiratory pump: mechanism which aids in the return of blood to the heart via the veins. During exercise breathing becomes deeper and causes pressure changes to occur in the thorax and the abdomen. Increases in pressure in the abdomen cause the large veins in that area to be compressed which squeezes blood back to the heart rapidly. This, together with the *muscle pump*, forms the *venous return mechanism* and helps to increase and maintain adequate blood flow during exercise.

response time: the time from the onset of the stimulus to the completion of the movement. The measurement includes the *reaction time* of the performer and the *movement time*. For example, when a water polo player attempts to score a goal, it would be the time taken to identify stimuli, assess the situation, make the decision and complete the shot. This can be expressed as:

reaction time + movement time = response time

reticular activating system (RAS): cluster of brain cells located in the central part of the brain stem, which maintains levels of *arousal*. It acts as a filtering mechanism, either allowing information into the brain or inhibiting it. People who are *extroverts* tend to seek higher levels of arousal as their RAS lacks stimulation, while *introverts* already have a higher level of stimulation, so they do not need as much excitement.

retro-active transfer: see *transfer of learning*

reversibility: principle of training which explains the deterioration in performance following the cessation of training or when a decrease in the intensity of training occurs. It appears that the physiological effects of training are lost once training ceases. The most noticeable deterioration occurs in aerobic efficiency, where a decrease in *maximum oxygen uptake* (VO_2max) of up to 27 per cent has been recorded. However, losses in muscle mass and therefore *strength* also occur, but at a much slower rate. It is also known as detraining, and sometimes regression.

reward: any event, which is pleasurable or satisfying to the individual receiving it. Rewards are often used as a form of *reinforcement* to shape behaviour and can be:

- tangible – e.g. cups, medals, certificates or money
- intangible – e.g. praise, personal bests, records or recognition.

Ringelmann effect: proposes that the performance of an individual may decrease as the group size increases. This is caused by a mixture of factors including low *motivation* and a lack of co-ordination within the group, leading to poor group *cohesion*. It could be categorised as a *faulty process*. For example, a footballer may perform better when playing five-a-side football than during a full game, because they feel lost within the team and their contribution in the latter may not be fully recognised, causing demotivation. See also *social loafing*.

risk is the possibility of incurring injury or loss or to expose oneself to *danger* or hazard. Outdoor and adventurous activities or outdoor pursuit activities pose situations of real and perceived risk.

- *Real risk* – risk from the natural environment such as a rockfall. Leaders need to be aware of the potential risks when planning routes and so on.
- *Perceived risk* – this is where the sense of adventure comes from and which leaders need to be aware of. However, if the perceived risk is too great for the ability level of the performer then feelings of anxiety could become too much.

There has been a considerable increase in the traditional (canoeing, rock climbing) and 'new' (jet skiing, snow boarding) adventure sports. The reasons why people seem to be seeking greater risks can be explained by:

- increasingly sedentary lifestyles, which make some people seek a more active and exciting leisure time (the pursuit of vertigo)
- increased accessibility of these sports
- the development of new and exciting technology sports
- the appreciation of the natural environment, particularly as a release from urban pressures.

ritual: any established form of religious or other ceremonial type of behaviour, consisting of a series of actions performed in a prescribed order. Most sports and pastimes had such associations particularly because they occurred on holy days and pagan festivals such as *Shrove Tuesday* and *May Day*. Rituals can be a way of expressing social bonding and serve to affirm an individual's commitment to the group. For example, the 'Hakka' is performed by the New Zealand rugby team at all international fixtures and originated as a *Maori* war chant.

role (social): the part played by a person in a particular social setting, influenced by the expectation of what is appropriate. Individuals may play various roles in their lives through their professional, family and other social relationships. Individuals learn their roles through *socialisation* and children often use their *play* activities to act out adult roles.

role (of the teacher/coach): the role of a physical education teacher is very different to that of a sports coach, even though they are both involved in teaching sporting activities. However, when a physical education teacher is involved with *extra-curricular* activities they are more likely to adopt the role of a sports coach. Below are the main differences between the two approaches.

Role of a physical education teacher	Role of a sports coach
Administration: comes under Government Department for Education and Skills.	Administration: comes under Government Department of Culture, Media and Sport.
Compulsory: this is a national curriculum subject.	Voluntary: children will have chosen to participate.
Range of activities: the national curriculum requires a variety of activities to be taught.	Specialism: the sport coach tends to have specialised in their activity and may coach to a higher standard.
Ability level: mixed ability classes are the norm for physical education lessons.	Ability level: performers will normally be taught according to their ability.
Children's needs: physical, psychological and emotional needs are developed and nurtured and take precedence over performance results.	Performance: the sport coach is often measured by the progress of their performers and therefore there is a concentration on results.
Values: values such as teamwork, sportsmanship and co-operation are encouraged.	Values: values such as commitment, dedication to training and competitiveness are encouraged.

role model: an individual whom a person admires in terms of skill, values or attitude. They are often termed, 'significant others' and can include parents, teachers, coaches, friends or heroes, who can have considerable influence during the socialisation and learning processes. For example, a young sportsperson may look up to and wish to imitate a player from their favourite or national team.

Romantic movement: the late eighteenth-century movement in literature and the arts which laid an emphasis on subjectivity and the individual. The work of the Romantic poets such as Wordsworth and Coleridge focused on the beauty of the Lake District and so had a considerable influence on recreation in the countryside; their poems made the countryside attractive to town and city folk. Initially the middle classes began to use the countryside for activities such as rambling and cycling, and gradually the working classes followed as their leisure time and affluence increased. These activities encouraged an appreciation of topography and local knowledge, and an aesthetic appreciation of natural beauty.

Rorschach inkblot test: form of personality test consisting of ten bilaterally symmetrical inkblots. The individual describes what they observe in each and their responses are analysed to form personality characteristics.

rotation: movement pattern which occurs in the horizontal or transverse plane about a longitudinal axis. Rotation of a joint occurs where the bone turns about its long axis within the joint and can produce movement either medially (towards the centre of the body) or laterally (towards the outside of the body). When performing the butterfly stroke in swimming for example, the humerus must rotate medially as the hands enter the water, also in preparation of a forehand stroke in tennis the humerus rotates laterally at the shoulder joint. (See appendix, page 270.)

rotator: muscle which causes *rotation*. For example at the hip, the gluteus medius and minimus rotate the hip medially, whilst the sartorius rotates the hip laterally.

rowing: the art of propelling a boat is practised as a sport in most countries. It began as a utilitarian activity when it provided power for war ships and transport in industrial towns. The River Thames provided one of the main highways in the *medieval era* in England; wealthy people had their own state barges and professional watermen plied for trade. By the eighteenth century there were over 40,000 watermen with frequent contests and wagering on the outcome was common. The standard of rowing increased in the nineteenth century as *professionalism* increased and rowing races attracted an enormous following and were widely reported in the press. Many rowers became coaches of amateur crews, but due to the powerful rise in *amateurism* and the power held by the middle class administrators, professionalism soon died out.

The Amateur Rowing Association was formed in 1882 but its strict social class discrimination meant the National Amateur Rowing Association in 1890 soon followed which based its amateur–professional rules strictly on monetary values rather than social class. See also *manual labour clause*.

rugby football: a form of football played with an oval ball in which the handling and carrying of the ball is permitted. It is purported to have originated at Rugby School in the nineteenth century having developed from the *mob game*. William Webb Ellis is said to have picked up the ball and run with it and the game was accepted as it conformed to the cult of *athleticism* and *muscular Christianity*. The adoption of the game by the northern working class led to a struggle for the possession of the game. The Rugby Football Union was founded in 1871 and became the custodian of the amateur game. However 'broken-time' payments and shamateurism (see *amateurism*) were to cause conflict within the administration and in 1894–5 there was a breakaway of the northern clubs and the Rugby Football League was formed, allowing *professionalism* to develop. In the twentieth century the distinction between amateurism and professionalism became increasingly blurred, and in 1996 all restrictions to payment were eliminated, allowing the game to become fully professional.

rules: a set of regulations or principles, governing behaviour. Rules for sporting activities used to be local in nature before they became codified, mostly in the nineteenth century, allowing fixtures to be played further afield. Nowadays, *international sport federations* decide on the rules for a sport and disciplinary action follows a breach of the rules decided by an official authorised to referee, umpire or judge the activity.

ruling class: the dominant group in society which controls the rest of society, either directly or indirectly. See also *dominant culture*.

rural sports: activities that originated in the countryside where the main economic activity was agriculture. They existed mainly before the *Industrial Revolution* though rural activities did survive in many areas, probably because of their isolation and lack of the outside influences, which were rapidly changing lifestyles in the urban towns. The seasons were important, as were the festivals and fairs for shooting and all kinds of animal hunting; the rivers provided recreation such as fishing and skating in the winter months. The occasional *mob game* reflected the harsh lifestyle of the agricultural worker.

sabbatarianism: a religious sect who strictly observe Sunday as the sabbath. Sabbatarianism had the effect of restricting the leisure activities of the *working classes* in the nineteenth century.

sacral vertebrae: region of the vertebral column consisting of five bones fused together to form the sacrum. It is the sacrum which fuses to the pelvis to bear and distribute the weight of the upper body. (See appendix, page 258.)

saddle joint: see *synovial joint*

saggital plane: an imaginary line which runs longitudinally through the body and limbs, dividing them into left and right parts. Movements such as *flexion* and *extension* which occur at synovial joints take place in this plane about the *transverse axis*. A knowledge of the planes of movement and rotation about axes is essential for the performer to know where their body is in relation to their environment. (See appendix, page 256.)

Samaranch, Juan Antonio: President of the International Olympic Committee (1980–2001). Some of his achievements include:

- loosening of the eligibility code, rule 26, of the Olympic Charter – professionals were now admitted. One effect of this was to outweigh the unbalanced nature of the superiority of the state-sponsored amateurs (*stamateurs*). However, it also created the travesty of the stars of the National Basketball Association of the USA competing against Angola, Lithuania and Croatia in Barcelona 1992

- increasing the *commercialisation* and marketing of the Games so they could continue on a more secure financial basis

- broadening *International Olympic Committee* (IOC) membership to include athletes, more members of the international federations and national Olympic committees and women!

- stabilising East–West, communist–capitalist relations in the run-up to the Seoul Games in 1988

- acceptance in 1992 of a team from the newly independent states from Russia

- drug programme improvements

- acceptance of South Africa back into the Olympic movement

- personal knowledge of most of the 172 national Olympic committees

- creation of an Olympic museum in Lausanne.

Samoa: a group of islands in the south Pacific, north-east of Fiji. It was an independent kingdom until the mid-nineteenth century when it was divided administratively into

American Samoa (east) and German Samoa (west). The latter was mandated to New Zealand in 1919 and then gained full independence in 1962 as Western Samoa. Before the Samoan culture was exposed to outside influences, the economy depended on agriculture, each individual was only as important as the household group and most activities were co-operative until it came to contests between rival districts. Prizes were not given though success was highly valued. Games involving teamwork did not appear in Samoan life until contact with Britain, America, Germany and New Zealand. *Cricket* was adopted readily as it appeared to reflect their own values – there could be hundreds on each side and a game could last for ten to twelve days in order to let everyone have a bat. *Rugby* and baseball were also initially modified to make them more compatible to the Samoan way of life. See also *primitive cultures*.

SAQ (speed, agility and quickness): a type of training designed to improve the *speed*, *agility* and quickness of a performer. It involves a range of training activities including ladder drills, *resistance* drills and *plyometric* drills. Speed, agility and quickness have been singled out as three of the most important components of fitness required for a whole range of sporting activities, but especially for games players. These drills should therefore form a central role in the fitness training for such athletes.

sarcomere: the contractile unit of skeletal muscle, consisting of two proteins: *actin* and *myosin*. It is the interaction between these two proteins that cause the muscle to shorten (see *sliding filament theory*). When viewed under a microscope, the striped appearance of skeletal muscle is a result of the overlapping of actin and myosin.

During contraction, shortening of the sarcomere generates great forces, for example, the shortening of the tricep brachii can generate sufficient force to push the body up when performing a press-up.

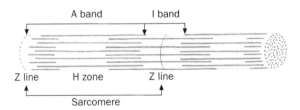

Saturday half day: was established in the nineteenth century. This was a dramatic change for the industrial *working classes* as they now had increased *leisure* time and improved income which led the way to the development of *association football* as a major spectator sport. The Birmingham chocolate firm Cadbury was the first company to implement this for their workers.

SCAT: see *sport competition anxiety test*

schema theory states that we store a generalised series of movement patterns that are modified to adapt to the current environment and situation. Therefore, when learning new skills or playing in a game, the performer will recall and alter stored motor programmes, such as jumping, catching, throwing, running and balancing to complete the task successfully. For example, a performer may modify the jumping schema to execute a high jump, gymnastic vault, basketball jump shot or volleyball block. The theory helps solve the problem of memory storage faced by the *closed loop theory*. The schema are initiated, evaluated and updated by two processes:

- Recall schema – start the movement based on two sources of information:

    1   Initial conditions or positional information, eg when completing a basketball shot, the position on court, the weight of the ball, location of defenders and the position of the player's own limbs are taken into account.

    2   Response specifications or information about the task to be executed. The basketball player formulates a motor programme deciding on the speed, power and direction of the shot as well as the specific technique that needs to be used.

- Recognition schema – control and evaluate the movement through:

    1   Response outcome or the end result compared with the intended aim. Knowledge of where the ball hit the backboard or the ring and whether it successful is stored. This is vital for the development of strong schema.

    2   Sensory consequences or the feeling during and after the movement. The player evaluates the feeling of the shot and the flight of the ball, and updates the memory stores for future performances.

In order to develop strong schema, practice must be varied to form a wide range of *parameters*. These need to be relevant to the game, challenging and progressive, with feedback provided to update the programmes for future reference.

scholarship: grant awarded to a student to gain financial aid. This is important for American college students and ranges from partial grants to full scholarships. There is a question over the equality with which they are granted; for example, do women and African Americans receive their fair share?

secondary socialisation: see *socialisation*

segregation: to set or be set apart from the main group. Segregation can occur on the basis of gender, religious or racial groups, disability or because of social class. Competitive sport has commonly been separated into male and female divisions. Segregation in this case is not illegal as it is exempt from the *Sex Discrimination Act* under section 44. Segregation is not necessarily divisive and can enable individuals to realise their potential under more appropriate conditions. See also *integration*.

selective attention: process that filters irrelevant information gathered by the *sensory system* and prioritises the *stimuli* that can affect that particular situation. For example, a badminton player will ignore the crowd, advertising boards and players on an adjacent court, and instead focus on their own and the opponent's position on court, actions that may indicate particular shots to be played, as well as the power and direction of the shuttlecock. This allows only the relevant information to pass into the *memory* system, allowing the execution of the shot to be faster.

The selective attention of a performer can be developed in a variety of ways, for instance, changing the intensity of the stimulus, increasing *motivation* levels and reaching optimal levels of *arousal* as well as directing *attention* to specific cues.

self-confidence: the positive attitude of an individual towards their ability to complete tasks. Performers with high levels of self-confidence tend to have higher levels of *motivation*. For example, an individual who is good at games generally will have the confidence in their ability when introduced to a new sport. However, this is not always the case, as self-confidence can be specific to certain situations (see *self-efficacy*).

self-directed relaxation: a technique in which the performer concentrates on specific muscle groups in order to relax each one in turn. Mastery of the technique takes time but when developed, it enables the performer to relax particular areas of the body during competition as they see fit. For example, if an athlete sensed their upper body was developing tension hindering their performance, they could attempt to concentrate on that area. See also *autogenic training* and *progressive relaxation technique.*

self-efficacy: the degree of self-confidence experienced by the performer when placed in a specific situation. Those performers with high levels of self-efficacy in a particular activity will tend to choose to participate, display good levels of *motivation* and perseverance, when compared with someone who has low self-efficacy and expectations. For example, a young basketball player may be happy to practice their shooting at home on their own, but may not be as confident of their skills when playing in a team situation.

Four factors influence an individual's level of self-efficacy;

- performance accomplishments – performers who have experienced success and enjoyment are more likely to develop high levels of confidence; for example, if the young basketballer scores several baskets during the game, they will have the confidence to continue to shoot

- vicarious experiences – performers who have watched others achieving the task will feel they are able to do so as well, especially if the model is of similar ability

- verbal persuasion – performers who receive encouragement about their abilities and actions, especially from *significant others*, will feel more confident about their actions or attempts

- emotional arousal – performers who are encouraged to perceive their physiological and psychological arousal before participation in a positive manner are more likely to develop high self-efficacy. For example, increased heart rate, respiratory rate and *cognitive anxiety* should be viewed positively, in terms of being ready to compete, rather than as indicating being ill-prepared.

Therefore, in order to develop positive expectations, performers should experience early success, observe competent others of similar ability, set realistic goals, be verbally encouraged whilst developing effective *stress management* and relaxation techniques.

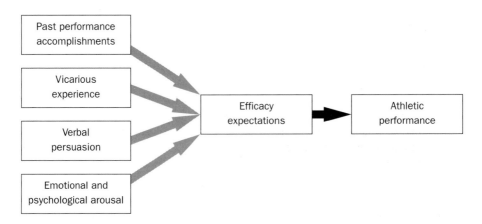

self-esteem: the value we place on ourselves as individuals based on an evaluation of our own abilities and performance when compared with others. This can contribute to our levels of *self-confidence* and *self-efficacy*, for example, a club standard gymnast may feel they are competent compared with other pupils in a class at school and possess a high self-esteem both as a gymnast and sports performer. It is important that individuals are given positive encouragement to develop high levels of self-esteem, as this can affect their *attitude*, *motivation* and participation in numerous activities.

self-paced skill: involves the performer initiating their actions based on their knowledge of the environmental conditions. They have control over when the movement has to be executed and control the rate at which the skill is performed. These types of skill are placed on the same *continuum* as *externally paced skills* and are often examples of *closed skills*. Examples include athletic throwing and jumping events, gymnastic moves and the serve during racket games.

self-serving bias: the tendency of performers to attribute their success to internal factors, such as effort and ability, and their failure to external influences, for example to bad luck and task difficulty. This allows the individual to protect their *self-esteem* and maintain levels of *motivation* for future performances. However, if they can attribute failure to internal factors, taking responsibility for their actions, they may be more motivated to correct faults in the future. See also *attribution theory*.

self-talk: involves the individual developing positive thoughts about their actions and performances. The aim is to eradicate any negative thoughts as they can be demotivating and increase *anxiety*. For example, a swimmer at the start of a race may alter thoughts such as 'am I ready for this?' to 'my training has gone well and I'm prepared!' Similarly a basketball team which are losing by four points near the end of a match may be told by their coach during a time-out, 'we've got plenty of time left' rather than 'we've only got two minutes left to win the game'. This technique can be combined with *thought stopping*.

semantic differential scales: questionnaire used to evaluate the *attitude* of an individual. The individual has to indicate their opinion, usually on a seven-point scale, with opposite words at either end of the scale. For example, to answer the question, 'do you feel exercise aids a healthy lifestyle?' the scale may range from 'beneficial' to 'harmful'. See also *attitude tests*.

semi-leisure: a concept developed by Dumazadier to refer to activities which are performed outside work but which may have a sense of obligation and compulsion attached to them. An example may be 'do-it-yourself' activities or playing for a club within a league structure each week. See also *leisure*.

sensory system: gathers information from the environment using various receptors, including sight, sound, touch and smell. This allows the performer to begin the *information processing* mechanism. There are three forms of receptors:

- *proprioceptors* – located on the nerves, muscle, tendons, joints and inner ear, which provide intrinsic information about the movement and balance of the body during the performance. This is commonly known as *kinaethesis*, allowing the performer to 'feel' the action; for example, the grip on a golf club, the force of a pass or the location of the body during a somersault

- *exteroceptors* – gather information from outside the body via the eyes, ears, nose and mouth. The most useful of these for a sportsperson are vision and audition, with the former being generally regarded as the most important form of receptor

- *introceptors* – pass information from within the body's internal organs such as the heart and lungs to the brain via the nervous system. This helps to regulate the various functions of the body and cater for the changing demands placed upon it.

The information collected by the different receptors is analysed by the process of *perception* which is then passed onto the *decision making* phase of the mechanism.

serial skill: composed of a number of subroutines, which need to be completed in the correct sequence. These skills may have discrete elements that may be isolated in practice conditions. This type of skill is placed on the same *continuum* as a *discrete skill*. Examples include athletic jumping actions, such as the high jump or triple jump, gymnastic routines, diving sequences and the basketball lay-up shot.

sesamoid bones: small bones situated within tendons, the function of which is to help in the smooth operation of two articulating bones. The largest sesamoid bone, the patella, enables a smooth action between the tibia and femur and prevents hyperextension occurring. Another exists in the knuckle of the thumb between the metacarpal and phalanx. Sesamoid literally means 'shaped like a sesame seed' as these bones are oval in shape.

Sex Discrimination Act (SDA): this Act of 1975 made sex discrimination unlawful in employment, training, education and the provision of goods, facilities and services. It stated that a female should be treated in the same way as a male in similar circumstances. However:

- competitive sport is excluded under Section 44 of the Act. Separate competitions are allowed for men and women 'where the physical strength, stamina or physique puts a woman at a disadvantage to the average man'. Problems have occurred where female referees and physical education teachers have been denied promotion on the grounds of being a woman, and some successful appeals have been made.
- private sports clubs can legally operate discriminatory policies under Sections 19 and 34.

sexism: the belief that one sex is inferior to the other, and is most often directed towards women. It is sometimes based on the idea that women are not best suited to roles that carry prestige and influence. Traditionally, women have been denied the same legal, political, economic and social rights enjoyed by men. If sexism occurs it can often be challenged by the *Sex Discrimination Act*. It is the more covert actions that occur due to sex stereotyping which are difficult to combat. For example, few women are in positions of power within the professional football structure.

shamateur: see *amateurism*

Sharpey's fibres: a tough connective tissue which anchors the tendon or ligament to the *periosteum* of the bone. They are therefore central to the interaction of the skeleton and the muscular system in causing movement. In cases of severe stress being placed upon these fibres, which is frequently experienced when the bones are still growing in length, damage can occur causing some discomfort when exercising. This is a medical condition known as Osgood Schlatter's disease.

shinty: a simple form of *hockey* originating in Scotland, played for centuries as part of the clan festivities. Rules were written down and an official association was formed in 1893 but it was not widely adopted in England because it was seen as a lower class activity, being violent and masculine, and was confined to a small geographical area. Hockey as a stick and ball game had already been started elsewhere.

short bone: type of bone found within the body, specifically designed for weight bearing, being compact in nature and often of equal width and length. The carpals of the wrist and tarsals of the ankle are examples of short bones and require great weight-bearing capacities when performing a handstand or withstanding the stresses of running and jumping.

short-term memory store: component of the *memory* process, which has a limited storage capacity for information, gathered by the performer. The store of between five and nine pieces of information, which have been transferred through the *short-term sensory store* and reduced via *selective attention*, can be retained for up to 30 seconds, before either being forgotten or passed into the *long-term memory*. Due to this limited capacity, performers often use the technique of *chunking*. For example, a rugby player may use a set call or number to remember a pattern of moves, rather than each section individually. This allows other relevant information to enter the system, such as the changing positions and actions of the opposition. Also known as *working memory*.

short-term sensory store: component of the *memory* process, with a huge capacity to receive information, but which can only be retained for up to 1 second before it is lost. Information must be constantly gathered and updated via the *sensory system* and any *stimuli* that are relevant are passed onto the *short-term memory store* by the process of *selective attention*. For example, a rugby player will receive information concerning everything around them in the *display*, including the position of players, the crowd, the referee, all sounds and weather conditions, but they will only process those stimuli that affect their performance at that particular moment.

Shrove Tuesday: the Tuesday before Ash Wednesday, therefore the last day of Shrovetide. Preparations were made for Lent and this was a time for feasting and fun. Recreations took place within a wide social pattern and activities included *mob football*, wrestling, animal *baiting*, skittles and *bowls*.

shunting: the redistribution of blood that occurs in the body when exercising. The distribution of blood around the body changes significantly during exercise. At rest, only 15–20 per cent of blood flow is directed towards skeletal muscle, the majority going to the liver and kidneys, however, during maximal exercise, blood is redirected to areas where it is required most. For example, a cyclist working maximally may have up to 80 per cent of *cardiac output* directed to muscles of the legs ensuring that these working muscles gain sufficient oxygen and other nutrients. This increased blood flow to the muscle results from a restriction of blood flow to the kidneys, liver and stomach. Also known as accommodation.

significant other: person that is held in high esteem by the individual. Such people can influence the actions of the performer either positively or negatively (see *social facilitation*) and they can considerably affect the *socialisation* process. Significant others may include family, members of one's peer group, teachers, coaches and *role models*.

simple reaction time: the time taken to respond when presented with one *stimulus* and one possible response. For example, it is the time taken for a sprinter to start moving off the starting blocks when the gun has been fired. See also *choice reaction time*.

simple skill: actions that have basic movement patterns or those with little decision-making requirements and can be performed with minimum conscious control. Examples are running, *swimming* and *cycling* or more difficult skills that are well learned, such as passing and receiving a ball. They are easy to perform successfully in comparison to *complex skills*.

single channel hypothesis: a theory which states that when processing *stimuli* from the *environment* the brain can only deal with one piece of information at a time. Therefore during a game, a performer must clear the first stimulus received before reacting to the second and clear the 'bottleneck' that has been formed. For example, a defending basketball player may initially think that the attacker is going to pass the ball and so moves to intercept, but at the last moment the offensive player keeps the ball and plays it in another direction. The defender cannot clear the first information quickly enough to react to the actual movement of the ball. This creates the *psychological refractory period*.

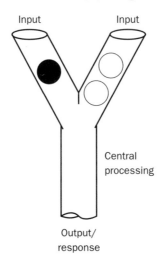

Input   Input

Central processing

Output/ response

sino-atrial node: a cluster of excitable cells within the heart which form the pacemaker. It is the sino-atrial node (SA node), which generates the heart rate by emitting impulses which are then conducted throughout the heart enabling blood to be pumped out and around the body. *Adrenaline* and *noradrenaline* are released prior to and during exercise by the *sympathetic nervous system* causing an increase in the rate at which these impulses are emitted from the SA node and therefore an increase in heart rate. This ensures that adequate amounts of oxygenated blood can be transported to the working muscles and blood high in carbon dioxide can be transported to and expelled via the lungs, to ensure optimum performance during exercise. See figure under *atrioventricular node*.

sit and reach test: a fitness test used to assess the *flexibility* of the hamstrings and lower back. The test can be easily administered and requires a sit-and-reach box. The subject sits on the floor with legs out straight, feet flat against the box and without bending the knees the subject reaches forward with arms outstretched and moves the cursor as far down the box as possible, holding the position for two seconds. The score is recorded and compared with standard tables.

skeletal muscle: a muscle of the body attached to a bone by a *tendon* and used primarily for movement. Skeletal muscle has several different properties which enable us to move and maintain posture:

- extensibility – the ability to lengthen, often whilst contracting
- elasticity – the ability to return to its normal resting length following stretching
- contractility – the ability of the muscle to shorten when contracting.

Skeletal muscle is voluntary and is therefore under our own control and this has important implications in the sporting arena as it is the individual who decides when each of their muscles contract. (See appendix, pages 260–7).

skeletal system: the bones and *ligaments* which form the skeleton. The term skeletal system covers all aspects of the skeleton including structure of bone tissue, types of bones, types of joint, as well as the *movement patterns* which can occur at these joints. It is therefore central to our study of movement. Major functions of the skeleton include:

- protection of vital organs
- production of red blood cells
- storage of minerals
- movement.

(See appendix, pages 257–9.)

skill: the learned ability to bring about pre-determined results with maximum certainty, often with the minimum outlay of time, energy or both. Performers who are said to be skilled often display similar characteristics including, consistency, efficiency, co-ordination, fluency, whilst completing a recognised technique allowing them to successfully achieve an end goal. Highly skilled performers are said to have reached the *autonomous stage of learning*. There are several types of skill including:

- *cognitive skills* – those involving mental processes; for example, problem solving, planning tactics and strategies to outwit an opponent during a game of hockey
- *perceptual skills* – those involving the interpretation of information entering the body via the sensory system; for example the position of players during the game and the possible options available to the performer
- *motor skills* – those involving the physical execution of the movement; for example, the passing of the ball or taking a shot at goal.

Skills are often classified using a continuum, with the most common being:

- *open – closed*
- *self-paced – externally paced*
- *gross – fine*
- *discrete – serial–continuous*.

skill-related fitness: those elements of fitness that involve the neuro-muscular system and determine how successfully a performer can complete a specific task. The difference between the skill-related components (which include *agility*, *balance*, *co-ordination*, *reaction time* and *power*) and health-related components (such as *strength*, *speed*, endurance, *flexibility* and *body composition*) can best be explained using the example of a tennis player. The performer may have the necessary physical attributes such as speed, stamina and strength to play a match, but if they possess poor agility and co-ordination they will not perform to a high level.

sliding filament theory: a microscopic process explaining how muscles contract. When viewed under a microscope, the process of muscle contraction can be explained by the complex co-operation of two proteins: a thick filament called *myosin* and a thinner filament known as *actin*. The figure on page 212 shows the structure of a muscle fibre when viewed under a microscope. The following events take place during contraction:

slow twitch muscle fibre

1   Upon the receipt of an impulse at the muscle fibre, calcium ions are released from the sarcoplasmic reticulum.

2   This removes the inhibitory effect of troponin and tropomyosin and exposes the binding site on the actin filament and allows the myosin crossbridge to attach to the actin forming the actomyosin complex.

3   Breakdown of *ATP* releases energy causing actin to slide over the myosin pulling the actin towards the middle of the *sarcomere*.

4   Since each actin filament is attached to 'z' lines the 'z' lines are pulled together, which shortens each sarcomere and so each muscle fibre.

5   It is the overlapping of the thick and thin filaments that is the key to the process of muscle contraction.

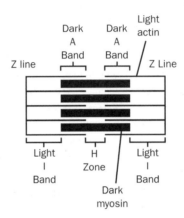

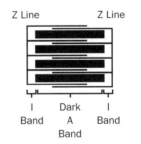

Z Line	= Marks the boundary of one sarcomere
I Band	= Actin only
A Band	= Actin and myosin
H Zone	= Mysosin only

slow twitch muscle fibre: fibres which are designed for endurance and are able to produce a large amount of energy using oxygen. They enable us to perform exercise over a long period of time and consequently there is likely to be a high percentage of slow twitch fibres in the legs of marathon runners and cyclists. Physiological characteristics include:

● high aerobic capacity

● high capillary density

- high myoglobin content
- high mitochondria density.

The fibres use glycogen and fat as fuels to produce contraction via the *aerobic energy system*. They are also known as 'type 1' muscle fibres. See also *fast twitch muscle fibre*.

smooth muscle: type of muscle which lies internally within the body and contracts in response to nerve impulses sent via the *autonomic (or involuntary) nervous system*. Smooth muscle is found within the muscular layer of the blood vessels, the intestines and the stomach. The blood vessels also act in response to other factors such as hormones, temperature and oxygen and carbon dioxide levels in the blood, and are essential for the smooth functioning of the body during exercise. For example, during exercise the carbon dioxide content within the working muscles increases, the chemo-sensitive areas of the blood vessels detect this and cause the blood vessel to dilate, enabling more blood to flow to the working muscle supplying oxygen and flushing away carbon dioxide. In this way the athlete can maintain optimal performance.

social classes: the divisions of a society defined on the basis of wealth, income, occupation and hereditary factors. Before the *Industrial Revolution* Britain had a two-tier structure – upper and lower class. With the development of society, increasing wealth through trade and education for all meant Britain became a three-tier social system – *upper*, *middle* and *working class*. Most people are found in the latter group. The upper classes tend to occupy the highest positions of wealth and status. It is increasingly difficult to differentiate between the middle and working classes, but generally the distinction is still based on the type of work done (manual or non-manual work).

social cohesion: the social interaction of group members, and how well they trust, communicate with and support each other. The *cohesion* of a group can be improved if both the social and *task cohesion* are good, although the group can be successful if only one of these elements is positive.

social control: the process whereby society seeks to ensure conformity to the dominant values and norms of that society. Formal and informal *socialisation* helps to ensure compliance. Sport has been used as a means of social control in many ways. See *athleticism* and *rational recreation*.

social facilitation: the influence of the presence of others on performance, which may be positive or negative. The *arousal* level of the individual increases, which could improve the performance of an experienced player or inhibit that of a novice (see *drive theory*). The 'others' include:

- the audience – those watching either at the event or at home via the media
- coactors – those performing the same task but not in competition
- competitive coactors – those in direct competition with the performer
- social reinforcers – such as a coach.

For example, in front of a large crowd a skilled gymnast will perform well with increased arousal levels, whereas the performance of a novice may decrease and they may experience *evaluation apprehension*. To reduce the negative effects of social facilitation the coach should encourage the individual to use *mental practice*, train in front of a crowd, develop their *selective attention* and reduce the importance of the event.

social inequality: the uneven distribution of resources in society which is reflected in an unequal distribution of prestige and feelings of superiority and inferiority amongst individuals. Examples in sport would be women, disabled and ethnic minority groups having less access to facilities and funding.

social learning theory proposes that people learn by observing others and then copying their actions. The repetition of an individual's behaviour is more likely to occur if *reinforcement* takes place, especially if it is received from a *significant other.* For example, if a young footballer observes a professional escaping a penalty or a booking after arguing with the referee they may feel this is acceptable behaviour. However, if the referee, disciplines the player and the child's parents agree that this decision was correct, the child will feel that this behaviour is unacceptable. Bandura suggested learning occurs in four phases:

- attention – the amount of notice taken by an individual while watching a model
- retention – the creation of a mental picture for future reference
- motor reproduction – if physically possible, the imitation of the model's actions by the individual
- motivation – the level of commitment to repeat the observed actions, which is often based on the reinforcement that is received and the importance of the task.

This form of learning is vital to the *socialisation* process within groups and society.

social loafing: the tendency of individuals to try to 'hide' when placed in a group situation and therefore not perform to their potential, because they feel their contribution is not being observed, evaluated or valued. It is important to eliminate such tendencies in order to develop the *actual productivity* of the group and improve group *cohesion.* Various methods can be employed to eradicate this situation, including:

- giving the performer a position of responsibility
- highlighting their specific role within the group
- evaluation of performance, feedback and praise
- variation of practice to maintain motivation
- avoidance of situations in which social loafing may occur
- development of team cohesion and social support from the peer group
- use of video analysis
- development of fitness, so performers don't need to 'take a break'.

See also *Ringelmann effect.*

social mobility: movements up or down the social class 'ladder'. The type of society can determine the extent to which movement is possible. For example, a *closed society* such as the Indian caste system is rigid and allows little, if any, movement of individuals. A democratic or *open society* is likely to be more fluid. Sport has often been an avenue of social mobility because:

- the emphasis on physical skills and abilities means that few formal qualifications are required
- sport may allow progression through the education system; for example, with sport *scholarships*

- occupational *sponsorship* may lead to future jobs
- sport can encourage values such as leadership and teamwork skills, which may help in the wider world of employment.

See also *stratification* and *upward social mobility.*

social order: the product of our adherence to society's rules and common ways of behaving. It is this that allows for predictability and gradual transitions in society rather than conflict, which can often bring about sudden change.

socialisation: the process whereby individuals learn the cultural *values* of their society. This is an ongoing process and individuals learn, via *social learning*, and they can expand, adapt or even reject the lessons learned. There are two types of socialisation:

- primary socialisation – where the family exert the greatest influence and which occurs in the early years
- secondary socialisation – where wider social agencies such as schools and the media operate. Conflict can occur if the learning in each differs.

See also *significant others.*

socialism: see *economic systems*

society: the totality of social relationships among organised groups of human beings and the distinctive cultural patterns and institutions they generate. A society will usually provide security, continuity and an identity for its members.

sociological theories: see *functionalist theory; interactionism; Marxism; symbolic interactionism.*

sociology: the study of the development, organisation, functioning and classification of human society. It developed as a field of study in the eighteenth and nineteenth centuries following the dramatic social changes around the scientific and *Industrial Revolutions*. It is a search for understanding and insight into the world that we inhabit.

somatic anxiety: refers to the individual's physiological responses when placed in a situation where they perceive an inability to complete the task successfully. For example, before a race a swimmer may experience increases in heart rate, sweating, *blood pressure*, muscle tension and feelings of nausea. All of which could hinder performance initially, but these symptoms often reduce when the event has started.

somatotype: method of classifying body shape. There are three extreme body shapes which have been identified:

- extreme endomorphs – characterised by a pear-shaped body, i.e. wide hips and narrow shoulders. They also tend to carry a lot of fat around their waist and limbs, for example a Sumo wrestler
- extreme mesomorphs – characterised by individuals with wide shoulders and narrow hips, rather like an inverted triangle, who tend to be much more muscular, for example a male gymnast
- extreme ectomorphs – characterised by individuals who are narrow at both the shoulders and the hips and tend to be very tall due to very long slender limbs; for example, a high jumper. Ectomorphs are generally very thin, possessing neither much fat nor muscle.

Although all extremes can be found, the majority of individuals are made up of all three body shapes. For example, a basketball player might have ectomorph characteristics since they are very tall, but also possess some mesomorph qualities as they also tend to be very muscular.

South Africa: a republic occupying the southern-most part of the African continent. British victory in the *Boer War* resulted in the formation of the Union of South Africa in 1910, but South Africa left the Commonwealth to become a republic in 1961. The controversial system of *apartheid* was implemented in 1948. Sport in South Africa is enormously popular and important with the games of cricket and rugby creating the most interest. They were both imperial games, were taught in the *public schools* which the officials and settlers attended and remained *amateur*. The smaller towns could not hope to compete with the *professional sports* in England, but in the amateur sports of rugby union and cricket they could compete with Britain on almost equal terms, with the *Springboks* winning their first test series in 1903. The triangular sporting exchange between Britain, South Africa and the Antipodes began at the turn of the century to become an established touring tradition following *World War I*. This all helped to emphasise the shared culture of the *British Empire*.

spa town: a place or resort where a mineral spring is to be found. Spa towns originated in Roman times and the *Tudors* established 'taking the waters' in the fashionable inland spa resorts because the water was considered to have beneficial healing properties. During the Georgian and *Victorian eras* the tradition continued of visiting the spas, which offered rest and relaxation away from the growing industrial towns. Some of the notable spa towns are Bath, Buxton and Harrogate.

spatial anticipation involves a performer attempting to predict what the actions of their opponent will be and formulating a response in readiness. For example, a batsman watches the bowler's action in preparation for the type of delivery they may receive. See also *temporal anticipation*.

specificity: a principle of training which suggests that any training undertaken should be relevant and appropriate to the sport for which the individual is training. For example, it would be highly inappropriate for a tri-athlete to concentrate solely on running as this is not relevant to the other two disciplines of *swimming* and *cycling*. The athlete would need to ensure that some training is undertaken in a swimming pool, some on a bicycle and some on the roads. In doing so the athlete will gain tremendous benefits by training all of the relevant muscles, types of fibre and energy systems, and of course improve technique.

spectator sport: a sport that attracts people as spectators rather than participants. The reorganisation of the population into large units during and following the *Industrial Revolution,* and the increased *leisure* time and income of the working classes, created the ideal conditions and market for mass entertainment on a commercial basis. Spectator violence has been a traditional aspect of some sports, particularly football. The rise in popularity of the sport and creation of rivalry between towns led to an increase in the number of *hooligans* and a corresponding rise in hooliganism. The development of the media, particularly television, created a new type of sports fan; the 'armchair enthusiast'. This term suggests that the participant takes no active part and is viewed as having both beneficial and detrimental effects on the participants and the sport. On the one hand it can increase interest in the sport but the lack of physical activity can have no physical benefits for the spectator.

speed: the maximum rate that a person can travel over a specific distance, and also how quickly a person can put body parts into action. A javelin thrower, for example, does not need to run at their maximum speed in their run-up but they do need to whip their arm through the centre line of their body as quickly as possible. Speed is classed as an *ability* that is largely genetically determined due to the physiological composition of the muscle, but it can still be improved through sprint *interval training* and *plyometrics*. *Biomechanics* and technique training are also essential in optimising the efficiency of the body's *lever* systems to improve speed of the body or body part.

sponsorship: the provision of funds or other forms of support to an individual or event for a commercial return. It is of mutual benefit to both parties. Sponsorship is now an intrinsic aspect of sports funding. Through the medium of television, business sponsors of sport can create the images they want, allowing identification with the sports and sportstars and introducing new audiences to their product.

The *Olympic Games* is one of the biggest global events in the world with sponsorship organised on a global basis. The Olympic Programme (TOP) involves approximately 44 companies, including Coca-Cola, Adidas and Kodak, and provides crucial, fundraising for the staging of the event.

Sponsorship has been a key factor in the redevelopment of many sports, providing capital for the sport and at the same time:

- securing an appropriate image for the sponsor, for example Gillette sponsors cricket, which creates an 'English' image for its product, while Coca-Cola sponsors the Olympics and school sport, conveying fun and liveliness

- achieving specific marketing objectives.

The disadvantages include:

- uneven development across some sports

- development of *elite* sport at the expense of *grass roots* sport

- male sport receives substantially more money than female sport.

sport: institutionalised competitive activities that involve vigorous physical exertion or the use of relatively complex physical skills by individuals whose participation is motivated by a combination of intrinsic and extrinsic factors.

Benefits of sport	Problems of sport
Acts as an emotional release	Can help to retain discrimination
Express individuality	Winning too important/financial rewards
Can help socialisation	Competition can be damaging
Individuals can achieve success	Spectatorism can outweigh participation
Can initiate social change	Dominated by media interest

Sport College status: the Sports College initiative was launched in 1996 with the first schools viable in September 1997. The government Department for Education and Skills lays down the guidelines and the *Youth Sports Trust* offers development and guidance. It is part of a specialised schools programme, which includes centres for technology, the arts and modern languages, an attempt to allow schools with particular strengths to build upon them and attract pupils with those interests. It was envisaged they would be centres for sport and physical education encompassing all sectors of the community. The objectives of the programme are to:

- extend the range of opportunities available to children which best meet their needs and interests
- raise the standard of teaching and learning for physical education and sport in schools
- develop characteristics which would identify the Colleges with their local communities and local schools
- be of benefit to local schools, within the 'family of schools network'
- attract local sponsors who should take an active role in the schools development
- show a 'vision' for each College in a document called a development plan.

sport competition anxiety test (SCAT): self-report questionnaire used to measure the *competitive trait anxiety* of a performer when placed in a pre-competitive sporting environ-ment (also known as Illinois competition questionnaire). It is used in an attempt to predict the anxiety levels of the individual in a specific situation. As a result the coach can develop appropriate *stress management* techniques to reduce high levels of anxiety. For example, if a sprinter knows they lose focus prior to the start of a race, techniques to improve concen-tration and self-confidence can be used. Further developments of this questionnaire produced the *competitive state anxiety inventory (CSAI-2)*, which measured both *cognitive* and *somatic anxiety*.

Sport England: the organisation responsible for leading the development of sport in England by influencing and serving the public, private and voluntary sectors. Its aim is to get:

- more people involved in sport
- more places to play sport
- more medals through higher standards of performance in sport.

Sport England came into being following the government report, 'Sport: *Raising the Game*' in 1997. The *UK Sports Council* oversees matters that need to be dealt with at the UK level, including issues such as *doping* control and decisions regarding the site of the *UK Sports Institute*. Sport England is accountable to Parliament through the Secretary of State for Culture, Media and Sport, who also appoints members of the Council of Sport England. There are ten regional offices across England which work with *local authorities*, sports *governing bodies*, plus regional and national organisations concerned with sport, recreation, education and the environment. The work of Sport England is jointly funded by grant in aid from the Exchequer, which pays for sport's infrastructure, and the National Lottery via the *lottery fund*.

Its *Sportsmark* and Sportsmark Gold award schemes also commit Sport England to improving standards of school sport, promoting the ideal of the minimum time for curricu-lum *physical education* as two hours a week.

Sport for All: a national and international campaign initiated by the *Council of Europe* which aims to increase the participation in physical activities of large population groups. It first appeared in Britain in 1972, launched by the then Sports Council. The Council of Europe published the *European Charter on Sport for All* in 1976. Sport in this instance covers activ-ities that come under the category of:

- *competition sport* and games
- outdoor and *adventurous activities*
- movement and *aesthetic* activities
- *conditioning activities.*

In Britain the aim is to:

- increase the participation rate overall
- improve performance at all levels
- provide facilities and resources that can be utilised as a social service
- promote awareness of a healthy lifestyle
- improve the quality of life.

Various campaigns were introduced to target specific groups, for example:

- Sport for All – Come Alive (1978)
- Sport for All Disabled People (1981)
- Fifty Plus – All to Play For (1983)
- Ever Thought of Sport? (1985)
- Year of Sport (1991).

Today two important campaigns are Football in the Community which links professional football clubs with facilities open to the public, and Action Sport which places an emphasis on inner city areas – this is popular with local authorities.

Sport Pour Tous: the French Sport for All campaign. In 1972 the French National Olympic and Sports Committees were given responsibility for a campaign to promote sport for all, following France's participation in the proceedings held by the *Council of Europe.* The campaign was intended to convince the public of the necessity of minimal participation in physical pursuits and sport and to enable their access irrespective of social status. It was specifically aimed at non-participating adults, with three levels at which intervention could occur:

- *leisure* time – adults were encouraged to practise a sport
- place of work – it was stressed that workers needed to be in better physical condition for their own safety
- place of residence – amenities were to be planned closer to places of residence.

The state finances sport in France to a greater degree than does the British system.

Sports Aid: set up in 1976 to enable top amateur athletes at both junior and senior level to train with similar privileges enjoyed by state-sponsored athletes abroad. It is a self-financing organisation, which draws its funds from commercial, industrial and private sponsors in addition to various fund-raising projects. Outstanding competitors usually receive the money according to their personal needs, cost of their preparation, training and competition, and are usually recommended by their *governing body*. Grants are also awarded through its charitable trust to talented athletes who are in education, on low income or disabled.

Sports Aid Foundation: see *Sports Aid*

sports medicine: the application of medicine to sport, and includes the services of, but is not limited to, athletic trainers, physicians, physical therapists, coaches, athletic administrators, exercise physiologists and nutritionists. The sports medicine professionals are involved with preventing injuries and developing training schedules.

Sports schools: schools that specialise in the development of young sport talent. Some British examples are Millfield, Kelly College, Reed's School and Lilleshall.

Advantages	Disadvantages
Quality coaching and education	Limits the pool of talent available
Accommodation and facilities	Exclusive
Medical science	Necessitates living away from home
Pooling of similar talent	High physical and psychological demand
Organised competition structure	*Burnout*
Links with professional clubs	

sports study sections (section sport etude): the French means of providing for talented youngsters within the education system. They provide special classes and schools specialising in certain sports. These have the usual advantages of *sports schools* – excellent facilities, coaching, medical and physiological tests and structured competition – while normal schooling continues. The pupils still work towards the *Baccalaureate* A, B, C, D or G and reach a certain level in their chosen sport. Movement on to specialist centres for specific sports excellence is possible but there is heavy competition for places.

Sportscoach UK: the organisation responsible for the development of coaching in Britain based in Leeds. It was established in 1983 to provide a range of educational and advisory services for all coaches and to complement the award schemes of the individual *governing bodies*. Its role has been to:

- develop sports science courses and generic courses rather than sport-specific ones
- produce coaching literature, videos, fact sheets and databases
- establish a Network of National Coaching (NCC) in higher education institutions
- make links with local authorities and national governing bodies
- develop coaching qualifications such as the Diploma in Professional Studies, Coaching for Teachers and progressive coaching course levels.

Its main sources of funding are from the *UK Sport*, earned income and other grant aid donations.

In 2001 the National Coaching Foundation was rebranded to Sportscoach UK. Membership reached 12,000 and achieved recognition from Sporting Equals for their work to support the development of coaches from black and ethnic minority communities. The Sportscoach UK mission statement is aimed at guiding the development and implementation of a coaching system, recognised as a world leader, for all coaches at every level in the UK.

The central theme of the mission statement is to describe what a world-class coaching system looks like. It is likely to include:

- coach development linked firmly to player development
- continuous learning and inclusive practice based on a strong foundation of research, continuous professional development and ethical practice
- central co-ordination by an organisation empowered to do so but 'owned' by everybody
- simplicity and flexibility, not hierarchy and rigid bureaucracy
- use of a common framework of agreed national standards
- shared strategic approaches with common generic components
- effective management of coaches (paid and unpaid) and their development through registers/licences
- not allowing organisations and/or individuals to opt out of the system
- a focus at all levels on adding value to the experience of the individual player/performer and the individual coach as well as the player–coach interaction.

sportsmanship: qualities displayed by a person or team that are highly regarded in sports such as fairness, generosity, observance of the rules and good humour on losing. This was one of the defining qualities of the *gentleman amateur* and *athleticism.*

Sportsmark: a scheme introduced in the government report Sport: *Raising the Game* in 1995, that recognises and rewards schools that provide the best *physical education* and sports provision to their pupils and the local community. The additional gold award is presented to those offering exceptional provision. To obtain the award, various criteria have to be achieved. Recently the *Activemark* and Activemark Gold scheme have been introduced to include primary, middle and special schools. See also *Active Sports Programme.*

Sportsmatch: the government's '£1 for a £1' business *sponsorship* incentive scheme which was established in 1992. It provides funding for *grass roots* development of sport and funds of over £3.7 million a year in the UK to match funds from the private sector. It is administered by the *Institute of Sports Sponsorship* in co-operation with *Sport England* and provides an excellent opportunity for sports bodies and sponsors to double the value of their project investment or to mount extra activities or events, which must be competitive, challenging and physically skilful. The awards panel is particularly interested in developing projects for rural and inner cities that lack sporting resources.

Springbok: an athlete who has represented *South Africa* in international competitions, especially in the sports of *cricket* and *rugby.*

S–R bond: see *stimulus–response bond*

S–R theories: see *associationist theories*

stable personality: a person who is calm, even-tempered, lively, controlled and reliable with good leadership qualities. They display traits linked to their autonomic nervous system, which responds slowly and minimally to stressful situations, causing the individual to be even-tempered and stable. They possess the opposite traits to those with a *neurotic personality* and are placed at the other end of the *continuum.* These characteristics can be measured using the *Eysenck personality inventory (EPI)* or *Cattell's 16 personality factors questionnaire.*

stacking: the disproportionate concentration of ethnic minorities in certain positions in a sports team, which tends to be based on the *stereotyped* view that they are best suited to roles which require physical skill rather than decision-making and communication qualities. In *American football* there has been a tendency to place ethnic players in running back and wide receiver positions rather than the pivotal position of quarterback. In baseball, until fairly recently they have tended to be placed in outfield positions. Also see *centrality*.

stages of learning: see *Fitts and Posner's stages of learning*

stamateur: see *amateurism*

Starling's law of the heart suggests that *cardiac output* is dependent upon the extensibility of cardiac muscle fibres. The more the cardiac muscle fibres are stretched during the diastolic (filling) stage of the *cardiac cycle*, the stronger the walls can contract and force blood into the circulatory system. The action is similar to filling a balloon with water: the more water that enters the balloon, the more the balloon stretches. Furthermore, during exercise the elasticity of cardiac fibres increases due to an increase in body temperature and the release of hormones such as *adrenaline* and *noradrenaline*, consequently causing *stroke volume* and therefore *cardiac output* to increase.

state: a term that encompasses all the major organisations which are agencies of the governing institutions in society. This includes, for example, the Royal family, Parliament and the civil service, the military, social security and education. State activity has increased during the twentieth century and this has meant an extension of state power. Also see *centralised*.

state anxiety: form of *anxiety* that occurs when the performer is placed in a particular situation that can vary from moment to moment. For example, an individual may become anxious immediately prior to the start of a race or match due to their perceived inability to cope with the situation. However, this may reduce when the event has started and increase again when faced with a new challenge, such as taking a penalty. Both *cognitive* and *somatic anxiety* may be experienced during this time. Also known as 'A state'.

state education: schools maintained by public spending, either through local education authorities or directly from central government as in the case of *grant-maintained schools*. State education began in Britain following the Forster Education Act 1870 (see *Education Acts*).

steady state: the plateau reached by of heart rate during sub-maximal, low-intensity exercise. If the heart rate is experiencing steady state, it is assumed that the oxygen demands made by the muscles are being met by the heart supplying sufficient quantities of blood. For example, a person jogging will be in 'steady state', whereas a sprinter during a 400-metres race will not. (See figure opposite.)

Steiner's model of group productivity: see *group productivity*

stereotype: a standardised image or concept shared by all members of a social group. In other words, certain behaviour traits are associated with particular types of individuals or groups. This usually involves negative images relating to gender and race. Our *attitudes* can affect our behaviour towards these groups or individuals. This is significant when it comes to issues like the expectations of teachers regarding the sporting potential of boys and girls.

stimulants: drugs or similar substances that increase physiological activity. An example of a stimulant is amphetamine. Stimulants are one of the most widely used manufactured drugs, being used to improve endurance performance, increase mental and physical alertness, decrease fatigue and increase metabolism, but they can lead to increases in heart rate and *blood pressure*. The more an athlete uses stimulants, the less effect they have on the body, so the athlete needs to take more. See also *doping*.

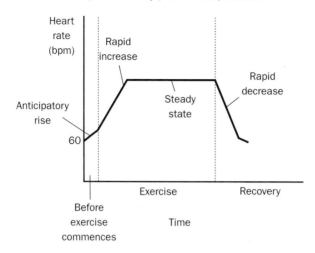

a) Low intensity (sub-maximal) exercise

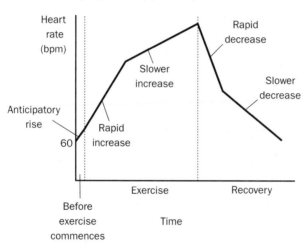

b) High intensity (maximal) exercise

Steady state

stimulus: any information that enters the body via the *sensory system*. Sports performers have to use the various stimuli presented to them from the *display* during *information processing*, often ignoring irrelevant details and focusing their attention on useful *cues*. The effective interpretation of this data can reduce *reaction time*. For example, the performer will note the location of themselves, team mates and opponents, the speed and direction of any object being used, the position and decision of the referee, the reaction of the crowd, the weather conditions, instructions from the coach as well as any pain or discomfort they may be experiencing.

stimulus–response bond: the relationship between a stimulus and the specific action that it initiates. These bonds form the basis of the *associationist theories* of learning. For example, when a badminton player sees their opponent at the rear of the court (stimulus), they may be conditioned to play their shot to the front (response).

stimulus–response compatibility: the degree to which the response to a given stimulus appears 'natural'. If a performer is presented with a situation in which they have been before and know how to react, their *reaction time* will be reduced. For example, if a table tennis player receives a shot that is high enough off the table to play a smash return, and through experience they recognise that option is available, the chance of a successful return will be increased. Similarly, if an opponent always returns the ball to the same place when playing a backhand stroke, the performer can learn to recognise this and execute their own shot more quickly when it occurs.

strategies: the plans and decision-making activities that are made in advance of sport performance. The type of strategy will depend on the nature of the sport being undertaken, for example:

- a *gymnastic activity* is about selecting or designing sequences that have varying levels of difficulty and also requires artistic interpretation
- an *invasion game* requires planning in advance as to how opponents are to be out-manoeuvred, but the strategy will need to be adapted depending on the opponents' play.

stratification: the division of society or any other group of people into layers based on biological, economic and social criteria, for example age, gender, race and *social class*. The *dominant culture* controls the more subordinate groups which can include women, ethnic minorities and the disabled. Wealth, status and hereditary factors can be influential, wealth and income being prominent in more modern societies. Those at the top have greater access to scarce resources compared with those at the bottom. Stratification in sport is inevitable when winning is highly valued. It is highlighted even more when monetary rewards are on offer. Also see *discrimination* and *social mobility*.

streamlining: the reduction in drag and promotion of *laminar flow* as a body or other object passes through air or water. For example, cyclists have attempted to streamline through the design of cycling helmets, shape of the bicycle and adopting more streamlined positions whilst riding. Swimmers attempt to minimise drag by wearing shiny swimsuits and swimming hats and shaving down (the removal of body hair), all of which allow the water to flow past the body more smoothly.

strength: the maximum force that can be developed within a muscle or group of muscles during a single maximal contraction. Strength is required in many activities but particularly in those that are *anaerobic* in nature and of high intensity such as weightlifting or *gymnastics*.

Several different types of strength have been identified, including:

- maximum strength – used in an all-out explosive event such as the shot putt
- elastic strength – evident in activities where a high speed of contraction is required such as in sprinting
- strength endurance – concerned with the avoidance of muscle fatigue and required in activities such as rowing and swimming.

Due to the diverse nature of strength, prescribing a training programme to encompass every athlete's requirements is obviously difficult. It is commonly agreed, however, that in resistance and weight training, to develop maximum strength the use of very high-resistance activities with relatively few repetitions is favoured, whilst strength endurance would involve the use of lighter resistance with a greater number of repetitions. Strength can be assessed by the use of dynamometers (the most common being the handgrip dynamometer) or by the one repetition maximum test (IRM).

strength training: a method of training used to develop *strength*. There are various varied ways to develop strength such as *circuit training* or *plyometrics*, but the most common is weight training. The use of weights can be adapted to meet the needs of specific individuals. For example, the weight lifter wishing to develop maximum strength will use heavy weights (high intensity – 90 per cent of IRM) and perform a low number of repetitions (six). The sprinter wishing to develop elastic strength will use medium to heavy weights (75 per cent IRM) with up to 12 repetitions. Whilst the rower wishing to develop strength endurance will use light to medium weights (50–60 per cent IRM) but perform a high number of repetitions (20).

stress occurs as a result of the individual perceiving an imbalance between the demands of a task and their ability to meet them. Stress can have positive or negative effects on performance. Those who seek out stressful situations and benefit from them experience *eustress*, while performers who react negatively to stress experience *anxiety*. For example, one person might enjoy the feelings created by diving off a high-board, while another may become very anxious at the thought of such a task. The various factors which facilitate such a response are known as *stressors*. These cause the body to undergo a series of sensations known as the *general adaptation syndrome*. It is vital that individuals are able to control their stress levels, employing appropriate *stress management* techniques to achieve an optimum level of performance. See also *type A personality* and *type B personality*.

stress management: techniques employed to lower the levels of *anxiety* experienced by an individual in order to improve performance. For example, the heart rate of a diver may increase while preparing for their final dive of the competition and they may worry about executing the sequence incorrectly. If they can control their breathing and think positively about their performance these symptoms of stress may decrease.

The techniques are generally sub-divided into:

- somatic methods – aim to decrease the physiological responses. They include *biofeedback*, breathing control or *centering* and *relaxation*
- cognitive methods – aim is to decrease the psychological worries. They include *goal setting*, *imagery* or visualisation and *self-talk*.

stressors: demands that are placed on the performer that initiate *stress*. For example, the nature of the competition, any threat to personal safety, conflict, frustration, pressure, the audience, the unknown and climate may trigger such a response.

stroke volume: the volume of blood ejected from the left ventricle of the heart per beat. Normal stroke volume at rest is approximately 70 ml of blood, but this can increase two-fold during medium- to high-intensity exercise. This increase is largely explained by *Starling 's law*, which suggests that the fibres of the heart muscle stretch during exercise, enabling the ventricles to fill with larger volumes of blood and causing the heart to contract with greater force. Resting stroke volume shows a significant increase following an endurance training programme, with highly trained athletes experiencing resting stroke volumes of up to 120 ml. This is largely explained by the enlargement of the heart that accompanies training, enabling the heart to fill with more blood due to a longer diastolic phase. Other factors affecting stroke volume include:

- age – stroke volume decreases with increasing age
- sex – females have a lower stroke volume due to having smaller hearts and lower testosterone levels.

structural functionalism: a form of *functionalist theory* associated with Talcott Parsons which views social structures in a positive light. That is, they exist for the good of society. However, it does not explain why structures such as criminal organisations exist.

Stuart era: period after the death of Elizabeth I, when James VI of Scotland became James I of England. He issued the *Book of Sports* as a result of the growing influence of the *Puritans*. His son Charles I was executed but Charles II returned as monarch in 1660. This was known as the Restoration period, as it was to restore many of the previously banned activities such as the *Dover Games*. Charles II was in favour of many sports and his court enjoyed a lifestyle of ease, affluence and leisure, occupying themselves lavishly on sporting pursuits and enjoying a revival of the 'courtly mould'.

subculture: a group in society which shares common values and attitudes that are based on social criteria (e.g. ethnicity) or on styles and trends (e.g. 'hell's angels'). These groups may well share some of the features of the *dominant culture* but may also be opposed to it in some manner. Examples within sport would include football *hooligans*, rugby clubs and surfers.

subjective: based on individual interpretation of behaviour, actions or events. Some testing methods, such as observation and interviewing, rely on the researcher's own interpretation of the results rather than interpreting them on the basis of *objective* data. For example, when observing a player during a hockey match who fails to receive a pass for several minutes, one person may feel they are being lazy or are *social loafing*, and not working to get the ball. However, another observer may conclude that simply play has not moved into that area of the field. The winners of some sporting activities are decided partly subjectively by a panel of judges, for example *gymnastics*, diving and skating.

subroutine: phase of a movement pattern which must be executed at the appropriate time in the sequence if the skill is to be successful. A series of subroutines combine to form an *executive motor programme*. For example, the high jump could be split into the run-up, take-off, flight and landing.

summer camps: see *camps*

superficial: structures or muscles of the body which lie closer to the surface of the body than others. For example, the soleus muscle in the calf lies above the tibialis posterior and is therefore classed as a superficial muscle.

superior: a structure above or closer to the head than another. For example, the superior vena cava lies above the inferior vena cava, entering the heart from above. (See appendix.)

supination: a movement pattern characterised by the rotation of the forearm laterally so that the palm of the hand faces upwards. Supination occurs in the horizontal or transverse plane about a longitudinal axis and occurs, for example, during the recovery phase of a breaststroke arm 'pull' or at the forearm of the right arm during a 'flick' in hockey. (See appendix.)

Swedish gymnastics: gymnastics that originated from Sweden under the name of Per Henrik Ling. The British school boards of the nineteenth century tended to favour Swedish gymnastics as being suitable for state schools for a variety of reasons:

- its free-flowing, free-standing exercises were cheap to implement
- its method of instruction was based on discipline which was considered suitable for *working class* children
- it drew on the knowledge of the human body available at that time
- its therapeutic effects were considered important for the working classes, who were generally in poor health.

swimming: a method of propulsion through the water. It is highly valued as both *recreation* and as an opportunity for vigorous physical activity. The sport goes back to ancient Greece and Rome, being considered an important part of warriors' training. Swimming was introduced into the Olympic programme in Athens in 1896. It became popular in Britain with the building of public facilities under the Public Baths and Washhouse Act in 1840, the publicity of feats such as Captain Webb swimming the English Channel, and the formation of the Amateur Swimming Association.

Syllabuses of Physical Training (1904, 1909, 1919, 1927, 1933): syllabuses outlining courses of exercises that were required by the *Board of Education* to be carried out in state schools. Due to concerns over the *model course* the Board of Education established these syllabuses since they provided prescriptive outlines that teachers who were generally unqualified to teach physical training (PT) found easy to implement. They stressed the physical and educative effects of physical activities:

- the therapeutic effect: the correction of posture faults and exercises to improve the circulatory system
- the educational effect: the development of alertness and decision-making ability.

They were a *centralised* policy.

symbolic interactionism: a concept, developed by Weber, that assumes we live in a symbolic world in which symbols have shared meanings. An example would be language or sport. It assumes that human behaviour involves choices based on the meanings that individuals attach to events, and these are transmitted down through the generations. This theory relies heavily of the concept of the self, individuals interpreting the connections between themselves and their social world and hence calculating the effects of their actions.

In a sporting context, symbolic interaction looks at how people see the world of sport; how they see themselves in relation to sport and what choices they make regarding, for example, their level of sport participation. This theory is useful when looking at various social groups and how and why they operate, but it does not help when looking at issues such as inequality in sport.

sympathetic nervous system: one of the two subdivisions of the *autonomic (or involuntary) nervous system* (the other being the *parasympathetic nervous system*) which is primarily in operation when energy is required. During exercise, its effects tend to oppose those of the parasympathetic nervous system, with the sympathetic fibres releasing *adrenaline* and *noradrenaline* which initiates the body's *fight or flight response*. This in turn produces many physiological effects designed to maximise performance. For example, both the rate and strength of contraction of the heart increase, blood vessels supplying skeletal muscle, cardiac muscle and the lungs all increase in size to ensure a greater volume of blood flow, the bronchioles dilate to ensure efficient exchange of oxygen and carbon dioxide and energy availability increases due to quicker conversion of glycogen to glucose. All these factors occur without us having to control them and are a natural response of the body.

synergist: a muscle which contracts to enhance the efficiency of the *prime mover* by preventing any undesired movement. It forms part of the co-operation or *antagonistic* effect of the muscles which work together to ensure that co-ordinated movement can take place. For example, when performing a bicep curl, the deltoids are synergists since they work to prevent any undesired movement at the shoulder, and in doing so enable the bicep to work as effectively as possible. Also known as neutralisers.

synovial fluid: a fluid rich in protein which is released from the synovial membrane of freely moveable *synovial joints*. It lubricates the ends of the bones as they move against each other (articulate) and nourishes the *articular cartilage* that covers the ends of bones. During exercise more synovial fluid is released which is soaked up by the articular cartilage, causing it to swell and offer greater protection and ease of movement.

synovial joint: joint which allows a wide range of movement and which is composed of two or more bones which exist in a joint capsule. The ends of these bones are covered in *articular cartilage* and are separated by a joint cavity filled with *synovial fluid*. Although all synovial joints are similar in structure and possess common features, variations do exist due to the shape of the articulating surfaces:

- hinge joint – the convex surface of one bone fits into the concave surface of another. Built for stability, movement only usually occurs in one plane and is limited to *flexion* and *extension*, for example the knee joint

- pivot joint – a rounded, peg-like structure of one bone that slots into a ring-shaped cavity of another to allow rotation. For example between the ends of the radius and ulna at the elbow, which enables *pronation* and *supination* of the forearm to occur and also at the neck

- gliding joint – the articulating surfaces in gliding joints are usually flat and often allow a small degree of movement in all directions, for example the bones of the carpals

- saddle joint – as the name suggests, one bone at this joint is shaped like a saddle whilst the other resembles a rider sitting in the saddle. This joint allows flexion, extension, *abduction* and *adduction* and only truly occurs where the carpal and metacarpal of the thumb meet

- ellipsoid joint – an oval-shaped end of one bone fits into an elliptical depression of another bone allowing movements in two planes (flexion, extension, abduction and adduction). An example includes the wrist joint where the radius meets the carpals

- ball and socket joint – a rounded head of one bone fits into a cup-shaped cavity, enabling the widest range of movement. For example, the shoulder joint enables flexion, extension, abduction, adduction, *circumduction* and *rotation*.

systemic circulation: component of the circulatory system which conducts oxygenated blood from the left ventricle to all the major organs of the body (excluding the lungs) and returns to the right atrium via the venae cavae. The distribution of blood throughout the systemic circulatory system alters significantly during exercise, so that more blood can supply the working muscles.

systole: the period of contraction of the heart during the *cardiac cycle*. 'Atrial systole' is the contraction of the *atria* forcing blood into the ventricles, whilst 'ventricular systole' is the contraction of both ventricles causing blood to exit the heart and flow around the body and to the lungs. Training can result in an increase in the force at which the heart can contract, due to the thickening of the cardiac muscle (*myocardium*) and therefore the systolic capacity of the heart.

What other subjects are you studying?

A–Zs cover 18 different subjects. See the inside back cover for a list of all the titles in the series and how to order.

Thomas Arnold: see *Arnold, Thomas*

thoracic vertebrae: the second region of the vertebral column containing 12 individual bones. Its function is to enable the 12 pairs of ribs to attach to the vertebral column so that the body's respiratory function can take place. The ribs pivot on the facet of the vertebrae enabling the rib cage to move upwards and outwards. In this way the lungs can inflate and *inspiration* can occur. (See appendix, page 258.)

Thorndike's laws of learning: three laws proposed by Thorndike which, if employed, were said to increase the likelihood of learning taking place during *operant conditioning*. The laws are:

- law of readiness – the performer has to be physically and mentally able to complete the task
- law of exercise – the performer must practice the task regularly in favourable conditions
- law of effect – the performer is more likely to repeat the task if their behaviour is followed by experiences of satisfaction (see *reinforcement* and *punishment*).

thought stopping: recognising and blocking worrying or negative thoughts about performance when they start to develop. As soon as this takes place a *cue*, action or word is used to redirect attention to positive thoughts. For example, a basketball player who has missed several shots and is beginning to worry might click their fingers or say 'focus' to themselves. As a result they concentrate on the action, technique or tactic for the next attempt, rather than think about the previous attempts. See also *self-talk*.

threshold: commonly used to identify the point at which one energy system becomes exhausted and another takes over. For example, the ATP-PC/lactic acid threshold will signify the point at which the *lactic acid* becomes the predominant system used in providing energy for resynthesis of *adenosine triphosphate (ATP)*.

Thurston scale: questionnaire to evaluate the *attitude* of an individual. It is composed of a series of favourable and unfavourable statements about the *attitude object*. The individual simply agrees or disagrees with each statement and the average is calculated to produce a score, which can be compared with others. See also *attitude tests*.

tidal volume: the volume of air inspired or expired per breath. A normal resting volume is approximately 500 ml but this can increase during exercise by using the *inspiratory* and *expiratory reserve volumes*.

Tidal volume can be calculated by dividing minute ventilation (volume of air inspired or expired in one minute) by the number of breaths taken per minute. See appendix, page 273.

tiers temps: a French term, which translated means 'one third teaching time'. This is a fixed weekly quota of 27 hours to be spent at school. Of these 27 hours six are supposed to be devoted to *physical education*. This can vary in practice depending on individual schools, their facilities and staff. They can be used for a block of teaching such as the *transplant classes*.

Title IX: federal legislation in the *United States of America*, under the education amendment of 1972, relating to the equality of opportunity for women in sport programmes. It made compulsory the equal treatment of men and women in education programmes that were in receipt of federal funding. The Department of Health, Education and Welfare released and enacted it in 1972. It stated that no *discrimination* should occur with respect to the programmes offered, the quality of teaching or the availability of facilities, medical services and travel allowances, and women could take a case as far as the supreme court.

Tom Brown's Schooldays: book written by Thomas Hughes, published in 1860, based at Rugby School. It expanded the ideals of manliness within the *muscular Christianity* movement.

Top Club: see *National Junior Sport Programmes*

Top Play: see *National Junior Sport Programmes*

Top Sport: see *National Junior Sport Programmes*

torque: the turning effect of a body or object. It is dependent upon the force and the length of the lever arm. The greater the lever arm or the larger the force, the greater the rotation. For example, a rower may increase their torque by their pulling harder or by lengthening the oar.

total lung capacity: the sum of residual volume, expiratory reserve volume, tidal volume and inspiratory reserve volume or, more simply, the volume in the lungs at the end of maximal inspiration. Because of the difficulty in measuring an individual's residual volume, it is difficult to give an objective figure to total lung capacity, but it averages around 6000 ml. Through endurance training, it may be possible to strengthen respiratory muscles and improve respiratory efficiency, and consequently increase total lung capacity. See appendix, page 273.

Tour de France: the first of the national stage races and the main professional event of the continental cycling season, founded by Desgranges in 1903. The yellow jersey was introduced in 1919 to distinguish the race leader at the end of the stage in which he takes the overall lead. The significance of the colour yellow is that it was the colour of the sponsoring newspaper 'L'Auto'.

tourism: the commercial organisation of tourist travel from a place of residence to a holiday destination or place of interest. Generally tourists stay long enough in a place to undertake some activities and use the local facilities. The most common motivations for tourism are rest and relaxation, visiting friends and relatives, business, attending festivals, exhibitions, conventions and sporting events. There are various sectors of the tourism industry including:

- transport, for example air, rail, ferry
- accommodation and catering, for example hotels and restaurants
- tour operators and travel agents
- visitor attractions and events
- services, for example financial, guides, tourist information
- tourism organisations, for example tourist boards.

The increased demand for tourism has gone hand in hand with the growth of *leisure* time generally. There are definite links between leisure and tourism, and sport has been and continues to be an area of high-priority spending for many people. Activities like *cycling*, walking and *golf* have helped to create new resorts, and events like the *Olympic Games* attract thousands of spending visitors. (See diagram on page 234.)

trabeculae: the criss-cross matrix of bony plates which makes up *cancellous bone*. Training (particularly *strength training*) can cause an increase in the density of these bony plates thereby strengthening the bones.

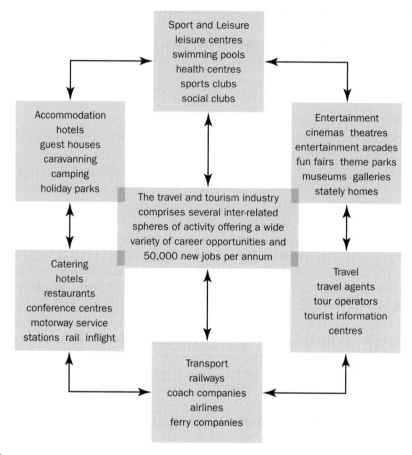

Tourism

trachea: an air passage forming part of the respiratory system extending from the larynx, directing air into the left and right primary bronchi. It is composed of 18 horseshoe-shaped rings of cartilage lined with a mucous membrane and ciliated cells which help to warm, moisten and filter the air ready for gaseous exchange in the lungs.

training zone: the rate at which the heart should beat during training to be of benefit to the cardiovascular system. This is best determined using the *Karvonen principle*, but can be calculated more simply as 60–85 per cent of *maximum heart rate (MHR)*.

trait: innate, enduring characteristic possessed by an individual that can be used to explain and predict their behaviour in different situations. Traits combine to form an individual's unique *personality*. For example, if a performer displays leadership qualities in one situation, they could do so in other situations. See also *trait theories*.

trait anxiety: the general disposition of an individual to perceive situations as threatening. If a performer possesses this characteristic they are more likely to become anxious in a wide variety of situations, experiencing a higher *state anxiety* than are those with low levels of trait anxiety. Such individuals may develop a high competitive state anxiety when placed in a challenging sporting environment. Also known as 'A trait'. See also *competitive trait anxiety*.

trait theories: theories that propose that the personality of an individual is made up of a number of characteristics or *traits*, which determine their behaviour in particular situations. After completing a *personality test* individuals are usually placed on two continuums:

* *extrovert – introvert*

* *stable – neurotic*

It was suggested that because of these specific traits, participation and performance in particular activities could be predicted. For example, extroverts would be more likely to play team sports, while introverts would be drawn towards individual activities. However, this has never been proven conclusively and critics of the theory argue it is too simplistic, failing to take account of the effect of environmental situations and learning experiences. Individuals may have core traits, but behaviour is specific to a particular situation. For example, a professional footballer may appear extrovert on the field, but in private be more introverted and reserved.

transfer of learning: the effect that the leaning or performance of one skill has on the learning or performance of another skill. The coach can apply this knowledge in order to reduce learning time and maximise the effectiveness of training time with the performer. For example, a basketball player might be encouraged to use their skills of handling, movement and spatial awareness when introduced to the game of netball. However the habit of performing certain skills may hinder their development, such as dribbling and shooting at the basket without the use of a backboard. Various forms of transfer exist as outlined below:

* positive transfer – previously learned skills that aid the learning of new skills, such as the basketball player utilising their passing skills when playing netball. To be effective practices should be relevant to those experienced in a game situation so that both skills and tactical decisions can be transferred. The performer should be aware of this form of transfer and possible links between skills should be encouraged

* negative transfer – previously learned skills that hinder the learning of new skills, such as the basketball player wishing to dribble the ball. Usually this is temporary and can be eliminated with careful construction of training practices, informing the performer of difficulties of which to be aware and allowing them the opportunity to reorganise their cognitive processes to adjust their movement patterns

* pro-active transfer – occurs when a skill currently being learned has an effect on a skill in the future. For example, the basketball player will learn the basic techniques of passing, footwork and dribbling before moving onto more advanced skills or implementing them in a game situation

* retro-active transfer – occurs when a skill currently being learned has an effect on one previously learnt. For example, the basketball player may develop new methods of dribbling the ball as they become more experienced and alter their initial technique, allowing them to execute more complex moves

* bilateral transfer – the transfer of learning from one limb to another, rather than task to task. The development of a skill with one limb will improve the performance of the opposite limb. There is no clear evidence as to why this occurs, but possibly the cognitive process of knowing how to complete the action and the creation of a generalised motor programme allows for adaptation. For example, games players are

encouraged to practice their skills with both the left and right sides of their body, such as passing, dribbling and kicking, in order to improve their overall performance

- zero transfer – occurs when the learning of one skill has no influence on the development of another skill. For example, the skills of a basketball player would not affect the skills executed during a rock climb

- near transfer – occurs when the performer experiences practices which are similar to the 'real game'. For example, the basketball players may have to shoot from outside a zone defence or practice moves to execute when confronted with a 2 v 1 option, which they may have to face in a match

- far transfer – occurs when the performer experiences practices that develop general skills or tactics, which may be used later in more specific situations. For example, a coach may use a variety of small-sided games to develop the handling and movement skills of novices, which may be transferred later to a game of basketball or other ball game.

transitional economies: see *economic systems*

translatory mechanism: see *decision-making*

transplant classes: classes in the French primary school educational system, whereby a whole class can be transplanted from its school to a place in the country. The children can spend two to three weeks away from home in three different types of classes:

- classes le vert – in the countryside
- classes le niege – snow classes
- classes le mer – water classes.

The varied climate and landforms offer excellent choices in outdoor pursuit activities and the classes encourage children to appreciate the *natural environment*. The teacher accompanies the children, to combine normal teaching in the morning with an outdoor activity in the afternoon.

transport revolution: the vast improvement made to the communication system in the nineteenth century. This included the expansion of the *railways*, canals and roads, which allowed people, ideas, services and goods to become mobile and spread around the country.

transverse axis/plane: an imaginary line running horizontally across the body, dividing it into superior (top) and inferior (bottom) sections. A person performing a tucked front somersault, for example, will rotate about the transverse axis. Also known as the horizontal axis/plane. (See appendix, page 256.)

triadic model: see *attitude*

trial and error learning: early theory of learning, proposing that responses that do not achieve the desired effect will be gradually eliminated and those that do are gradually strengthened. Also known as *operant conditioning*.

trochanter: a very large protrusion found on the surface of a bone. The best examples include the greater and lesser trochanter found on the femur.

trust funds: the means for an amateur athlete to receive money from their sport. They are managed by *governing bodies* and accept money from subventions, advertising services or as participation money. They will be held until retirement from sport, but funds for athletic expenses can be withdrawn before retirement.

Tudor period: the era between 1485 and 1714. England changed rapidly during the time of the Tudors, and under the rule of Henry VIII there was greater prosperity and more time for cultural pursuits like music, literature and the theatre. He was a great sports lover and created one of the liveliest courts in Europe. He participated in all-day hunts, wrestling and ordered his own real tennis court to be built at Hampton Court. Access to education, equipment and facilities allowed the upper classes the privilege of exclusive recreational activities. Under Elizabeth I, England prospered leading to the age of the Renaissance gentleman who was knowledgeable, took part in physical activities and was appreciative of art forms, while the mass of the population enjoyed their traditional pastimes of *mob games* and *animal sports.*

type A personality: a set of personality characteristics which when present together increase the risk of stress-related heart disease. Performers who may fall into this category are often competitive, self-critical, feel they are working against the clock, often multi-tasking and avoid delegation, prefer to complete the work themselves. Some Type A performers are capable of achieving success and appear to be fully in control of situations.

type B personality: a set of personality characteristics which may indicate a lower reaction to stressful structures. In comparison to *type A personality* performers, they are more relaxed, less competitive, delegate tasks easily, more tolerant and calmer when dealing with problem situations.

Do you know we also have A–Zs for:

- Biology
- Geography
- Travel and Leisure
- Health and Social Care?

Ask for them in your local bookshop or see the inside back cover for ordering details.

UK Sport: the organisation responsible for developing *elite* sport in the United Kingdom. Its main aim is to provide the best sportsmen and women with the support they need to compete and win at the highest level, with the express aim of achieving sporting excellence on the world stage. It takes the lead among the sports councils (England, Northern Ireland, Scotland and Wales) in all aspects of sport which require co-ordination or representation for the benefit of the UK as a whole. It is a small organisation with only 33 members of staff and a budget of £11.6 million. It holds the Royal Charter, meaning it is supposedly free from political control, and has a range of objectives:

- to encourage and develop higher standards of sporting excellence in the UK
- to identify sporting policies that should have a UK-wide application
- to identify areas of unnecessary duplication, overlap and waste in the way that sport is administered in the UK
- to develop and deliver appropriate grant programmes developed by the governing bodies with a UK or Great Britain remit in conjunction with the home country sports councils
- to oversee policy on sports science, sports medicine, drug control and coaching
- to co-ordinate policy for bringing major international sporting events to the UK
- to represent the UK internationally and increase the influence of the UK at an international level.

It delivers these objectives via four key directorates:

- Performance Development
- *UK Sports Institute (UKSI)*
- International Relations and Major Events
- Ethics and Anti-doping.

UK Sports Council: see *UK Sport*

Union National de Sport de Scolaire (UNSS): the organisation responsible for school sport in *France*. It forms part of the *centralised* policy, taking the organisational and financial responsibility away from the individual schools. It is based on the multi-sport federation and ensures a pyramid structure for promoting talented performers.

United Kingdom sport system: the sport system in the United Kingdom started from the *grass roots* level and the formation of *clubs*. Groups of clubs then developed *governing bodies* to administer their affairs. Thus there was initially no government involvement and the UK has managed to restrict the power of politicians compared with countries like

France, the *United States of America* and *Australia*. There is little sport legislation and the *Central Council of Physical Recreation*, *Sport England* and the *British Olympic Association* remain autonomous. (See figure below.)

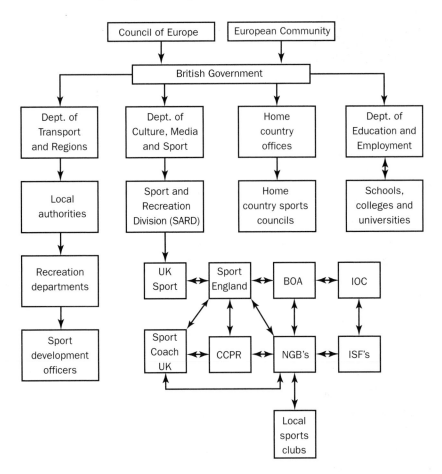

United Kingdom sport system

United Kingdom Sports Institute (UKSI): series of regional satellite centres co-ordinated by Central Services in London with the purpose of developing *elite* performers. The idea of an Institute was raised by the government in its policy statement Sport: *Raising the Game*, in July 1995. The views of sports administrators, coaches and elite athletes were sought with the concept being to focus on the needs of top level performers and those with talent and commitment to succeed. As well as providing world class training facilities, UKSI also provides a support structure including coaching, sport science and medical expertise. The responsibilities of the UKSI are sub-divided:

- *UK Sport* – co-ordinates central services, who administers the medical insurance scheme Athlete Career and Education Programme (ACE UK), Coach Development Programme and Web-based Access training

- home country sports councils – co-ordinate regional satellite centres.

United States of America (USA): the world's fourth largest country composed of 52 states based on a federal system, where the powers of government are divided between both national state and provincial governments. It is an *egalitarian*, *pluralistic* and multi-cultural society, where the dream of success is made possible whatever your social background.

See also *United States of America sport system* and the figure below.

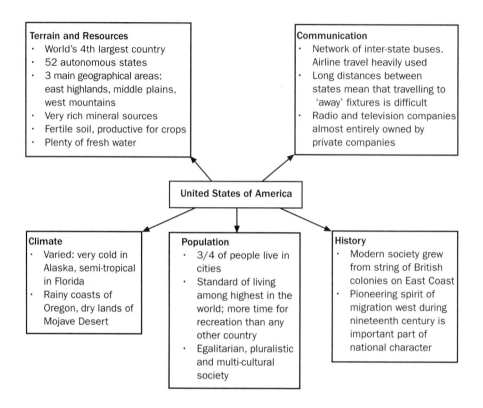

United States of America sport system: this system operates at four main levels:

● high school – interscholastic competition

● collegiate and university – the large institutions are controlled by the *National Collegiate Athletic Association*

● amateur – individual governing bodies control their sport, for example the Amateur Athletic Union (AAU)

● professional – each professional sport has its own association, for example the National Basketball Association. Professional sport is the ambition of most sport performers where they can earn lucrative lifestyles.

See figure on page 241.

upper class: a term used to denote the dominant group in society but traditionally concentrates on the aristocratic families who held power up until the first half of the twentieth century.

Federal Government

Department of
Education

Department of
Fish and Game

Parks and recreation
commissions

National Olympic Committee

Individual
governing
bodies
of sport

National
federation
of SHSAA

NCAA

AIWA

NAIA

Regional conferences

State associations
in each sport

High school
athletic
associations

Local
subdivisions

United States of America sport system

upward social mobility: movement of an individual from a subordinate position in society to a higher or more powerful one. Education and sport are both avenues of *social mobility*.

urban areas are usually characterised by a high-density population living in towns or cities with people mainly occupied in manufacturing and service jobs. These areas grew considerably during the *Industrial Revolution*.

urban revolution: *see urbanisation*

urbanisation: the process whereby the mass of a population changes its lifestyle from living in villages and rural areas to living in towns and cities. This was one of the greatest legacies of the *Industrial Revolution* in the nineteenth century.

validity: the ability of a test or measurement to produce accurate results that can be relied on. There are two forms of validity:

- internal validity – ability of a test to produce the required data, with all possible variables kept to a minimum

- external validity – ability to apply the data produced to a wider population. Often research conducted in laboratory conditions has lower external validity when compared with that completed in field experiments using a larger section of the population.

For example, the *sit and reach flexibility test* can be said to have both internal and external validity, as it measures the flexibility of the athlete's hips, which can then be graded in comparison with other performers.

values: the moral principles and beliefs of a person or social group. Within society the accepted values are often determined by the *dominant culture*. Examples include respect for property and honesty, while in a sporting environment, the concept of *sportsmanship* is encouraged. Individuals or groups can accept or reject such values, consequently influencing the formation of their *attitude*.

variable practice: type of practice in which the coach develops the skills of the performer using a mixture of *massed* and *distributed practice* methods. The choice of practice will vary depending on the nature of the group, task and situation. This will not only maximise learning but also maintain *motivation* and reduce fatigue when appropriate. For example, a coach may use massed practice for passing drills, but later use distributed practice to develop set moves performed at high intensity.

vasoconstriction: the narrowing of blood vessels, resulting in increased *blood pressure* and hence the speed at which the blood flows round the body. It is central to the process of blood *shunting* during exercise, where blood is diverted towards the working skeletal muscles.

vasodilation: the widening of blood vessels, resulting in decreased *blood pressure*. Vasodilation occurs after exercise, leading to a drop in blood pressure to its normal level. It is also essential to the process of blood *shunting* during exercise to ensure that optimal volumes of blood and nutrients can reach the working muscles.

vector quantity: a biomechanical term referring to a quantity which has both size (magnitude) and direction. For example, the difference between speed and *velocity* is that *speed* can occur in any direction whereas the velocity of a body must have a specified direction. Velocity is therefore a vector quantity.

vein: a blood vessel which conducts blood away from *skeletal muscle* and other tissues back to the heart.

velocity: the rate at which a body moves in a specified direction. It is calculated by:

$$\frac{\text{displacement}}{\text{time}}$$

and is measured in metres per second (m/s).

Velocity can occur in a straight line (linear velocity) or with rotation (angular velocity), and is a fundamental element of many sporting activities. These include the 100 m sprinter whose aim is to cover the distance of 100 m in a straight line in the shortest possible time, and the trampolinist performing a triple back somersault who must ensure sufficient rotation and angular velocity to complete the task successfully.

venous return mechanism: the process by which the blood returns to the right side of the heart via the *veins*. At rest the venous system (veins) contains up to 70 per cent of the total volume of blood. This is very important since it acts as a reservoir of blood for when it is needed, for example during exercise.

The body relies upon its venous return mechanism in order to ensure an adequate supply of blood during exercise. This is because the more blood that returns to the heart the more blood can be pumped out. Essentially there are two 'pumps' involved in this process: the *muscle pump* and the *respiratory pump*. The muscle pump consists of the contracting skeletal muscles squeezing the veins and forcing the blood held within them towards the heart. Pocket valves within the veins ensure that blood flows only one way towards the heart, without any back flow. The respiratory pump relies upon the changes in pressure that occur in the thoracic cavity during inspiration and expiration. This can cause compression of the veins, resulting in blood being 'sucked' into the heart.

verbal guidance: see *guidance*

Veroff's stages of achievement motivation proposes that the *achievement motivation* of a performer develops in three distinct phases:

- Autonomous competence stage – occurs during the first five years of a child's life when they master basic skills, only evaluating their actions against their own intrinsic goals, not those of other people. For example, the repeated throwing and catching of a ball to themselves until competent.

- Social comparison stage – occurs from the age of five onwards, when individuals compare their actions and performance with those of others in their peer group. Some individuals will continually seek out competition to evaluate their skills, either in terms of end result or performance, and when content, progress to the final stage.

- Integrated stage – occurs at any age, depending on the experiences and development of the individual. It is based on both internal and external standards. It allows the performer to alter their level of motivation depending on the requirements of different situations.

vicarious experiences: see *self-efficacy*

Victorian era: the period of the reign of Queen Victoria from 1837 to 1901. Under her reign there was a period of dramatic social change that was reflected in the structure and organisation of games and sports. The social changes that occurred during this era include:

- social reformers campaigned for improvements in the physical and mental health of workers in society

- Parliament passed many Acts such as the Ten Hour Act 1847 and the *Municipal Reform Act 1835*

- *half day Saturday* and early closing Wednesday began, increasing the leisure time of the working classes

- *rational recreation* developed rapidly

- the working classes became entitled to free education following the *Forster Education Act 1870* (see *Education Acts*).

Victorian Institute of Sport (VIS): a sporting establishment in the state of Victoria, Australia with the responsibility of promoting sporting *excellence*. It was established in 1990. Each state has its own Institute, each of which is supported financially by the government and private sectors. Individual sports bodies can apply for admission and, if successful, the athletes will have access to advanced coaching – fitness, skill, tactical and psychological aspects of their chosen sport; competitive opportunities – national and international events; career development – personal skills, education and future employment prospects.

visual guidance: see *guidance*

visualisation: see *imagery*

voluntary associations: and association which individuals choose to belong to, and usually freely donate their home, skills and money towards the running of the organisation. An example would be a sports club. The *United Kingdom sports system* is based on this foundation.

volunteers in sport are individuals who helps others in sport through formal organisations such as clubs or governing bodies, whilst receiving no remuneration except expenses.

There is universal acceptance of the important contribution and vital role volunteers make to the development of sport, as coaches, administrators, managers and officials. The estimated number of volunteers is three times that of those working in paid employment in sports-related activity. For major sport events, such as the Commonwealth Games, it is not unusual for competitors to be outnumbered by volunteers.

Do you need revision help and advice?

Go to pages 274–287 for a range of revision appendices that include plenty of exam advice and tips.

wakes: watch or vigil held over the body of a dead person before burial and sometimes accompanied by festivity. Also, in England, a vigil kept in commemoration of the dedication of a parish church. The latter type of wake consisted of an all-night service of prayer and meditation in the church. These services, officially termed 'vigiliae' by the church, appear to have existed from the earliest days of Anglo-Saxon Christianity. Each parish kept the day following its vigil as a holiday. Activities such as bull baiting, bear baiting, dog fighting and cock fighting were common.

Wakes soon degenerated into fairs; people from neighbouring parishes journeyed over to join in the merrymaking, and the revelry and drunkenness became controversial. The days usually chosen for church dedications being Sundays and Saints' days, the abuse seemed all the more scandalous. In industrial England wakes became an annual holiday in various towns in northern England, when the local factories would close down. Community holidays to places such as Blackpool became the norm and later holiday camps like Butlins helped to foster a similar community spirit.

warm-up: period of light activity and stretching exercises undertaken prior to the commencement of any exercise. Not only does a warm-up ensure that the body is ready for exercise, but it also prevents injury and muscle soreness. Where possible warm-ups should be specific to the activity that follows and prepare the appropriate muscles and the energy systems. A warm-up consists of three stages:

- Stage 1 – a period of light continuous activity, such as jogging, which raises heart rate and body temperature and prepares the body for stage 2.

- Stage 2 – stretching activities can follow, now that the muscles are warm. Stretches should aim to take the muscles through their full range and each should be held for a minimum of 15 seconds. It may be necessary to replicate movements from the activity that follows to ensure that the muscles are fully prepared. For example, a long jumper may perform some bounding exercises.

- Stage 3 – skill-related practices should form the basis of the third stage, which works the neuromuscular mechanisms. For example, shooting baskets in basketball, practising turns in swimming or serving in tennis.

wars: see *World War I, World War II* and *Boer War*

Washhouse Act: legislation under the Public Baths and Washhouses Act (1846), which was to increase the provision of public baths. The main aim was to clean up the working classes. Large towns would have separate baths for the different social classes, they were called 'penny baths' because there was a fixed limit on charges for the second-class facilities. Swimming, water polo and diving were developed as a result of these social changes.

wave summation: method of increasing the force of contraction of a muscle that results when stimuli (nerve impulses) arrive in rapid succession. On receipt of a nerve impulse a muscle fibre will go through a period of contraction followed by a period of relaxation. This is known as a *muscle twitch*. If a second impulse arrives at the muscle fibre before it has had time to relax, the muscle responds with a stronger contraction since the effect of the second stimulus is added to that of the first. This is known as wave summation and is illustrated in the figure below. In order to overcome great forces such as in weightlifting, the brain must constantly fire impulses to the muscle to ensure that the contraction is strong enough to overcome the resistance.

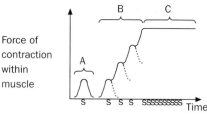

Force of contraction within muscle

A = Muscle twitch
B = Wave summation
C = Tetanus
S = Stimulus

weight training: see *strength training*

Weiner's model of attribution: see *attribution theory*

West Indies: an archipelago off Central America extending over 1,500 miles in an arc from the peninsula of Florida to Venezuela, separating the Caribbean from the Atlantic. The largest island is Cuba. It is classed as an *emergent culture* using sport to create a *national identity*, for example cricket.

Western European sport: sport that has developed in Western Europe, where it is run by both governmental and non-governmental organisations. Thus it is a result of private and public interest and activity.

White Australia policy: an Anglo-Celtic creation to keep Australia free of immigration from the East, and it was not until the 1950s that large numbers of people from Europe and Asia were accepted. This policy also limited the amount of friction between different religious sects and was mainly restricted to the Protestant and Catholic divide.

whole method practice: practice method in which the performer attempts to complete the entire movement, after observing a demonstration or being given verbal instructions. This form of *practice* has the advantage of helping the individual to experience and develop the feel or *kinaesthetic* awareness of the whole action, allowing them to begin to understand the relationship between the different phases. It can be used when learning to catch and throw a ball, swing a golf club or throw a javelin. It is advisable to use this method when the performer is motivated, experienced and possesses high levels of attention, or with skills that are simple, discrete, ballistic in nature and comprised of easily interlinked subroutines.

whole-part-whole method practice: a combination of the *whole* and *part methods of practice*. This format utilises the benefits of each, allowing the performer to gain experience and understanding of the complete skill, before refining specific subroutines. For example, a long jumper may be taught the basic technique and after several attempts complete drills to develop the take-off and flight phases.

wilderness areas: tracts of land that are uninhabited, uncultivated and isolated. Countries like the *United States of America*, *France* and *Australia* all have such geographical features whereas the United Kingdom, which is relatively small and densely populated, does not. This type of land provides access for outdoor pursuit activities in extreme conditions. Within Britain the equivalent would be the *National Parks*.

win ethic: see *Lombardian ethic*

Wingate cycle test: fitness test designed to measure *anaerobic* capacity. This test involves the subject pedalling as fast as possible on a cycle ergometer, for 30 seconds (against a resistance which has been adjusted for body weight – usually 75 g/kg body weight). The number of revolutions pedalled by the subject per five seconds of the test are counted. The test is able to determine:

● mean power – the average work output over the 30-second test period

● peak power – the highest power output in a 5-second period

● fatigue index – the difference between peak power and the lowest output of 5 seconds divided by peak power.

The Wingate cycle test is of use to the exercise physiologist or coach, since it can assess an athlete's maximum capacity over a 30-second period. If, for example, an athlete fatigues rapidly after 15 seconds the coach may need to adjust the training programme to accommodate more endurance-based work. More recently, the Wingate cycle test has been developed to assess the anaerobic capacity of the arms, which is obviously of benefit to performers such as swimmers and rowers.

women in sport: an issue that focuses on the role of women in sport. Traditionally, women have participated in sport to a lesser extent than men, even though they comprise approximately half the population. This has occurred in most cultures, and is an issue that extends far beyond the world of sport and into society generally. The major basis for sexual *discrimination* in sport have been biological differences (women are deemed less well suitable physically and physiologically to certain sports than men); sexual *stereotyping* and the domestic role of women which has left them less *leisure time* in which to pursue their sporting interests. Efforts to counter the problems include:

● Equal Pay Act 1970

● *Sex Discrimination Act 1975*

● *Title IX*

● *Brighton Declaration on Women and Sport.*

Women's Sport Foundation (WSF): a voluntary organisation promoting the interests of women and girls in sport and recreation. There is a network of regional groups and a wide range of activities and events are organised. Their regular publication is 'Women in Sport Magazine'.

working class: the position in the social structure occupied mainly by manual labourers. This is changing as machinery takes over the need for physical labour. Traditionally this class within society has been linked with *low culture*.

working memory: see *short-term memory*

work-to-relief ratio: method of expressing the length of the rest or recovery period during an *interval training* session. A work-to-relief ratio of 1:3, for example, means that the resting interval is three times longer than the work period.

World Class England: linked to the *National Junior Sport Programme,* with the aim of providing opportunities for young people to try a sport for the first time and to have structures in place to allow them to reach international success. It operates on four main levels:

- World Class Performance – enables national *governing bodies* to give the best possible training and support to the country's elite athletes and players

- World Class Events – a scheme to attract the cream of international competition and sporting events to this country

- World Class Potential – provides support for governing bodies to identify and help talented youngsters develop their skills

- World Class Start – consortia of *local authorities* and other providers to help put in place coaching schemes and support programmes to give children the best possible sporting start.

World War I: the war (1914–18) fought mainly in Europe and the Middle East, in which the allies (France, Russia, Britain, Italy and the United States after 1915) defeated the central powers (Germany, Austria, Hungary and Turkey). Millions were to die in static trench warfare. Also known as the Great War. *Nationalism* came to the fore, and public school men were enthused with idealism about the coming conflict as if it were a football match. The football match between Britain and German soldiers at Christmas 1914 set the tone for the role of sport during the entire war. Football grounds were used extensively for recruiting though eventually the *Football League* bowed to moral pressure to stop fixtures for the duration of the war. Following the war there were hopes of a more equal society but this was not immediately realised.

World War II: the war (1939–45) in which the allies Britain and France declared war on Germany as a result of the German invasion of Poland. After this war there was an extensive rebuilding programme and new sports facilities were more sophisticated than ever before. The *therapeutic* effect of recreational activities was once again highlighted. Commando training during the war had developed the use of obstacle training, and the first apparatus began to appear in schools.

The *movement approach* was adopted in physical education lessons in schools, with the *Butler Education Act* (see *Education Acts*) reforming education in Britain.

wrestling: individual *combat* activity; strength, skill and stamina combine to make it one of the most basic sports. Its origins are ancient and are illustrated in wall paintings in ancient Greece, Egypt and China. In Britain it was popular from the village green to the Royal court.

Nations developed their own styles of wrestling. Britain was no exception. Notable ones were:

- Cumberland and Westmoreland – commence chest to chest, 'take hold' round the body. Competitors were allowed to use all legitimate means to throw.
- Devon and Cornwall – bouts controlled by three judges called 'sticklers'. The wrestlers wore jackets and had to hold collar and sleeve.

This activity took place at fairs, as part of the *prizefight* and in music halls. Later developments included safety considerations, with the introduction of weight categories, rules, training, preparation and control of and referee.

Do you need help with the synoptic element of your Physical Education course?

Go to page 274 for tips and advice.

Yerkes and Dobson's theory: see *inverted U theory*

Young Men's Christian Association (YMCA): a non-sectarian, non-political Christian lay movement that was established in London in 1844. Its aims were to develop high standards of Christian character through group activities and improve the spiritual, social, recreational and physical life of young people. The games of *basketball* and volleyball developed directly through this organisation in the *United States of America* in the nineteenth century. They were designed to enable young and middle-aged men to enjoy using indoor facilities. Later a similar association was established specifically for women, the YWCA.

youth movements are organisations providing leisure activities for young people, often associated with a church. During the nineteenth century the invention of adolescence as an age-defined social cohort segregated the young from adult status and created a social problem whose solution became the provision of adult-supervised leisure pursuits. The middle classes were to use the combination of Evangelical Christianity, public school manliness, militarism and imperialism to instil their values in the middle class. The gradual loss of control by the established church led to the middle class organising the leisure of adolescents. Youth movements were seen as a way to curb juvenile restlessness. Examples of such movements were The Boy's Brigade, the Church Lads Brigade, the Scout movement and the Girl Guides.

Youth movements helped to:

- smooth the way for upper-working class and lower-middle classes into the urban industrial order of British society
- instil religious, moral and militaristic values
- provide an opportunity for the working classes to experience something of the elite public school education and values
- provide a mass leisure outlet for working class adolescents controlled by middle class adults
- provide opportunities for outdoor activity
- promote acceptance by young people of social order.

Youth Sports Trust (YST): a registered charity set up in 1994 to improve sporting provision for young people in the United Kingdom. Its mission is to develop and implement a linked series of quality sports programmes, known under the umbrella term as the *National Junior Sports Programme*. The Trust also works alongside the Department for Education and Employment (DfEE) to support maintained secondary schools that are applying for Specialist Sports College status.

Zajonc's theory: see *social facilitation*

zero transfer: see *transfer of learning*

zig-zag test: fitness test designed to measure *agility*. Similar to the *Illinois agility run test* it requires the athlete to run a course in the shortest possible time. A rectangle measuring 10 feet by 16 feet is marked out by four cones with one cone placed in the centre of the rectangle. The subject starts at cone 1, runs to the centre cone, then on to cones 2 and 3, back to the centre cone, and finally to cone 4 and back to cone 1. Times to complete the course are compared with standard tables. Some coaches prefer this test as the total distance covered is shorter than the Illinois course and therefore fatigue does not become an issue.

zone of optimal functioning: the unique level of *arousal* for an athlete, which allows them to perform with maximum concentration and effort. Within a team, each player may have a different optimal arousal level and must work in conjunction with the coach to find how to reach and maintain this zone to function effectively in the match. See also *inverted U theory*.

What other subjects are you studying?

A–Zs cover 18 different subjects. See the inside back cover for a list of all the titles in the series and how to order.

A
B
C
D
E
F
G
H
I
J
K
L
M
N
O
P
Q
R
S
T
U
V
W
X
Y
Z

TERMS OF DIRECTION AND PLANES OF THE BODY

Directional terms for humans

Terms	Etymology*	Definition
Left		Toward the leftside
Right		Toward the rightside
Superior	L, higher	A structure higher than another (usually synonymous with cephalic)
Inferior	L, lower	A structure lower than another (usually synonymous with caudal)
Cephalic	G, *kephale*, head	Closer to the head than another structure (usually synonymous with superior)
Caudal	L, *cauda*, a tail	Closer to the tail than another structure (usually synonymous with inferior)
Proximal	L, *proximus*, nearest	Closer than another structure to the point of attachment to the trunk
Distal	L, *di-* plus *sto*, to stand apart or to be distant	Farther than another structure from the point of attachment to the trunk
Medial	L, *medialis*, middle	Toward the middle or the midline of the body
Lateral	L, *latus*, side	Away from the middle or midline of the body
Anterior	L, before	The front of the body (synonymous withventral)
Posterior	L, *posterus*, following	The back of the body (synonymous with dorsal)
Ventral	L, *venter* or *ventr-*, belly	Toward the belly (synonymous with anterior)
Dorsal	L, *dorsum*, back	Toward the back (synonymous with posterior)
Superficial	L, *superficialis*	Toward or on the surface (not shown in figure)
Deep	OE, *deop*, deep	Away from the surface, internal (not shown in figure)

*Origin and meaning of the word −L, Latin; G, Greek; OE, Old English

Source: Seely, Stephens, Tate − *Anatomy & Physiology* 3rd ed., Mosby 1995.

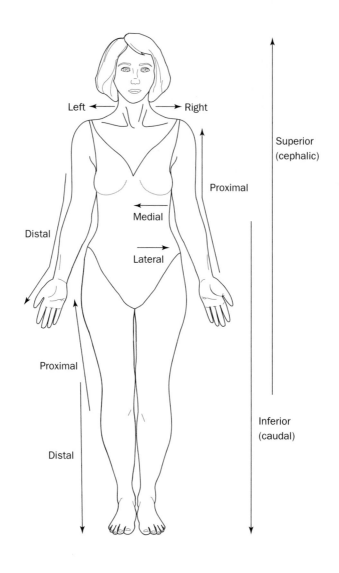

Left ← → Right

Superior
(cephalic)

Proximal

Medial ←

Distal

Lateral →

Proximal

Inferior
(caudal)

Distal

Figure A1.1 Directional terms for humans (continued on page 255)

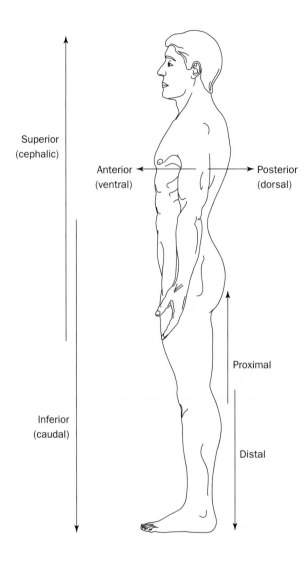

Superior
(cephalic)

Anterior
(ventral)

Posterior
(dorsal)

Proximal

Inferior
(caudal)

Distal

Figure A1.1 (continued)

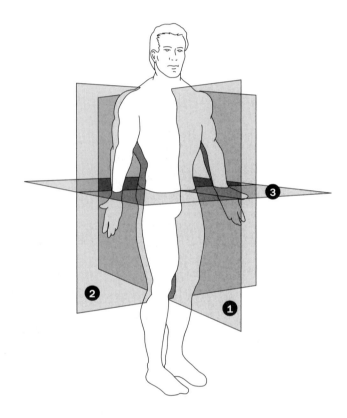

Figure A1.2 Three planes of motion

1 = Median plane/saggital plane

2 = Frontal plane/coronal plane

3 = Horizontal plane/transverse plane

Source: Aaberg: Muscle Mechanics Human Kinetics *1998*

THE SKELETON

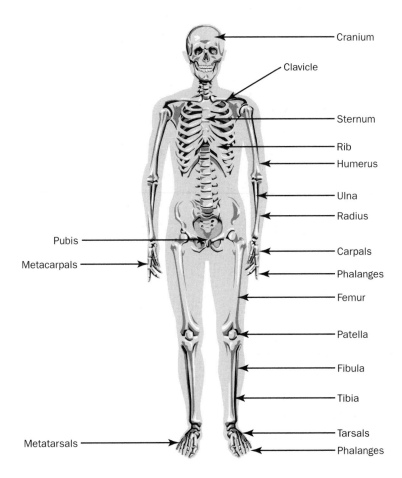

Figure A2.1 The skeleton: anterior view

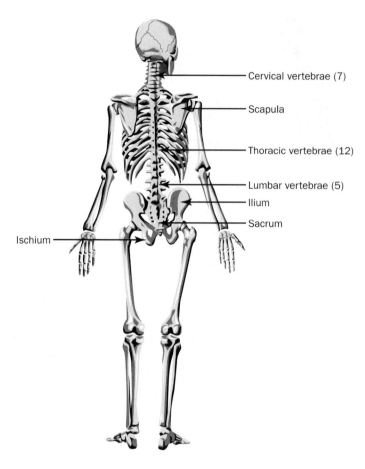

Figure A2.2 The skeleton: posterior view

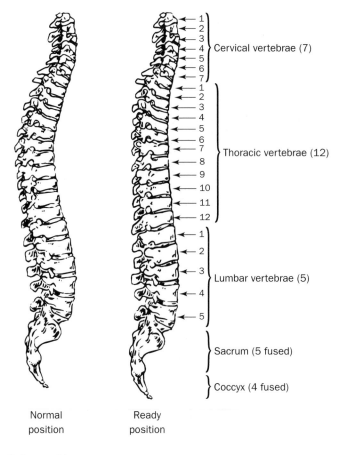

	Cervical vertebrae (7)
1 2 3 4 5 6 7	
1 2 3 4 5 6 7 8 9 10 11 12	Thoracic vertebrae (12)
1 2 3 4 5	Lumbar vertebrae (5)
	Sacrum (5 fused)
	Coccyx (4 fused)

Normal   Ready
position   position

Figure A2.3 Spine positions

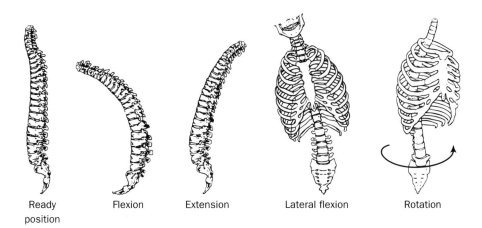

Ready   Flexion   Extension   Lateral flexion   Rotation
position

Figure A2.4 Spine positions during exercise

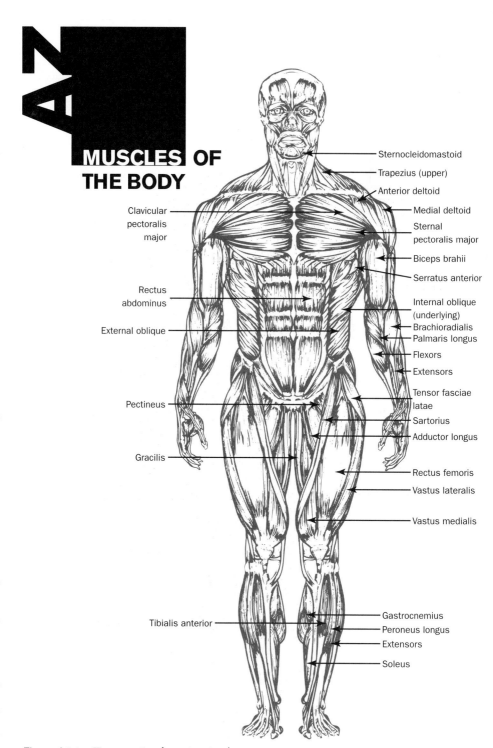

A7

MUSCLES OF THE BODY

Sternocleidomastoid

Trapezius (upper)

Anterior deltoid

Clavicular pectoralis major

Medial deltoid

Sternal pectoralis major

Biceps brahii

Serratus anterior

Rectus abdominus

Internal oblique (underlying)

External oblique

Brachioradialis

Palmaris longus

Flexors

Extensors

Tensor fasciae latae

Pectineus

Sartorius

Adductor longus

Gracilis

Rectus femoris

Vastus lateralis

Vastus medialis

Gastrocnemius

Tibialis anterior

Peroneus longus

Extensors

Soleus

Figure A3.1a The muscles (anterior view)
Source: Aaberg: Muscle Mechanics Human Kinetics 1998

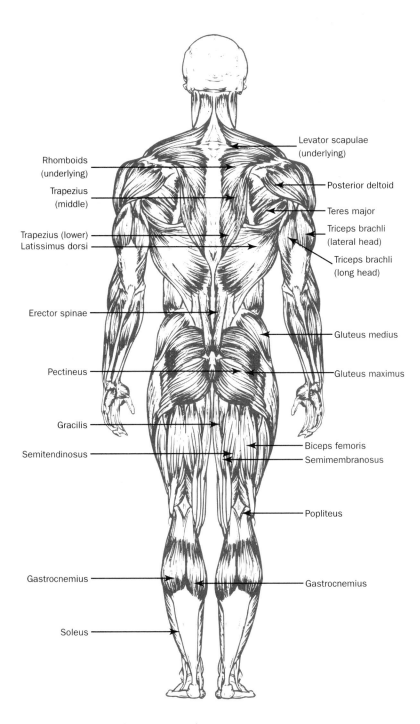

Levator scapulae
(underlying)

Rhomboids
(underlying)

Posterior deltoid

Trapezius
(middle)

Teres major

Triceps brachli
(lateral head)

Trapezius (lower)
Latissimus dorsi

Triceps brachli
(long head)

Erector spinae

Gluteus medius

Pectineus

Gluteus maximus

Gracilis

Biceps femoris

Semitendinosus

Semimembranosus

Popliteus

Gastrocnemius

Gastrocnemius

Soleus

Figure A3.1b The muscles (posterior view)

Shoulder Flexion Median Anterior deltoid
Pectoralis major
Coracobrachialis

Extension Median Posterior deltoid
Latissimus dorsi
Teres major

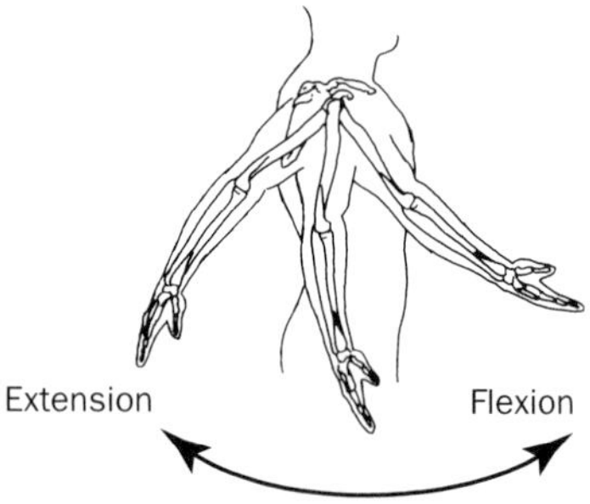

Extension   Flexion

Adduction Frontal Latissumus dorsi
Pectoralis major
Teres major
Teres minor

Abduction

Adduction

Abduction Frontal Medial deltoid
Supraspinatus

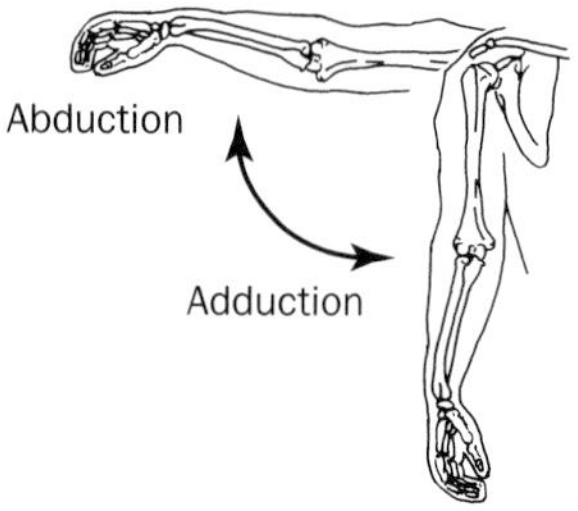

Horizontal Horizontal Pectoralis major
adduction Anterior deltoid

Adduction

Horizontal Horizontal Posterior deltoid
abduction Trapezius
Rhomboids
Latissumus dorsi

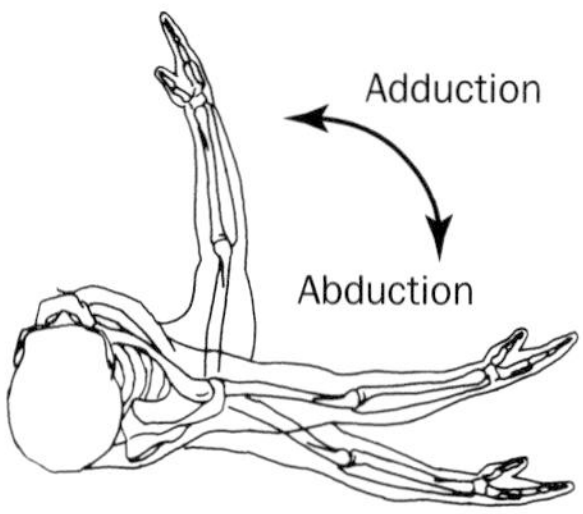

Abduction

Medial
Lateral

Medial Horizontal Subscapularis
rotation

Lateral Horizontal Infraspinatus
rotation Teres minor

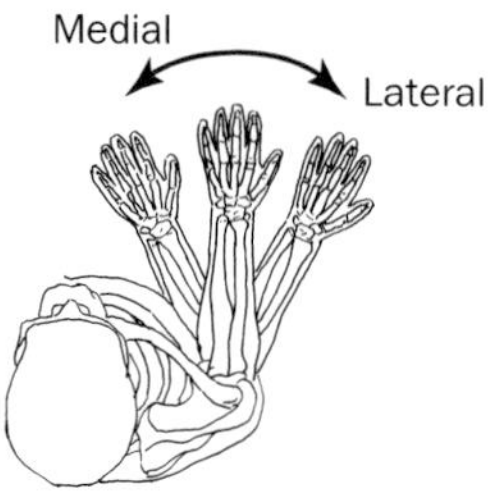

Elbow	Flexion	Median	Biceps brachii
			Brachialis
			Brachioradialis
	Extension	Median	Triceps

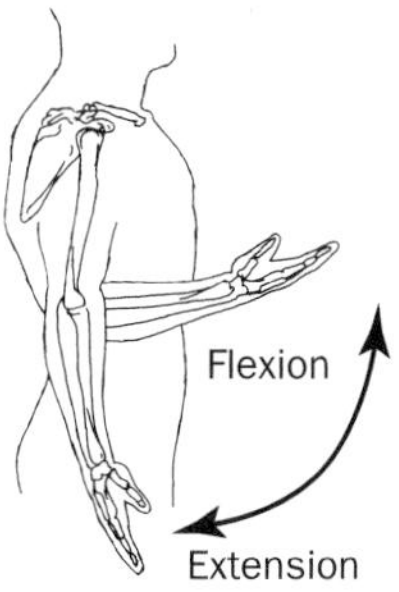

Flexion

Extension

	Pronation	Horizontal	Pronator teres
			Pronator quadratus
			Brachioradialis
	Supination	Horizontal	Biceps brachii
			Supinator

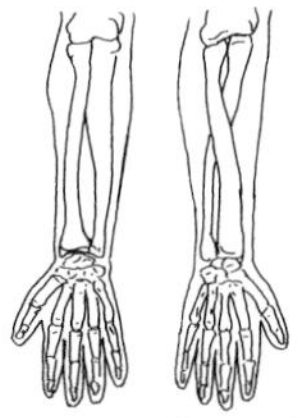

Supination   Pronation

Wrist	Flexion	Median	Wrist flexors
	Extension	Median	Wrist extensors

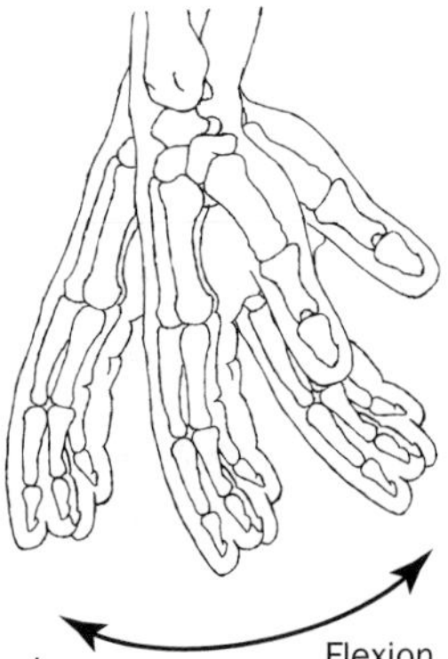

Extension   Flexion

Movement of the trunk	Flexion	Median	Rectus abdominus
			Internal obliques
			External obliques
	Extension	Median	Erector spinae
			Iliocostalis
			Spinalis

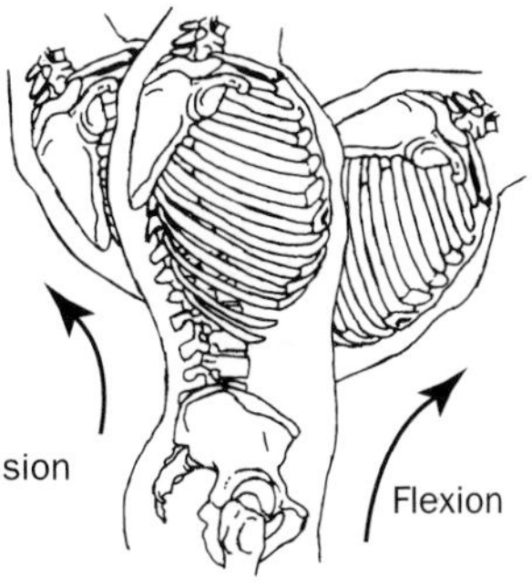

Extension   Flexion

Lateral flexion	Frontal	Internal oblique Rectus abdominis Erector spinae Quadratus laborum	

Lateral flexion

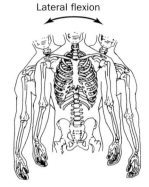

Rotation	Horizontal	External oblique Rectus abdominis Erector spinae	

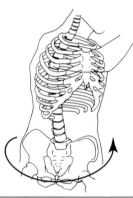

Movement of the scapulae	Elevation	Frontal	Levator sapulae Trapezius Rhomboids

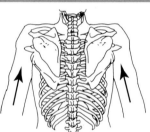

	Depression	Frontal	Trapezius (lower) Pectoralis minor Serratus anterior (lower)

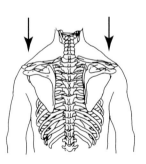

| Protraction | Frontal | Serratus anterior | 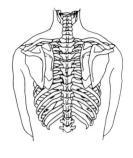 |

| Retraction | Frontal | Rhomboids
Trapezius | 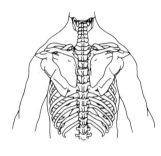 |

| Upward
rotation | Frontal | Trapezius (upper)
Serratus anterior | 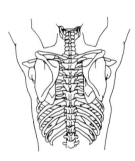 |

| Downward
rotation | Frontal | Rhomboids
Levator scapulae | 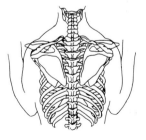 |

MOVEMENT ANALYSIS

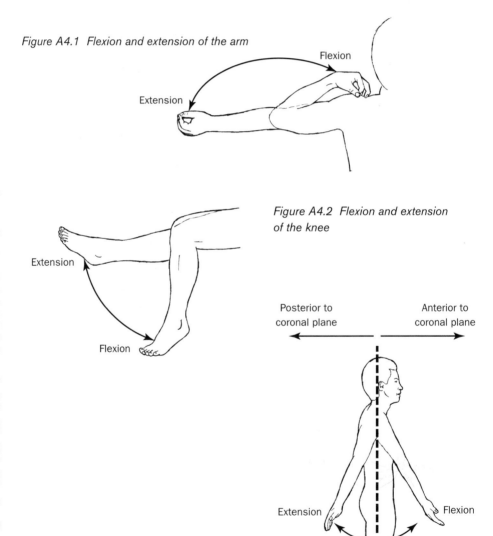

Figure A4.1 Flexion and extension of the arm

Flexion

Extension

Figure A4.2 Flexion and extension of the knee

Extension

Flexion

Posterior to coronal plane

Anterior to coronal plane

Extension

Flexion

Figure A4.3 Flexion and extension of the shoulder

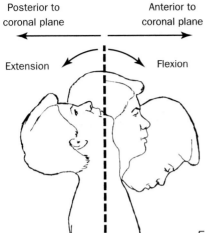

Posterior to
coronal plane

Anterior to
coronal plane

Extension

Flexion

Figure A4.4 Flexion of the neck

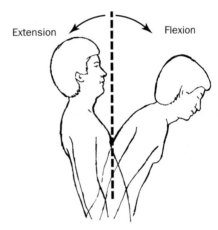

Extension

Flexion

Figure A4.5 Flexion and extension of the
trunk

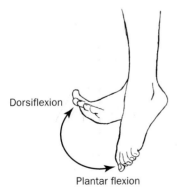

Dorsiflexion

Plantar flexion

Figure A4.6 Plantar flexion and dorsiflexion of the ankle

Abduction

Adduction

Figure A4.7 *Abduction and adduction of the upper limb*

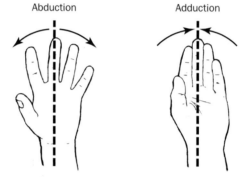

Abduction

Adduction

Figure A4.8 *Abduction and adduction of the fingers*

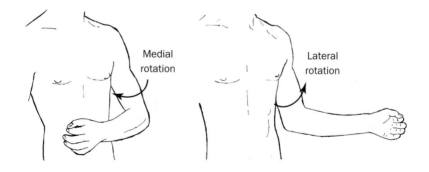

Medial rotation

Lateral rotation

Figure A4.9 *Medial and lateral rotation of the humerus*

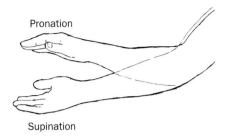

Pronation

Supination

Figure A4.10 Pronation and supination

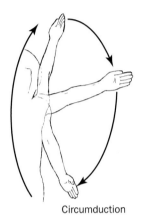

Circumduction

Figure A4.11 Circumduction of the shoulder

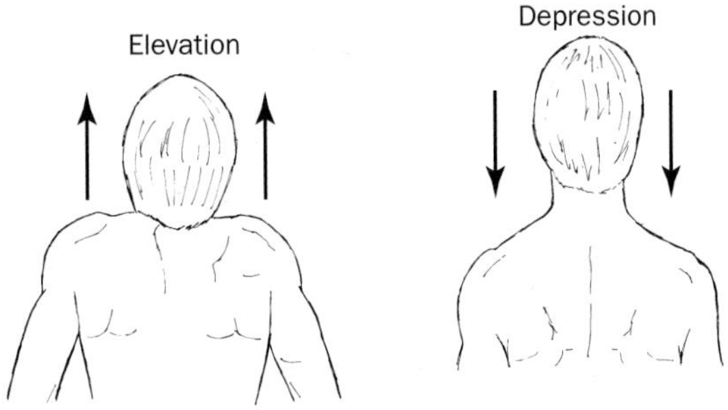

Figure A4.12 Elevation and depression of the shoulder

Elevation

Depression

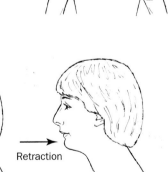

Protraction

Retraction

Figure A4.13 Protraction and retraction of the jaw

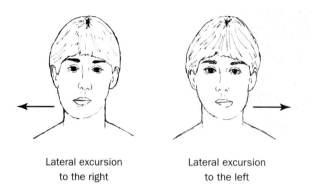

Lateral excursion
to the right

Lateral excursion
to the left

Figure A4.14 Lateral excursion of the jaw

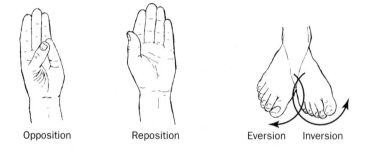

Opposition   Reposition   Eversion   Inversion

Figure A4.15 Opposition and eversion of the thumb

LUNG VOLUMES

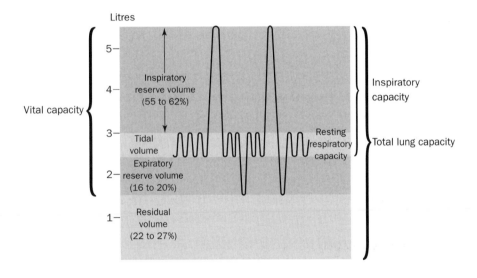

Litres

Vital capacity

Inspiratory reserve volume (55 to 62%)

Tidal volume

Expiratory reserve volume (16 to 20%)

Residual volume (22 to 27%)

Resting respiratory capacity

Inspiratory capacity

Total lung capacity

ADVICE ON REVISION

The following pages offer advice on revising for AS and A levels in Sport and Physical Education. First, you will find some general guidance assessment, including hints on how to revise and definitions of examiners' terms. Then revision lists are given by examination boards and specific modules.

Synoptic assessment

From September 2000, all A level specifications have included the phrase: 'synoptic assessment'. This term means that a section within the examination will test your understanding of the subject as a whole, not simply small sections of the subject. It will also test your ability to interlink and relate different subject areas to each other. In all subjects, this part of the examination must take place at the end of the course (i.e. A2 only, not AS) and account for 20 per cent of the total marks for the A level. The government believes this will be a better test of your knowledge and understanding and be one of the most challenging sections of the course.

Sport and Physical Education courses have a wide variety of topics that need to be assimilated and linked to practical examples. As such it is important that you do not compartmentalise each section from the beginning of the course. Instead you should try to see how one part might relate to another; for example, when discussing 'abilities' required for a specific activity a link could be made to the methods of training that may be suitable to improve abilities and enhance performance. Further links could be made to the availability of facilities to complete the training and the role a governing body plays in developing a route from participation level to excellence.

Examiners recognise that the skills requiring you to think 'synoptically' are very demanding. It is not so much what you know that is the problem, but knowing what you know and applying it correctly! If you are to be successful in the synoptic sections you will need to develop the skill of bringing together different aspects of the course.

Synoptic revision

Within your synoptic revision you will be required to bring together different aspects of the course and relate this knowledge to practical situations. The examiners will test this by creating questions that demand an integrated solution. Each examining board will have its own unique style of questioning and you should become familiar with their particular requirements before you devise your revision programme. The following revision methods will need to be adapted accordingly and should be used after your normal revision has taken place.

When answering questions, candidates need to plan quickly what is involved in different parts of the topic. As an example, shown below is a spider diagram that outlines possible factors to discuss when looking at the development of excellence. The arrows show the broad relationships that can be further expanded as required.

Having completed the spider diagram, it is useful to develop each 'leg' a stage further, in order to extend your thoughts using a planning hierarchy, as shown below. The final stage of the process involves looking at how the different elements relate to each other. This is represented by the dotted lines.

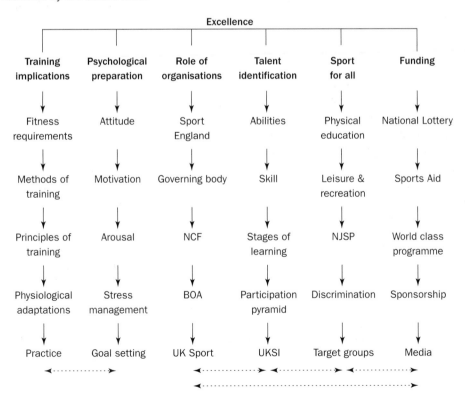

Once you have studied how to use these methods, attempt to complete another theme taken from the suggested list at the top of the next page. It may be advisable to complete one per day leading up to the synoptic examination.

Don't forget to make use of your *A–Z Sport and Physical Education Handbook* in your synoptic revision. Carry out the exercise without help initially. If you encounter difficulties, try looking up the key words and look for cross-references in the handbook to add greater detail.

Suggested topics:

- the value of developing 'sport for all' policies
- the effects of the media on individuals and their sport
- the effects of commercialisation on performers, spectators and sport
- the use of world games for political purposes
- the implications of doping for performers, spectators and sport
- the value of developing 'talent identification programmes' for the athlete, sport and country
- the value of developing assessment structures within sport
- discrimination within sport in different cultures and countries
- the functions of play, leisure, physical education and sport within a society
- the benefits of developing technology to optimise performance
- the analysis of activity categories using the following terms: structural, strategic, technical, physical and psychological.

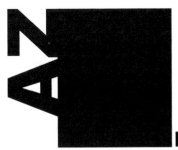

EXAMINERS' TERMS

To maximise your examination performance it is vital for you to understand the nature of the question and its requirements. This will help you to structure your answers and not waste valuable time on questions that only require short answers.

Study the terms below so that you are familiar with their meanings and attempt to locate them in the question before constructing your answer.

What are the advantages ... ?

This requires a description of why one situation/factor is better than another. Often this requires evaluation, justification and explanation.

Calculate

This requires a mathematical calculation, including relevant workings and correct units.

What are the characteristics ... ?

Here you need to list the common features that identify a term, process, situation or structure. A question asking for characteristcs normally requires short answers, but take care not to repeat yourself with similar terms.

Define/What is meant by ... ?

This requires a statement outlining the meaning of the term. Usually a formal definition is not needed, only key words to demonstrate a clear understanding.

Describe

Here quantitative or qualitative information should be used to demonstrate an understanding of the topic and any relationships that may exist.

Describe how you ...

The onus is placed on you as the student, drawing on experiences within school, college or other relevant situations, to explain an understanding of the specific topic.

TOP REVISION TERMS

Key terms underpinning the subject

Concepts of physical activity

Popular and rational recreation

Industrialisation

Education

Olympic Games

Equal opportunities

Commercialisation

Kinesiology

Newton's laws of motion

Cardiac cycle

Principles of training

Energy systems

Fitness and measurement

Skill and ability

Information processing

Arousal and motivation

Anxiety and stress management

Guidance and practice

Personality

Groups and leadership

AQA   Module 1 (PED1) – Physiological and psychological factors which improve performance

ability

blood pressure

cardiac cycle

conditioning theories

feedback

fitness

gaseous exchange

guidance

health

Hick's law

information processing

kinesiology

levers

measurement of fitness

memory

motivation

motor programme

observational learning

practice

reaction time

schema theory

selective attention

skill

stages of learning

synovial joint

teaching styles

transfer of learning

venous return mechanism

AQA   Module 2 (PED2) – Socio-cultural and historical effects on participation in physical activity and their influence on performance

active sports programme

analysis of activities

athleticism

Best Value

Boer War

British Sports Trust

Disability Sport England

discrimination

ethnic group

gender

governing bodies

industrial revolution

leisure

military drill

mob games

moving and growing

muscular Christianity

National Curriculum

outdoor education

outdoor recreation

participation pyramid

physical education

physical recreation

play

public school

racism

sport

Sport England

Sport for All

stereotype

syllabuses of physical training

Women's Sport Foundation

World War I/World War II

AQA Module 3 (PED3) – Analysis and evaluation of the factors which improve performance

circuit training

continuous training

cool-down

Fartlek training

interval training

multi-stage fitness test

plyometrics

principles of training

sit and reach test

training zone

warm-up

weight training

Wingate cycle test

AQA Module 4 (PED4) – Physiological, biomechanical and psychological factors which optimise performance

achievement motivation

adenosine triphosphate

aerobic fitness

aggression

altitude training

angular motion

anxiety

arousal

assertive behaviour

attitude

attribution retraining

attribution theory

catastrophe theory

Chelladurai's model of leadership

cognitive dissonance

cohesion

energy systems

Fiedler's contingency model

frustration–aggression hypothesis

goal setting

group dynamics

group productivity

interactionist theory

inverted U theory

lactic acid

leadership

learned helplessness

linear motion

maximum oxygen uptake

motor unit

muscle spindle apparatus

Newton's laws of motion

oxygen debt/EPOC

periodisation

periodisation

personality

persuasive communication

PNF

profile of mood states

recovery

Ringelmann effect

self-efficacy

social facilitation

social learning

social loafing

stress management

trait theories

AQA Module 5 (PED5) – Factors affecting the nature and development of elite performance

academies of sport	INSEP
amateur	media
British Olympic Association	National Lottery
centralisation	Olympic Games
commercialisation	professional
contract to compete	sponsorship
decentralisation	Sportcoach UK
Department for Culture, Media and Sport	sportsmanship
deviancy	title IX
doping	UK Institute of Sport
French sports system	UK sport
gamesmanship	United States of America sports system
governing bodies	world class programme
hooligan	

AQA Module 6 (PED6) – Analysis and critical evaluation of factors which optimise performance

no direct theoretical content

OCR Module 1 (2562) – The application of physiological and psychological knowledge to improve performance

Section A	Section B
blood pressure	ability
cardiac cycle	conditioning theories
cool-down	feedback
fast twitch/slow twitch muscle fibres	information processing
gaseous exchange	memory
kinesiology	motivation
levers	motor programme
Motor unit	practice
Newton's laws of motion	reaction time
strength	reinforcement
synovial joint	schema theory
venous return mechanism	skill
warm-up	stages of learning
	transfer

OCR Module 2 (2563) – Contemporary studies in physical education

amateur

coach

Disability Sport England

emergent society

governing bodies

National Lottery

outdoor education

outdoor recreation

participation pyramid

physical education

physical recreation

play

professional

sport

Sport England

Sport for All

Sportscoach UK

sports college

UK Sport

United Kingdom Sports Institute

Women's Sport Foundation

OCR Module 3 (2564) – Performance and its improvement through critical analysis

no direct theoretical content

OCR Module 4 (2565) – Physical education: historical, comparative, biomechanical and sport psychology options

HISTORICAL

cricket

melting pot

mob games

model course

moving and growing

planning the programme

popular recreation

public school

rational recreation

real tennis

syllabuses of physical training

COMPARATIVE

United States of America sports system

American Football

baggataway

baseball

basketball

ice hockey

summer camps

title IX

French sports system

INSEP

le plein air

transplant classes

Australian sports system

Aborigines

Aussie rules

Aussie Sport

Australian Institute of Sport

BIOMECHANICAL

acceleration

air resistance

angular motion

Bernouilli effect

centre of gravity

levers

linear motion

moment on inertia

momentum

Newton's laws of motion

SPORT PSYCHOLOGY

achievement motivation

aggression

anxiety

arousal

attitudes

attribution theory

Chelladuri's multi-dimensional model of leadership

cohesion

cue utilisation theory

Fiedler's contingency model of leadership

group dynamics

group productivity

leadership

personality

self-efficacy

social facilitation

stress management

OCR Module 5 (2566) – Exercise and sport physiology and the integration of knowledge of principles and concepts across different areas of physical education

adenosine triphospate

energy systems

ergogenic aids

lactic acid

oxygen debt/EPOC

periodisation

principles of training

OCR Module 6 (2567) – Improvement of effective performance

no direct theoretical content

Edexcel Module 1 – The social basis of sport and recreation

Section A – UK and European Context

Active Sports

British Sports Trust

church

commercialisation

governing body

industrialisation

National Junior Sport Programme

participation pyramid

physical education

public school

Sport England

Sport for All

stereotype

target group

United Kingdom Sports Institute

Section B – Olympic case study

Baron Pierre de Coubertin

Brundage, Avery

deviancy

ethnic groups

Olympic Games

Paralympic Games

race

Samaranch, Juan Antonio

sponsorship

women in sport

Edexcel Module 2 – Refining performance
Section A – Acquiring skill

ability

conditioning theories

feedback

information processing

memory

motivation

motor programme

practice

reaction time

reinforcement

schema theory

skill

stages of learning

transfer

Edexcel Module 3 – Exercise and training

blood pressure

cardiac output

cool-down

fast twitch/slow twitch muscle fibres

fitness

hypokinetic disorders

kinesiology

lactic acid

maximum oxygen uptake

measurement of fitness

periodisation

physical activity readiness questionnaire (PAR-Q)

principles of training

synovial joint

warm-up

Edexcel Module 4 – Global Trends in International Sport
Section A – World Cultures

Argentina

Asian Games

Australian sports system

Kenya

New Zealand

South Africa

United States of America sports system

Section B – Synoptic analysis of trends in international sport through global games

academies of sport

amateur

apartheid

centrality

commercialisation

East German model

ping pong diplomacy

professional

stacking

Edexcel Module 5 – Refining performance

no direct theoretical content

Edexcel Module 6 – Scientific principles of exercise and performance

Section A – Exercise and energy systems

energy systems

ergogenic aids

fatigue

glycogen

oxygen debt/EPOC

recovery

sliding filament theory

Section B – Option A – Sports mechanics

acceleration

air resistance

angular motion

Bernouilli effect

centre of gravity

levers

linear motion

moment on inertia

momentum

Newton's laws of motion

velocity

Section B – Option B – Sports psychology

achievement motivation

aggression

anxiety

arousal

attitudes

attribution theory

Chelladuri's multi-dimensional model of leadership

cohesion

cue utilisation theory

Fiedler's contingency model of leadership

group dynamics

group productivity

leadership

personality

self-efficacy

social facilitation

stress management

EDEXCEL REVISION LISTINGS

287

USEFUL WEBSITE ADDRESSES

Organisation	Website
AQA Examination Board	www.aqa.org.uk
British Olympic Association	www.olympics.org.uk
Central Council of Physical Recreation	www.ccpr.org.uk
Commonwealth Games Federation	www.commonwealthgames.com
Dept. of Culture, Media and Sport	www.culture.gov.uk
Disability Sport England	www.euroyellowpages.com/dse.dispengl.html
Edexcel Examination Board	www.edexcel.org.uk
International Olympic Committee	www.olympic.org/uk/index
International Paralympic Committee	www.paralympics.org
Lawn Tennis Association	www.lta.org.uk/lta.htm
OCR Examination Board	www.ocr.org.uk
Physical Education Association	www.teleschool.org.uk/PEA
Sport England	www.sportengland.org
Sportscoach UK	www.sportscoachuk.uk
UK Sport	www.uksport.gov.uk
Women's Sport Foundation	www.wsf.org.uk